CW01213241

PRAISE FOR CYNDI'S FIRST BOOK,
THE SCIENCE OF PERSONAL COACHING

⭐⭐⭐⭐⭐ **Like having access to a personal coach whenever you need one!**

Reviewed in the United States on 2 April 2020

Verified Purchase

I got WAY more value out of this book than what I paid. When I find myself stuck in a rut, I do some of the exercises and they help me pull myself out of it. The exercises make me take the time to think about the issue I'm experiencing, which creates the space I need to reconnect with my motivation, vision, and what's possible.

What's also cool about this book is that it incorporates a genius system where you earn points for doing the exercises, which helps you stay accountable to yourself and feel rewarded. This makes the book even more effective because it makes sure I don't skip any of the questions that I may not feel like thinking about at the time, but need to. ;-)

If you ever feel stuck and have a hard time getting motivated, I would highly recommend you buy this book and go through it as instructed. You'll be glad you did!

Kahu

⭐⭐⭐⭐⭐ **Great insights**

Reviewed in Australia on 22 November 2022

Verified Purchase

Being a coach I found this book gave great assistance in how to structure coaching sessions. And if ready to make a change would be so helpful and very possible in coaching yourself.
😊

PRAISE FOR
CYNDI'S ONE-ON-ONE COACHING

Cyndi was able to help me clarify some goals in an area that has been causing me some distress. It was a real life challenge, and her coaching was incisive and produced real life results in a short amount of time.

Jim Catalano, PhD
Clinical Psychology

CEO, The Catalano Group
New York, NY

PRAISE FOR
CYNDI'S ONE-ON-ONE COACHING

A personal message on facebook Messenger

3/29/17, 12:41 AM

I wanted to give you a quick update. Everything in my relationship has changed. The man I've been seeing has finally opened up and has said "I love you" for the first time last month. He was afraid of allowing anyone to be close to him again and fears being rejected. We've been able to talk about absolutely anything and everything now. I'm really grateful to you for your program. It will only work if people are willing to take the steps you've outlined so they have to be open to that. I just wanted to let you know what had transpired. Have a great day today! -

3/29/17, 4:16 PM

Your message really made my day,

If you are comfortable with it, would you allow me to remove your identity (no name and picture), and use your quote as a testimonial?

If not, no worries.

✨☺️✨

3/29/17, 11:16 PM

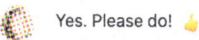

Yes. Please do! 👍

THE ONLY BOUNDARIES BOOK
YOU'LL EVER NEED

THE BOUNDARIES HEALTH CHECK

CYNDI D. McCOY

CONVOSIQUE

Published by Convosique Pty. Ltd.

CONVOSIQUE

The Boundaries Health Check: The Only Boundaries Book You'll Ever Need
Edition – First
ISBN: 978-0-9756468-3-0
Publisher name: Convosique Pty. Ltd.
Website: www.convosique.com
Email: hi@convosique.com
The Boundaries Health Check™ and The Boundaries Dashboard™ are trademarks of Convosique Pty. Ltd.

LEGAL STATEMENTS

To make the lawyers happy, we've made sure to include some important legal disclaimers here.

The author and publisher of this book can't be held responsible for the consequences of any actions taken as a result of information provided in this book.

Just because someone is quoted in this book as a testimonial, endorsement, or as a reference, it does not mean that the person agrees with every idea or belief contained in this book.

Every effort has been made to obtain permissions, properly credit, and acknowledge sources for the content of this book. If any permissions, credit, or acknowledgments have been overlooked or omitted, or any rights overlooked, it is unintentional. Please notify the publisher, and it will be rectified in future editions.

The Boundaries Health Check: The Only Boundaries Book You'll Ever Need. Copyright © 2024 by Convosique Pty. Ltd. All rights reserved. No part of this book may be used or reproduced in any manner whatsoever without written permission, except in the case of brief quotations embodied in critical articles and reviews.

This book may be purchased for educational or business use.

For questions, please contact the publisher using the information above.

Editorial work provided by: Sean Thomas
Minor editing provided by: Capstone Editing (capstoneediting.com.au),
Ian Mathieson Editing (ianmathiesonediting.com)

DEDICATION

To my dad,

who deserves this dedication

for being my #1 most consistent source

of laughs and lightheartedness throughout my life.

No matter how far apart we live in this world,

you remain closest in my heart.

TABLE OF CONTENTS

INTRODUCTION		3
SCIENTIFIC RESEARCH		9
WHY I WROTE THIS BOOK		13

PART ONE	**GET IN THE DRIVER'S SEAT**		**17**
CHAPTER 1	INSTRUCTION MANUAL		19
CHAPTER 2	WHAT ARE BOUNDARIES?		33
CHAPTER 3	BOUNDARIES HEALTH CHECK		49
PART TWO	**CHECK THE LIGHTS**		**79**
CHAPTER 4	INTRO TO THE FOUR DASHBOARD LIGHTS		81
CHAPTER 5	OIL CHECK (SELF-CARE)		89
	EXERCISE PART 1: SELF-CARE SCORES		109
	EXERCISE PART 2: COLOR OF YOUR DASHBOARD LIGHT		119
CHAPTER 6	FUEL CHECK (MOTIVATORS)		121
	EXERCISE PART 1: MAKE BELIEVE		127
	EXERCISE PART 2: COLOR OF YOUR DASHBOARD LIGHT		131
CHAPTER 7	BATTERY CHECK (CONSENT)		135
	EXERCISE PART 1: YOUR CONSENT SCORE		141
	EXERCISE PART 2: COLOR OF YOUR DASHBOARD LIGHT		145
CHAPTER 8	TEMPERATURE CHECK (EMOTIONAL STATE)		147
	EXERCISE PART 1: TEMPERATURE FORECAST		175
	EXERCISE PART 2: COLOR OF YOUR DASHBOARD LIGHT		183

boundariescheck.com | ix

PART THREE	GET ROADWORTHY	**189**
CHAPTER 9	INTRO TO YOUR VEHICLE INSPECTION	191
CHAPTER 10	TERRITORIES DIAL	195
	EXERCISE: TERRITORIES DIAL INSPECTION	207
CHAPTER 11	TREASURES DIAL	215
	EXERCISE: TREASURES DIAL INSPECTION	219
CHAPTER 12	TOOLS DIAL	227
	EXERCISE: TOOLS DIAL INSPECTION	239
CHAPTER 13	TOPICS DIAL	247
	EXERCISE: TOPICS DIAL INSPECTION	257
CHAPTER 14	THIRD PARTIES DIAL	265
	EXERCISE: THIRD PARTIES DIAL INSPECTION	273
CHAPTER 15	TIME DIAL	281
	EXERCISE: TIME DIAL INSPECTION	285
PART FOUR	**MAP YOUR TRIP**	**293**
CHAPTER 16	RELATIONSHIP ROADMAPS	295
CHAPTER 17	MY ROAD LENGTH	305
	EXERCISE: MY ROAD LENGTH	311
CHAPTER 18	MY DESTINATIONS	313
	EXERCISE: MY DESTINATIONS BRAINSTORM	321
CHAPTER 19	SHARED ROAD LENGTH	327
	EXERCISE: SHARED ROAD LENGTH	331
CHAPTER 20	SHARED DESTINATIONS	333
	EXERCISE: SHARED DESTINATIONS BRAINSTORM	343
CHAPTER 21	MY RELATIONSHIP ROADMAP (EXERCISE)	351

PART FIVE	PLAN YOUR NEXT STOP	367
CHAPTER 22	AN INTRODUCTION TO YOUR NEXT STOP	369
CHAPTER 23	GET HOOKED INTO YOUR GOAL (EXERCISE)	373

PART SIX	USE THE GLOVE COMPARTMENT	387
CHAPTER 24	COMMUNICATING BOUNDARIES	389
CHAPTER 25	GOVERNING STYLE	405
CHAPTER 26	MY TAKE ON TOXICITY	409
CHAPTER 27	DATING BOUNDARIES	413
CHAPTER 28	FALLING IN LOVE OR FALLING IN EXPECTATION?	425
CHAPTER 29	FINAL WORDS	431

ABOUT CYNDI D. MCCOY	435
ACKNOWLEDGEMENTS	439
ENDNOTES	443

boundariescheck.com | xi

FOREWORD

Cyndi's boundaries program builds you up like the human spine – beginning with a strong foundation, vertebra by vertebra, to create a strong, flexible human being.

Her theory uses simple and helpful metaphors to explain complex concepts. Her program in this book is challenging, thought-provoking, and most importantly, is based equally on both self-respect and respect for others.

The strong framework in her theory helps you know where you are in the process of managing boundaries, and she guides you through that process.

I know Cyndi, and this work of hers speaks deeply of who she is and how she does life.

Jo Gore, Psychotherapist
Sydney, Australia

Jo has been practicing as a psychotherapist since 1996 and a clinical supervisor since 2001.

Jo's main modes are emotion-focused therapy and existential therapy, working largely with adult survivors of childhood trauma and adoptive parents.

INTRODUCTION

(5 minute read)

So, who is on your mind right now?

Who slows your brain's processing power down to the speed of a clunky old laptop with too many applications running?

Who is it?

Is it a parent? Sibling? Partner? Friend?

Is it a client? Boss? Coworker?

Maybe it's not an individual, but a group or organization.

Is it your family? The company you work for? A religious organization? A group of people at the office?

Or maybe the relationship on your mind is your relationship with *you*. In the very back of your mind, there are looping videos of promises you've made to yourself, your deepest wishes, and your honest yet neglected needs. Maybe that is the relationship that has been sitting on the back burner, urgently waiting for your attention, and all the while, guilt is leaking into all areas of your life because you have put it off for so long.

Whoever it is that is on your mind, it's a human relationship that needs your attention. You know it does....

But now you have in your hands a revolutionary tool to empower this relationship. The Boundaries Health Check™ gives you a measurable way to start understanding and prioritizing healthy and life-giving boundaries in any human relationship – romantic, family, professional, social, political, your relationship with yourself (or "your relationship with you" as I like to call it), and any other human relationship category that exists.

Here's how the Boundaries Health Check works. It introduces standardized metrics to measure your sense of health and satisfaction in any human relationship – quantifiable and trackable, so you know in what direction you're headed.

You might say that, until right now, you've had an inconsistent form of checking your boundaries. Rather than naming, measuring, and tracking what's going on inside of you, you let it hide in your nervous system.

In your human relationships, your nervous system has been flashing green, yellow, and red lights throughout your life, but until now you haven't known a reliable way to name those lights or identify what to change in order to keep them glowing green.

When it comes to that relationship you thought of earlier – the one that needs your attention – think of all of your decisions about boundaries in this relationship as "dials" on a dashboard, and imagine how you think and feel about this relationship as red, yellow, and green status lights on that dashboard. In this book, you will walk through naming and measuring all of those things to arrive at a total Boundaries Health Check score.

The boundary decision dials, the lights, and the score all belong to what I call your "Boundaries Dashboard."

Introduction

Every time you complete a Boundaries Health Check, your results impact the dashboard and help you see the direction that you're headed on the road of this relationship.

By reading this book, you have now sat down in the driver's seat, and the steering wheel in front of you represents the actions that you will personally take in this relationship from today forward.

The "road" you're driving on symbolizes both the direction of this relationship and everything that you share in it. Most importantly, each person on the road of this relationship is a driver of their own car, each one responsible for driving and maintaining their own vehicle.

Like a teenager sitting down behind the wheel to learn to drive for the very first time, you're about to grasp the inspiring power and capability you have on the road.

Behind the steering wheel where you sit, there's your boundaries dashboard, and you can see it has only two sections.

In one section of the dashboard, you see six control dials that you can turn up or down. They look like volume dials, and they represent your decisions about what you choose to share or not share in this relationship. Turning them up or down dictates your personal sense of health, joy, peace, and satisfaction in this relationship.

On the road of this relationship, there are two parties – the other person (or group of people) and you. You control *your* decisions, and the other person controls *their* decisions. The relationship road involves two people negotiating how to travel it together; otherwise, the road ends.

Next to the six control dials, in the second section of your dashboard, you see four display lights. Their only purpose is to tell you the health status of your car or, in other words, your personal health status in this relationship.

Based on the color of the light, you know when your sense of health, joy, peace, and satisfaction in this relationship is at risk, and with that information, you can use the six control dials to make new and better decisions.

At any time, day or night, one or more of the four lights may turn red (unhealthy), yellow (warning), or green (healthy). To make a red or yellow light turn green again, you simply adjust your control dials or, in other words, adjust your personal decisions. Simply turn up or down any of the six dials to change your health and happiness status.

In this book, I'll introduce you to the names of each of these dials and lights, and you'll identify the settings for each of them for this relationship through exercises.

And those six dials and four lights are your "Boundaries Dashboard." The lights tell you when to make a change in this relationship, and the control dials tell you what you can change to move from a red or yellow to green. Whenever you complete your Boundaries Health Check, you will discover which lights have changed color.

When it comes to the relationship that's on your mind right now, what dashboard lights are flashing for you? As a result, what personal decisions do you need to make right now? The exercises in this book aim to gently pull those answers from deep inside of you and train you to maintain daily awareness of your power to make positive change happen.

Daily awareness? Yes, daily. Whether you realize it or not, the Boundaries Dashboard™ is there all day long as you drive on the road of this relationship, and any moment you ignore its warning lights, you risk finding yourself in a ditch with $5,000 or more worth of damage.

That $5,000 figure comes from a real incident where I ignored my "dashboard lights" in a relationship. After spending time with that person, I

Introduction

hopped in my car to drive home, but my emotional state distracted me from paying attention to other cars on the road. Consequently, I ended up crashing my beautiful car, and my insurance required me to pay $5,000 out of pocket for repairs.

Although the kinds of crashes may vary from person to person, from physical to emotional or mental, each of us is capable of doing the same, or so much worse, on the metaphorical road of our human relationships. This book is about keeping you driving with high performance and great satisfaction, avoiding the ditches and staying aware of other cars on the road.

So, for a safe and high-performance relationship, please carefully read this book from beginning to end.

To make it easier for you to plan and fit this into your schedule, I have included under each chapter title an estimated number of minutes that it will take to read.[1]

But before we get started, would you like to know the science behind why the Dashboard matters?

boundariescheck.com | 7

SCIENTIFIC RESEARCH

(4 minute read)

Feeling satisfied in a human relationship is something "nice to have," but it's not essential to life or health, right?

It's a luxury, but not a necessity, right?

Research appears to be shouting a loud "Wrong!" from across the room. It looks like quality relationships, characterized by healthy emotional patterns, are as crucial to your physical health as vitamins.

If you haven't heard the news, recent breakthroughs reveal that, in human relationships, our feelings of satisfaction wield a power beyond our imagination; they're not just important, they are life-preserving and life-extending. In other words, high quality human relationships have been shown to provide abundant health benefits.

One of the major studies to shed light on this is the Harvard Study of Adult Development. It's one of the world's longest studies on living humans ever conducted.

The Harvard Study has been going on for over 80 years. At the time I'm writing this, there have been over 45 million views of the TEDx Talk that introduced this study to the world.[2] And as many of you already know,

Harvard is an Ivy League University ranked #1 in the world for its academic reputation, so this knowledge is not to be taken lightly.

The study validated something that many of us need to know – the quality of our human relationships impacts our mental and physical health, and this quality is a better predictor of health than genetics, social class, or even IQ.[3]

One of the many specific findings in this study, as shared by Robert Waldinger, psychiatrist and director of the study, was that "the people who were the most satisfied in their relationships at age 50 were the healthiest at age 80."[4]

Dr. Waldinger also shared from the study how "good relationships don't just protect our bodies, they protect our brains." He went on to explain that:

> *It turns out that being in a securely attached relationship to another person in your 80s is protective, that the people who are in relationships where they really feel they can count on the other person in times of need, those people's memories stay sharper longer. And the people in relationships where they feel they really can't count on the other one, those are the people who experience earlier memory decline.*

And here's one more worthy quote from Dr. Waldinger's same talk: "It turns out that living in the midst of conflict is really bad for our health…. And living in the midst of good, warm relationships is protective."

Satisfaction. Secure attachment. Warmth. Feeling you can count on another person. Those emotional states and other satisfying feelings can predict the health of your brain and body.

That Harvard study is not the only one to show the importance of high-quality human relationships.

Scientific Research

A fifteen-year study led by physician and researcher Stewart George Wolf on a community in Pennsylvania, USA, used medical records, physical exams, and lab results, to find out that "unconditional interpersonal support counteracts life stress and thus preserves life."[5]

An additional study published by the *American Journal of Public Health* looked at the same community in Pennsylvania and confirmed the link between human relationships and physical health and longevity.[6] This 50-year study again showed how high-quality human relationships keep people alive and healthy far more than the other factors we typically think of, like diet and exercise. Fried food, alcohol, and unfiltered cigarettes apparently aren't as detrimental as we may have thought compared to the impact of human relationships.

A widely cited paper is "Social Relationships and Health: A Flashpoint for Health Policy," published in the *Journal of Health and Social Behavior* in 2010. It analyzed findings from 148 studies and found that individuals with strong social relationships have a 50% increased likelihood of survival compared to those with weaker social ties.[7]

A 2023 advisory publication by the U.S. Surgeon General is full of research and findings regarding the direct impact of the quality of human relationships on physical health. One of many key statements worth noting is this:

> *Furthermore, evidence suggests that individuals with higher purpose and perceived emotional and practical support from their social networks are more likely to engage in health-promoting behaviors, such as the use of preventive health care services.*[8]

The above sources are only among the most popular ones, but there are more if you do a little research. Science is unveiling what's important to our health.

Science now shows what most of us felt deeply but could not articulate or validate. The quality of our human relationships is one of the most important factors in our health and longevity.

And if that's the case, then perhaps the most important thing you can do this very moment is to begin evaluating your personal emotional patterns in the human relationships in your life. Avoiding this subject could be detrimental to your health, as research powerfully suggests.

Have you heard of sayings like "Feelings aren't facts" or "Don't let your emotions cloud your judgment"? While those two statements carry some important truths and good intentions, it's crucial not to misinterpret them to mean that feelings are irrelevant to your health or that feelings are unworthy of thorough examination or consideration. Your feelings are worthy of attention, and as a matter of fact, they're an indicator of the direction of your health.

So, it's time to update the sayings we are unsuccessfully living by. A more relevant, practical, smarter, and healthier saying would be "*Unexamined* feelings aren't facts" or "Don't let your *unanalyzed* emotions cloud your judgment."

Giving time and attention to the most emotionally impactful relationship in your life right now isn't just "a nice thing to do." Your life and vitality apparently depend on it, and *The Boundaries Health Check* is your tool to help keep that life and vitality in check.

WHY I WROTE THIS BOOK

(3 minute read)

In this book, I introduce what some might say is an unprecedented way to measure the health of your human relationships. I once called it the "Human Relationship Dashboard," but now I call this theory the "Boundaries Dashboard," and I share groundbreaking methods to put the theory into practice, notably through the "Boundaries Health Check" and "Relationship Health" score.

Because I believe that the Boundaries Health Check is the most important idea for you to remember from this theory and that you should practice it regularly, I made it the title of the book.

Before writing this book, several options crossed my mind about what to do with these three ideas. I could have kept the Boundaries Dashboard, Boundaries Health Check, and Relationship Health score as my own little secrets that give me superpowers, or I could have enrolled in a doctoral program in psychology to develop this as a doctoral thesis. Although a doctoral research process was tempting, I decided that I'd verify the value of this theory on my own time, in my own way, and in a spirit of conversation.

So, that's what I've done. I've written this book in a non-academic style of discussion, using examples from my own life, from reputable sources and experts that you can find online, and from references pulled widely from pop culture.

Here are three more reasons that went into my decision to write this book.

First, I wondered if my theory would help other people as much as it helped me, so as a test, I turned it into an online workshop. I referred to it as a boundaries workshop, incorporated professional coaching tools and techniques, filmed myself in an empty spare bedroom, and produced a series of prerecorded videos with a workbook. I treated the whole thing lightly, only wanting to test the waters. My favorite part was the bloopers.

Forty-five people signed up for that boundaries workshop, and when I saw a total feedback rating of 4.6 out of 5 stars, I suspected I had something worth building on.

Second, I earned credentials from the International Coaching Federation as a life, business, and career coach, so I was able to test the same theory in a new context with five very different people through one-on-one professional coaching conversations. All five clients reported back to me a significant, measurable increase in their sense of health, peace, joy, and satisfaction in their relationships. They came to me with a wide assortment of human relationships to work on – some family, some romantic, and some professional.

The results from my theory when it was delivered in one-on-one coaching conversations blew my mind. Their feedback made my life feel more meaningful.

Third, a couple of professional therapists reviewed and endorsed my theory, with one of them saying that they started using it in their own personal life. I thought, "Wow, a seasoned, licensed therapist uses my theory. It also worked wonders for my coaching clients. Strangers from the internet loved it, too. This must mean something for the world."

I also had informal conversations with friends and acquaintances in which I helped them with human relationship boundaries based on my theory, and it seemed to produce consistent "aha!" moments of clarity. Those felt great, too.

The consistently positive feedback from such a demographically diverse group of people gave me the belief that there are possibly millions of others in the world whom I could also help. Seeing a 100% success rate in all three of the above test cases inspired me to convert my video script from the boundaries workshop into a book with further refinements and improvements, all with the hope that the same results can be replicated and multiplied throughout the world.

On top of all of that, I felt a strong sense of moral obligation to share my theory when I found best-selling books about boundaries have confusing and impractical ideas in them. No wonder people feel stuck when it comes to boundaries! I must set the record straight and clear. So, let's get started.

PART ONE

GET IN THE DRIVER'S SEAT

Part One: Get in the Driver's Seat

CHAPTER 1

INSTRUCTION MANUAL

(15 minute read)

Instruction manuals come with everything – printers, stereos, shavers, hairdryers, and other electronic devices. They have several annoying pages of small print with warnings, step-by-step directions, and specifications. "Do not operate while driving," "Intended for users 16 years and older," and several other instructions that most people don't care to read, even when there might be death-risk warnings.

However, there are some instructions that I'm sure you and I will be much more motivated to follow than others. For example, you'd probably have an exceptionally strong desire to carefully follow step-by-step instructions for your parachute when diving out of a plane; it could mean the difference between a tragic accident and a safe landing on your own two feet.

Please treat this first chapter with the same care as you would a parachute lesson. Each one of the following instructions can and will be the deciding factor for a successful "jump" into a new world for you and the relationship that you're working on.

This chapter is like an instruction manual for this book. It will prepare you to get behind the wheel of the Boundaries Dashboard™ and make it the ride of your life.

SAFETY FIRST

Throughout the course of our lives, there will be people who endanger our mental, emotional, physical, and/or financial well-being, and they can show up in our immediate family, workplace, romantic life, social group, or anywhere in our community at large.

If someone does endanger your safety, please do not use this book as an attempt to mend or continue that relationship. Instead, find the appropriate professionals or local authorities to help you. None of the information, advice, tips, exercises, and ideas throughout this book are meant to replace support from a medical professional, psychiatric professional, or any other relevant experts and authorities.

SECOND, ONLY ONE RELATIONSHIP PER READ-THROUGH

I designed every chapter of this book to work on only one human relationship per read-through. In other words, you can read this book as many times as you need, but each chapter and exercise are structured for one relationship from beginning to end. Throughout the pages of this book, I will continually refer to your relationship with that person (or group) as "this relationship."

All chapters work together to build a vision for you in your relationship with that other person or group. So, it will not make sense to start with one person in the beginning and then change halfway through. Quite frankly, it would be a mess.

"This relationship" doesn't have to be a relationship between you and an individual. The relationship may be between you and a group of people of any size. If that's what you choose to do, then everywhere in the book where I refer to the "other person," please think of the name of that group of people instead.

The human relationship you work through may be your relationship with an individual or a group or company or organization. For example, you may want to work through this book with "people I talk to on dating apps" as the name of your group or "workmates at the office" or "my parents."

At the same time, you'll be looking at "your relationship with you," as I like to say, and how that impacts your relationship with the other person or group.

I have been seeing video and images from an Australian government-funded mental health ad campaign called "Dear mind," and one of its slogans is, "Create a healthier relationship with your mind." Some of the scenes show people journaling or sitting alone looking out into the distance, indicating that they are having an inner dialogue with their own mind. It was deeply satisfying to see our relationship with ourselves being taken so seriously by the government of a country.

This book is equally as concerned with the health of your relationship with your mind as it is with the health of your relationship with the other person.

Whichever relationship you focus on, know that once you have finished the entire book with that one person (or group) in mind, feel free to go through the book again with the next person or group that you want to work out. Remember that this book is designed so that its exercises only make sense by sticking to one relationship from beginning to end.

Side note: when I refer to the other person in your relationship, I might sometimes use the term "themself" or "themselves." This is a growing trend in grammar to use gender-neutral pronouns when it makes sense to do so. I find in many contexts, it makes writing easier for me, too; so, I do it in this book. I'm mentioning it here so that you know it's intentional.

THIRD, SCORE AT LEAST AN EIGHT

Can you remember a time in your life when you desperately desired something? Maybe that time is right now. Maybe it was last year. Maybe you haven't desired something in a very long time.

Imagine a scale from 0 (zero) to 10 (ten). A score of 0 means that you could not desire it less. A score of 10 means that you could not desire it more. What does a desire level of 10 feel like for you? Maybe you'll have to travel back through your memories to a moment from childhood or school days to recall what level 10 desire felt like.

Maybe you greatly desired buying your first car. Maybe you greatly desired spending time with a best friend. Maybe you greatly desired a romantic relationship or accomplishing a specific dream. Whatever it was, and whenever it was, take a moment to remember what that level of intensity felt like, then consider that desire a score of 10.

Some of my "10" scores from childhood or school days were to go to a rave or to sit behind my crush in geography class. As an adult, one of my level-10 desires is the feeling of 955K people viewing a funny or inspiring video that I made on social media (yes, that happened!). A 10 for me can also be a peaceful desire rather than euphoric, like the heart-warming desire to wrap myself in a blanket on the couch and have nothing else to do. Ah, the warm fuzzy feeling of cozy comfort!

Chapter 1: Instruction Manual

OK, let's come back to you, to this present moment, and to this book.

Think about the relationship you're looking to improve. On a scale of zero to ten, how much desire do you have to make a positive change in this relationship?

What is your score?

This is a revealing moment because your score is going to tell you whether you're going to continue working on this relationship right now or not.

If your score is an eight or above, then you're ready to keep working on this book with that same person in mind.

If your score is a seven or below, then your level of desire is not great enough for you to make significant change happen in this relationship.

So, if your score is a seven or below, consider *another* relationship you've been thinking of working on; start with that one instead, assuming it's a score of eight or above.

FOURTH, CREATE A SAFE SPACE

Every time you sit down with this book, create a safe and comfortable space for yourself, or at least as best as you can. By "safe and comfortable" I mean an environment where you feel both physically comfortable and free to think and read in privacy, without interruptions. Reducing external activity around you helps you become far more aware of the internal activity within you – your honest thoughts and feelings.

Feeling physically comfortable and ensuring a sense of privacy allows you to more easily access your genuine ideas and emotions, which is a critical state for you to benefit from this book.

For the period of time that you plan to sit and read, consider turning your phone on airplane mode. If others are around at home, try sharing with them a fun form of "Do Not Disturb" message, like "Wellness Reboot Underway: See you in 40 mins" or "Mental Recharge Time: See you in 20."

A quiet external atmosphere will help you hear what is going on in your internal atmosphere, and that is the level of listening you need to get the best results.

FIFTH, HAVE YOUR DIARY WITH YOU

Starting in Chapter 3, every time you sit down to read this book, be sure to have a dedicated diary with you. I call it your Dashboard Diary, which is short for Boundaries Dashboard Diary. Find a blank digital or physical notebook and dedicate it to the work that you're about to do throughout this book.

In your Dashboard Diary, you'll be answering key questions that this entire book builds upon and they are necessary for getting clarity and taking action on your boundaries.

Your Dashboard Diary is critical if you want to see powerful shifts in your life and relationships through this book.

Just as a bank keeps a record of your constantly changing balance, the Dashboard Diary will show you what's going in and out of your relationship. You'll use this diary as a kind of relationship accounting record.

Another and perhaps even better way to understand the importance of your Dashboard Diary is to see this book as a paint brush and your

Dashboard Diary as the canvas where your painting will appear. This book and the words you read are only a tool like a paint brush, your genuine thoughts are the paint, and the diary is the canvas.

This book is the tool in your hand, your ideas are the paint colors, and your Dashboard Diary is the final product.

So, what kind of diary would you like to use for this – paper or digital? Smartphone or iPad? Laptop or paper notebook? I suggest going to get your diary right after you put this book down today, and then have your diary ready to go every time you read this book.

SIXTH, FEEL AWAKE

Whether you're snuggled on a couch, sitting on a train, cozy in the corner of a café with a hot cup of something, or sitting in your bed propped up with a pillow, make sure you feel awake and mentally alert.

If you feel sleepy or low energy while reading, then you will not be able to concentrate, and your brain won't recollect important memories or generate new ideas as easily. So, do at least one thing to feel awake whenever you sit down with this book and your Dashboard Diary.

Maybe take a power nap before you start or sit outside or on a balcony somewhere in a comfy chair with a cup of homemade something.

Or maybe you want to sit down with this book after a short exercise session, when powerful brain chemicals are firing.

The point is to feel enough energy, whatever it takes, as long you are being good to yourself.

Part One: Get in the Driver's Seat

SEVENTH, BUILD MOMENTUM

Each chapter of this book is written to make sense when you read it in sequential order. This isn't the kind of book in which you can randomly open to any page and start reading, and that's because new concepts build on previous chapters.

In other words, the exercises in this book are designed to be cumulative, meaning that each chapter and exercise builds up on the answers you gave in the previous exercises. The answers in your Dashboard Diary that you write down from early chapters become an essential part of all later chapters.

If you skip a chapter or exercise, you'll also miss the definitions of new concepts, and so new words or content will likely confuse you. It's best to start from the beginning, not skip anything, and wait no longer than one week between each chapter or exercise.

If you wait more than one week between exercises, you will likely forget new concepts, lose momentum, feel drained of emotion to some degree, and lack what's needed for solid progress. The connectivity between answers will lose strength if you wait too long.

So, to keep momentum, consider marking your calendar or setting up a reminder to continue reading within the next few days or no more than seven days from today.

EIGHTH, MASK YOURSELF FIRST

If you've ever been on an airplane, you have seen the passenger safety instructions. There is usually an illustration of an emergency scenario where masks drop down from the ceiling and a passenger is putting on her own oxygen mask before putting one on her child.

Pretty scary drawing when you first saw it, right? What good parent would put her own life before her child?

However, the truth is this: in this scenario, if the mother doesn't take care of her own needs first, she risks losing both her life and her child's life. "Putting the child first" risks both lives. The science behind it is that if she doesn't have oxygen, she will pass out before she can save her child.

Ironically, putting your needs first is often how you can best help others; otherwise, you may not be able to show up for them at all. So, throughout every exercise in this book, we're focusing on identifying your needs, not only for your sake but for the sake of the relationship.

And you're the only person who can do it. Your needs are your responsibility. If your tooth needs a root canal, your friend can't go and get a root canal on your behalf. They can recommend a dentist, but you are the only one who can sit down in the dentist's chair to make your mouth healthy again. So, you have an essential role to identify and take care of your needs.

Other people do not have the capability to hear all of the many unexpressed thoughts and feelings inside of you, but you can observe that kind of activity within yourself. I'm here to help you identify and speak up for your needs.

The tools on the dashboard create awareness of your needs – emotional, mental, physical, and even financial states. In this relationship, the other person has their own dashboard for their needs. In this book, we concentrate solely on yours.

Part One: Get in the Driver's Seat

NINTH, RELINQUISH CONTROL

The Boundaries Dashboard™ is your own personal control panel. It allows you control of the controllables.

Controllables is a helpful word I've heard a few times, and it refers to things that you can control in life. For example, you may not control the weather today, but you can control the decisions you make in response to the weather.

As you will learn in upcoming chapters, your "controllables" are the six dials on the Boundaries Dashboard, and each of those dials represent your personal decisions about your boundaries in the relationship. The other person has their own dials to manage their decisions, too.

This book looks at ownership of your personal decisions and actions in this relationship. I believe that is how we act with integrity, as well as create sincere relationships and a better world overall.

One of my favorite motivational speakers and fitness coaches, James Smith, was asked by one of his fans, "Is there any way to gently push a partner into a hobby I believe they would be awesome at?"

James responded, "Things you control: Your actions. Your emotions. Things not to try to control: Their actions. Their emotions."[9]

I believe the point that James made was that any amount of "push" still means you're exerting control. Even when the push is "gentle," it's still a push.

Any amount of "push" requires force. Have a job that you need the other person to do? Rather than push them, inspire the other person by sharing a vision of the end goal. Acknowledge the skills or strengths you see in them that can help make the vision happen. Invite them. Check in that they're able and willing.

Whether it's a professional or personal relationship, I have a high level of sensitivity when someone attempts to exert any amount of verbal or emotional force on me. My nervous system detects it in a matter of what feels like nanoseconds, and it immediately raises red flags. My nervous system also detects the opposite; when someone invites me, asks me, checks in with me, or inspires me, it raises green flags.

It also feels equally revolting for me in moments when I become conscious of myself exerting verbal or emotional force on others. Becoming conscious of it is key; sometimes I'm not aware of it.

When people want to know how something works, they like to see a demonstration. Your healthy decisions and actions for yourself in this relationship are demonstrations of healthy boundaries for the other person and anyone watching.

You don't control anyone but yourself, but you can train people how to treat you by what you accept. In other words, you can adjust the controllables on your personal control panel. You can turn the dials of your boundaries.

TENTH, BEWARE OF BRAIN GLITCHES

Instruction manuals prepare you for just about anything; so, here's one danger that you hopefully won't encounter, but I'll play it safe and include it here.

I trust that when someone genuinely wants you to be healthy, they will support any of your decisions and actions that you intend to improve

Part One: Get in the Driver's Seat

your emotional, mental, physical, or financial health.

However, occasionally your healthy decisions and actions might unexpectedly trigger anger in another person. While anger can happen for many reasons, a few popular reasons are guilt and envy.

The other person may exhibit either a subtle or obvious outlash, and this can come from guilt over their own self-neglect or envy of your new change. They may be neglecting their own need to make healthier decisions, and so they create a false story to move their internal blame and focus onto you.

It's like a malfunction of mental software; things stop making sense.

That's because during anger or fear, part of the human brain becomes hijacked. The part of the brain responsible for reasoning is biologically impaired. This is referred to as the "amygdala hijack" in the book *Emotional Intelligence* by psychologist Daniel Goleman, PhD.[10]

In an airplane hijack, the hijacker takes over the airplane's behavior and disregards the pilot altogether. Similarly, during fear or anger, the emotional part of the brain (amygdala) takes over the person's behavior and disregards the "pilot" part of the brain that controls rational decision-making.

A popular and dangerous mental hijack technique is called gaslighting.

Gaslighting is like a subtle form of anger. It's when someone convinces you to start doubting your own sanity. It can be expressed in several ways. For example, the other person may persuade you to doubt what "healthy" means for you. They might accuse you of using boundaries as a weapon against them. They might incorrectly frame your need for a healthy boundary as a demand or ultimatum, even though it's your own personal decision that you're making for yourself.

So how do you respond to that?

As a professionally trained personal coach, I hold clients accountable to identify, clarify, and then achieve goals but I do not diagnose mental health conditions or provide treatment for mental abuse, so when it comes to gaslighting or verbal mistreatment, I recommend a licensed therapist.

However, I can say that in that situation, my own immediate response is to protect my brain from emotional hijack in the moment by exiting the conversation until I can put my own sense of reason back into the pilot's seat. Otherwise, both of us will be speaking from hijacked brain states.

It is like a software glitch of the brain. And as most software developers will tell you, it takes lots of patience, calmness, and logical troubleshooting to fix a bug. If it happens often, it's just not safe or worth it for me to maintain interaction with that person, unless a professional can help, or a miracle takes place.

ONE MORE THING

Time will tell, but I am convinced this book will significantly change your life if you read it entirely and finish the exercises.

However, as you read this, if you feel like you need extra help, motivation, or positive guidance at any point, or if you want to supercharge your progress, I can offer a few forms of support. I earned my credentials as a professional personal coach, and so here's a little shameless plug.

Professional personal coaches are trained to help you find motivation and then stay motivated, focused, and accountable for any kind change that you want to make in life, and that also includes boundaries and

Part One: Get in the Driver's Seat

human relationships. We do this through confidential one-on-one conversations using specific coaching conversation skills and techniques.

I wish I could do a one-on-one coaching session with each and every person who reads this, but if my schedule is booked, then I can refer you to a professional personal coach who I recommend or an accountability group that I organize.

So, whether it's one-on-one coaching or a group thing, you're covered. My brand of personal coaching is Best Kinda Friend™. A Best Kinda Friend will supercharge your decision-making and action-taking in any area of life and especially while working through this material.

The website is **BestKindaFriend.com**.

And that completes the instruction manual for the Boundaries Dashboard. You can now safely start playing with the six dials and four lights and have a look around. I'll introduce their names in the next chapter.

CHAPTER 2

WHAT ARE BOUNDARIES?

(17 minute read)

What do you share in this relationship? What do you not share?

All human relationships are defined by what a person shares and doesn't share in that relationship.

All. Human. Relationships.

I share the Earth with all of humanity, but I don't share my time with 99.998%[11] of them.

I share the same national laws with my countrymen, but I don't share the same local laws with them.

I share a smile with a stranger on the street, but I don't share my drinking straw with them.

I share my dating goals on my dating app profile, but I don't share my home address with my profile visitors.

See how the list can go on?

Part One: Get in the Driver's Seat

And on?

And what do we mean exactly when we say "share"? Throughout the world, we use the word "share" to mean a few different things. Most commonly, we mean to divide something physical and portion it out, like breaking a candy bar in half.

"Share" also means either having or using something in common, like sharing spaces – digital or physical.

Third, it means to participate in or partake in an experience together to any degree. That experience can involve anything – a financial or material exchange, an emotional exchange of any kind, or a sharing of understanding, abilities, or interests.

In a professional relationship, you might share your skills or knowledge in exchange for payment. In an intimate partnership, you might share your body and affection in exchange for the same from the other person. In a family relationship, you might share your physical effort and assistance freely, with the hope of only their well-being and safety in return.

By sharing anything with another human – a physical thing, a physical or digital space, or an experience – you are participating in that relationship.

This book looks at what you choose to share or not share in a particular relationship. What you share and don't share defines the health of that relationship.

If you put together all of the stories of everything that you share with the other person, that becomes the journey of your relationship. Throughout this book, I use the metaphor of a road to represent that journey.

You and the other person are like two cars driving on a road, and whatever stops you make together along that road are the experiences you share.

These experiences consist of different amounts of six relationship elements: your time spent, your energy invested, your physical spaces shared, the impact of your other human relationships, the tools you use to communicate, and the topics you talk about and think about. Your sense of health, peace, joy, and satisfaction in any human relationship depend on how much or how little of those six things you choose to share. For the purposes of this book, let's refer to them as your six "boundaries."

Of course, there are plenty of other metaphors that I could use to represent a human relationship other than a road with two cars. Here's one that is ultra-simple, using only two circles.

Picture two empty circles next to each other. You are one circle, and the other person is the other circle. Now imagine the two circles moving closer and overlapping each other. Can you see in your mind how the overlap creates a third space? This third space is shaped like an oval, pointy on the top and bottom.

The overlap represents everything that you and the other person share. The more you share, the larger the overlap and the more of your life the other person consumes. The other person consumes a portion of those six parts of your life, as you do theirs.

The more of your life the other person consumes, the less you can invest in other human relationships.

Just because you have a large overlap with someone else, it does not mean that what you share is healthy or that it is high quality. You can share significant parts of your life, and it can still be dangerous to your health.

The good news is that this book will help you look at how you manage the health and quality of the six boundaries that you share.

Part One: Get in the Driver's Seat

So where do we begin? There are only six rules to how the six boundaries work.

As a matter of fact, if human relationships are defined by what you share (and don't share), then these six rules can be titled "The Six Rules of Every Human Relationship."

And so, here are those six rules.

RULE #1
THERE ARE ONLY SIX BOUNDARIES

There are six rules of human relationships, and the first rule is that "there are only six boundaries." Easy to remember, right?

In every human relationship, there are only six parts of life that you share or don't share with the other person (or group of people), and they define your sense of health, peace, joy, and satisfaction in the relationship. Everything in our known universe that can impact the health of a relationship falls into one of these six.

In a creative attempt to help you memorize all six, I put each one into a line of the poem I wrote below.

My frequency of hours and minutes,

My physical space and everything in it,

My physical investment – strength, money, or things,

My mode of communication – a text, an app, or song that I sing,

The topics I say or don't, 'cause it makes a big difference,

And those people who impact this relationship's existence.

Those are the six boundaries, making us closer with distance.

Another creative attempt to help with memorization was to give each one of the six boundaries a name beginning with the letter T.

TIME

This boundary refers to the hours and minutes you share with that person and the frequency of those blocks of time. For example, maybe you spend 30 minutes at a frequency of twice a day. Maybe you spend two hours at a frequency of twice a week. Maybe you spend one hour at a frequency of once a year. The Time boundary also includes the timing (the sequence or chronological order) that you choose to share your time. For example, you might choose to complete personal errands before spending time with a friend, or as another example, you may choose to first go to the gym before going to work. In each decision you make, your timing impacts your relationships.

TERRITORIES

This boundary refers to the environments that you share or don't share with the other person, and it breaks down into two kinds. First, it refers to your physical environment – the geographic location, the four walls around you (if any), and anything inside of that shared environment – people, sounds, smells, textures, and visuals. The second kind of territory refers to the way you use the space or distance between your physical bodies, or what I call "body boundaries."

Treasures

This boundary refers to the investment of your energy, physical strength, and your material or financial resources. Treasures are any action you perform for the sake of the other person or for the sake of the relationship. Treasures can be given with no expectation of something in return or they can be traded with the understanding that it's an exchange of some sort.

Tools

This boundary refers to any tool that can be used to communicate – your own mouth, a pen and paper, body language, and even little audio messages you can send on Facebook. They are all tools.

The tricky part of this boundary is that there are two groups that can be managed differently. The first is sending tools – the ways you choose to say something or send a message to the other person. The second tool type includes the ways that you receive communication back from the other person. For example, you can receive a message through email (receiving tool), but then respond by calling them on the phone (sending tool). There are also two sub-groups for both sending and receiving – verbal and nonverbal.

Topics

This boundary refers to the topics (and subtopics) you talk about and don't talk about. This includes every possible topic in the universe such as your emotions, your worldview, what you ate for dinner, or even this book.

Third Parties

This boundary refers to any relationship outside of this one that influences your ideas, feelings, thoughts, and behaviors toward the other person to any noticeable degree. You may or may not share this human relationship with the other person. Third parties to your relationship can be the acquaintance you chat with at the local grocery store, a shared family member, a therapist, a coworker, or any other human relationship that noticeably impacts this one in any way.

Yes, anything in the universe that you can share in a human relationship will fall into one of those six categories.

RULE #2
BOUNDARIES CONTROL PERSONAL PEACE, NOT THE OTHER PERSON

Boundaries are about self-control, not control of anyone else. They are about making sure that you are first taking good care of everything that is in your own personal realm of control, so that you are in a great and healthy state to give your best to others.

Boundaries are about control of your personal peace, not coercion or force of the other person. An example is politely stepping away from what might be, for you, an unhealthy conversation instead of forcing or expecting others to stop discussing it. Another example is turning the phone off, rather than telling people not to call you.

There are ways to assert your boundaries that do not involve demanding an action from someone else. Controlling your personal peace carries a sense of safety, protection, calmness, and learning, as opposed to demanding, controlling, or forcing a behavior from the other person.

Of course, if the other person fully agrees to hand over control of their decisions or actions, then it is no longer forceful, controlling, or coercive. But without expressed consent or a clear agreement, commands feel like acts of brute force or even just bullying.

A forceful intention can happen very subtly, even "politely." For example, attempting to control someone can sound like: "You need to stop, please." Adding a "please" sounds nice, but a sentence like that can communicate a tone of a demand rather than a request.

I am certainly guilty of a demanding form of "please," and when I notice it in myself (usually after it slipped out of me), I cringe at what I've done.

I believe in adding the word "please," but I also recognize it is meaningless if we feel any intention to control another person when we say it. They notice – even if unconsciously.

Controlling personal peace, rather than the other person, means using the magical word "I", rather than the word "you."

The switch from "you" to "I" tends to wonderfully strip out a large degree of cringey forcefulness and passive aggressiveness.

Instead of "You need to stop," you can switch to: "That doesn't feel right or healthy for me, so I need to either respectfully end this conversation or move on to a different topic for now." In that statement, you would not be demanding anything of the other person; rather, you would be exercising control over your choice to participate in the conversation.

Another option is: "I don't like talking about that. It brings me down, so how about we move on to a new subject?" This is an act of extending an invitation. You are inviting the other person to continue interaction and conversation, while protecting your peace.

Controlling the other person may sound like, "Hurry up, move more quickly, and be done by 5:00 pm." In contrast, controlling personal peace starts with "I", as in, "I'll be leaving at 5:00 pm because I have things to take care of. I hope you'll join me."

Control of others sounds like, "Don't ask me to do that for you." Controlling personal peace means starting with "I" and saying, "I'd be happy to do that for you if I felt right about it, but I don't."

Control of others sounds like, "Get out or I'm throwing your stuff on the front lawn." Controlling personal peace means saying, "I'm comfortable sharing this home with you, if you're willing and able to help with the cost."

What another person says or does is up to them; we don't control their behavior. We can invite, request, negotiate, make a plea, or suggest something, but if we want a genuine and healthy connection, then force isn't an option. Forcefulness puts a sense of psychological, physical, financial, or other form of pressure on a person to do or say something at your command that may go against their wishes or values. If you desire sincere willingness from the other person, then invading and capturing like an army probably won't win their heart; rather, try creating a space and inviting them to join.

Yes, your decisions and actions will impact the other person, and the other person's decisions and actions will impact you. Yet, our primary role is to manage what is healthy for us individually in the relationship and to express it so that the other person knows who you are and what keeps your peace.

I am in love with the saying: "It's time to start being loyal to your own peace of mind." It's a powerful way to live, and life started making so much more sense to me when I started living by it. I even put that quote into my "to do list" so that I'd keep it in mind as I plan my days.

Part One: Get in the Driver's Seat

RULE #3
BOUNDARIES CAUSE EMOTIONS

I think of emotion as our complex internal software that runs the dashboard, sending us notifications when a boundary is working and when it needs adjustment. Since you are the only one who lives inside your body, it's primarily up to you to look for those internal green, yellow, and red notifications, then categorize them, and own them.

In short, emotions can be thought of as signals that help identify when a boundary is healthy or not.

The boundary is the input, and the signal is the output.

In other words, boundaries cause emotions.

I can't say that I have ever experienced emotions in any other order of events, and I've never seen anyone else experience them any other way, either. When we're using the word "boundaries" to refer to everything and anything that you can share in a human relationship, from conversation topics to places to time itself, it's easy to see how everything and anything can impact emotion.

Emotions are not a boundary; rather, they are the sign or signal of the health of a boundary in the same way that a red engine light on a car's dashboard is a sign or signal of the health of the engine.

Another way to think of the relationship between boundaries and emotions is the relationship between a recipe's ingredients and the healthiness of a dish – it is the ingredients of a recipe that produce its healthiness. Likewise, it's the boundaries "recipe" that produces the healthiness of an emotional state.

Your environments cause emotions. The time you spend or don't spend causes emotion. The topics you talk about or don't talk about make you feel a certain way. The things you do or don't do for the sake of the relationship cause feelings. It's the tools you use to communicate (or don't use) that can make or break an emotional bond. It's the influence of other people that can either empower or destroy.

When it comes to human relationships, yes, perhaps there are unknown or not-yet-known causes of emotions beyond the six boundaries; but if they are not yet known and immeasurable, then they do not (yet) have a dial on the Boundaries Dashboard. When it comes to emotional states, everything currently unknown and immeasurable belongs outside the realm of your personal control panel.

RULE #4
BOUNDARIES MEAN SURVIVAL

Consider a fish. In its natural state, a fish cannot survive for long beyond the boundary of an ocean or lake. They need a certain amount of water to flow into their gills to survive. All living things have a similar story about specific boundaries that keep them alive.

We, humans, can't breathe beyond roughly 20,000 feet above sea level. There's just not enough oxygen for our lungs to continue working.

The reason why boundaries mark life and death is that boundaries consist of dosages, and the dosage of everything that goes in and out of a living being determines its lifespan. Living beings die when they have too much or too little of anything.

Water is life-giving, but it can also be deadly if you're given too much or not enough. More than three or four days without water, and you'll die.

But if you have too much water, your sodium levels drop, and you can also die. The dose makes the poison, and it also makes the healing.

Yes, the most life-giving natural resource in the world can kill you. Immerse your entire body in water for too long, and you'll stop breathing. Drink too much, and you drown your internal organs.

In the natural world, the amount or volume – aka the dose – changes everything, and the same goes for the boundaries of human relationships.

The dose makes the poison.

You can destroy emotional bonds with some conversation topics. You can end a relationship over a misunderstood text message. You can wear each other out by spending too much time doing the same thing or by being in the same place without a break. You can feed each other's unhealthy habits and then both end up sick and exhausted.

So, when does a human relationship turn toxic? When you do not do or say what is life-giving and healthy for you in the relationship.

The dose also makes the healing.

You can find conversation topics that turn pain to laughter or compassion. You can choose a way to communicate that finally shows your true intention. You can reduce or increase amounts of time spent interacting until it's just right. You can pick environments or environmental elements that nourish the bond and connection you have. You can surround yourself with people who model what is healthy.

And with this book, you will take vital time to stop and identify boundaries that are life-giving and healthy for you in this relationship.

RULE #5
BOUNDARIES ARE RELATIONSHIP-SPECIFIC

The boundaries of your relationship with your medical doctor are most likely very different from the boundaries of your relationship with your romantic partner and different from your boundaries with your local grocery store clerk.

Boundaries are relationship-specific, meaning that your boundaries will change depending on which relationship you're talking about. Your boundaries in your relationship with your pet will be different from the boundaries of your relationship with your parents. Your relationship with your electronic devices will be different from the relationship you have with your coworkers.

But the scope of this book is human relationships, so my point here is that the human you interact with can be incredibly different from one to the next with different and even opposing needs.

Everyone's neurology is different; the way that different parts of your brain are connected can be significantly different for the other person. We each think, learn, and behave differently every day because the brain is like a big puzzle, and each piece represents a different skill or ability, like memory, language, and problem-solving. Some people might have certain pieces that are bigger or more connected than others.

Every person has their own different sets of unique needs. The same thing that makes one person feel ill makes another person feel euphoria. I've met people who feel like vomiting when they smell coriander (also called cilantro), while for me, it feels like a stimulant, and I can't get enough of it. And what about those who are allergic to it?

Same leaf, but potentially violently different reactions.

Part One: Get in the Driver's Seat

While we're all human, each person in your life has multiple strengths and weaknesses that differ vastly from one to the next. These strengths and weaknesses are due to biological, neurological, physical, intellectual, social, legal, and financial reasons.

People also have different roles to play in your life, and they have only agreed to the tasks of their specific role, nothing else. This, too, marks different boundaries for each person.

So, for each of the six boundaries, your specific dashboard settings will change depending on the uniqueness of the relationship. The same six general categories of boundaries will be in every human relationship, but they will look very different with each person, and each boundary will be healthy in different measures.

In this book, you're about to walk through the boundaries of one relationship in your life. These boundaries are like volume dials that you can turn up and down, and their settings determine your health in your relationship.

For each relationship in your life, you will turn most of those dials differently.

RULE #6
BOUNDARIES ARE WHAT YOU SAY YES TO

The statement "Boundaries are what you say no to" is a half-truth.

Rather, boundaries are equally what you say yes to and what you say no to. I may say yes to meeting a first date at a public location, and I may say no to meeting a first date inside their home. The yes and no are both boundaries.

Boundaries mark danger, but they also mark safety. They mark the end of bad things, and they mark the beginning of wonderful things. They mark where oppression ends and liberation begins.

A refugee's relationship with the country they are escaping and the new country they seek is a great example of how human relationship boundaries can be oppressive and restricting, or they can be liberating and full of opportunity.

Asylum seekers from countries around the world regularly risk their lives to escape their relationship with the governments and nations where they were born.

They are fleeing oppressive Topic boundaries, such as death for speaking out a political opinion; dangerous Territory boundaries, such as severely neglected infrastructure or undrinkable water; Treasure boundaries, particularly national spending that does not prioritize the health and welfare of its people; and other unhealthy boundaries in their relationship with their government.

They hope to find life-giving opportunities within the borders of a new country where they can feel safe to share topics under greater freedom of speech, where they can enjoy healthier and more reliable water systems and transportation, where there is more financial investment in citizens' health and welfare, and other healthy boundaries.

Being within the boundaries of their new country, refugees find liberation, more job opportunities, a higher chance for a longer and higher quality life, and so much more.

In their old country, refugees had boundaries. In their new country, they still have boundaries. The difference is that one collection of boundaries oppresses or takes life, and the other boundaries give life.

Consider a couple who move into the home of their parents or in-laws to save money to buy a home. The presence of parents might hamper or subtly oppress the couple's romantic connection. They don't feel free to talk about the same subjects. They don't feel free to be romantic or sexual because, well, they feel restricted with their parents around. They may not feel free to be as loud, fun, and playful.

However, the temporary shared environment with the parents and in-laws provides the couple financial liberation. This situation frees the couple from spending money on rent that will never be returned to them. Once the couple saves enough money, they move into their own home, and suddenly they feel a new sense of freedom financially, conversationally, and sexually.

Their new-found sexual freedom may even result in giving the parents and in-laws a grandchild. And everyone is happy.

As important as it is to identify what you say no to, it is equally important to identify what you say yes to, and both of these are equally decisions about boundaries that shape the health, peace, joy, and satisfaction of every human relationship.

Part One: Get in the Driver's Seat

CHAPTER 3

BOUNDARIES HEALTH CHECK

(31 minute read)

THE SATISFACTION SCALE

We now know that a sense of satisfaction in human relationships impacts physical health as much as, and potentially far more than, other factors previously considered to be most important, like diet and exercise. In this chapter, you'll put a number to your satisfaction in this relationship.

What I'm talking about here is a scaling question, where you give yourself a score as a measure of how you feel on a scale from 0 to 10 (zero to ten).

Medical doctors often use a self-reporting score for critical decisions; they will ask you a scaling question and use the score you give as medical data about your physical pain or mental health. Your score can help them figure out how serious a condition may be or a category of diagnosis.

Part One: Get in the Driver's Seat

For example, if you just came out of surgery, your doctor may ask you to give them a number from 0 to 10 for how much pain you feel, with zero meaning "no pain" and 10 meaning "the worst possible pain." This is widely known as the Numeric Rating Scale (NRS) in the medical world. Doctors make medical decisions with the help of your self-reported score.

If you go to the doctor for a mental health check and say you feel depressed, your doctor may ask you, on a scale from 0 through 10, how often you think negative thoughts, with zero meaning "never" and "10" meaning constantly. They make diagnosis decisions with the help of your self-reported score.

It's a subjective measurement, and yet it is taken seriously. That is because only you know how you truly feel inside. Since you're the only one in the world who lives inside of your body, the world depends on you to report how you feel the best you can.

So, when it comes to any human relationship, how do you report your sense of relationship health in a measurable, actionable way?

Allow me to introduce you to the Boundaries Health Check. The Boundaries Health Check uses a satisfaction scale that you can use for any human relationship. I'll be asking you to give me a number on a 0 to 10 (zero to ten) scale for the relationship you are working on with this book. A score of 10 means it couldn't get any better, and a score of 0 means it couldn't get any worse or that you detect no satisfaction at all within you.

It's like the medical world's pain-level questionnaire, but rather than a "10" meaning worst-case scenario and "0" meaning best, the Boundaries Health Check treats a "10" score as best-case scenario and "0" meaning worst. Measuring your health and satisfaction on a 10-point scale is similar to a "five-star rating" in marketing, where the more stars you score, the better the experience.

Some of you reading this may need help with putting a score to a feeling. You may wonder what a "10" feels like. If that's you, then simply take a few minutes to think of something in your own past (it can be recent or from many years ago) when you felt a great level of genuine satisfaction (great health, peace, or fulfillment), and consider that a score of 10.

If scaling questions are what doctors use when your medical and mental health depend on it, then I trust they're also a good idea when measuring your health in this relationship.

And in this next section, you will determine your score using the Boundaries Health Check.

Part One: Get in the Driver's Seat

THE FIRST MOST IMPORTANT FORMULA

There are ten scaling questions that make up the Boundaries Health Check, and together they add up to an overall score. Below is the formula.

There's no division or multiplication; it's just a matter of adding up the numbers from each of your ten scaling questions to get one total number:

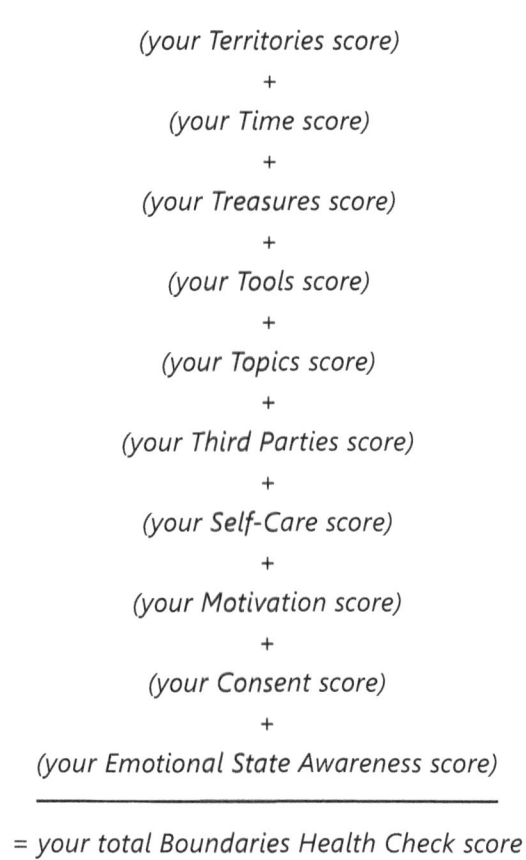

(your Territories score)
+
(your Time score)
+
(your Treasures score)
+
(your Tools score)
+
(your Topics score)
+
(your Third Parties score)
+
(your Self-Care score)
+
(your Motivation score)
+
(your Consent score)
+
(your Emotional State Awareness score)
―――――――――――――――――――
= *your total Boundaries Health Check score*

Each word in the formula beginning with the letter "T" represents one of the six boundaries. The other four parts represent the four dashboard lights on your Boundaries Dashboard.

The total you calculate from this formula represents the health and quality of this relationship for you. Since there are ten ratings in the formula and each has the highest possible score of 10, the highest overall Boundaries Health score you can receive for yourself is 100 points.

As you know from the research I mentioned earlier in this book, it looks like your sense of health and satisfaction in this relationship is going to impact your physical health and longevity, so this score is not something to be taken lightly.

Apparently, this score may be far more significant than the number of digits in your income, how much exercise you've had this week, or even how many fatty pieces of bacon you had for breakfast.

THE SECOND MOST IMPORTANT FORMULA

What about the other person? It takes two to tango, right?

If the other person reads this book and calculates a Boundaries Health Check score for themself in their relationship with you, then you can add their score to yours for a total Relationship Health score.

your total Boundaries Health Check score
\+
their total Boundaries Health Check score
_____
= *your total Relationship Health score*

Part One: Get in the Driver's Seat

In your personal Boundaries Health Check score, the highest number you can each score is 100, so if you add both of those scores, the highest total Relationship Health score equals 200.

A Relationship Health score between 180 and 200 falls into the highest category of the most healthy, flourishing, and powerful human relationships you can have.

However, this book is about you and your health. So, what is most essential right now is for you to personally take inventory of your own side of the relationship, which includes the six dials that you personally control, the way you make your decisions in this relationship, and the way you feel.

By the end of this book, you may see so much improvement in the relationship that you don't feel a need to seek out a Relationship Health score. However, inspiring the other person to read this book and calculate their Boundaries Health Check score could perhaps start the healthiest relationship conversation you've ever had.

But first things first. This is all about your own personal dashboard. And only you can do this work.

Ta-da! Now I have presented to you the first and only mathematical formula in the world to quantify and measure all aspects of a human relationship in a standardized way, for you individually and for both of you as a whole. I say it's "standardized" because the six boundaries apply to every human relationship on Earth, and so that means we can systematically rely on the same Boundaries Health Check scoring system no matter who it is.

Now you're probably wondering: "OK, when and how do I get my Boundaries Health Check score?" Good question! Read on.

YOUR BOUNDARIES HEALTH CHECK

Do you remember the Instruction Manual section at the beginning of this book? I hope you read it and that you now have a Dashboard Diary.

If so, it's time to grab your Dashboard Diary so you can complete the first exercise. Remember that your Dashboard Diary is pivotal if you want to make this book work for you and see significant results. I'll call it your "Diary" from this point.

Open your Diary, whether it's a physical or digital notebook, and write (or type) today's date at the top of the page and the title: Boundaries Health Check.

Underneath the date and title, the next thing to write in your Diary is the heading "Time Frame." Next to Time Frame, write the number of days, months, or years that you would like to look back on as you evaluate this relationship. You'll use this same time frame to answer each of the ten Boundaries Health Check questions.

Have you known this person for more than one year? If this is your first time completing the Boundaries Health Check for this relationship and you have known this person for more than one year, then I suggest you stick with evaluating only this past year since this is a reasonable amount of time for people to show new patterns.

If you choose to evaluate the past year, then write down "Time Frame: one year." And then, for each question, you'll be evaluating only the past 365 days of this relationship.

One year is also good for an evaluation because you will likely remember your feelings better over the past year vs. over the past five or more years.

Have you known this person for less than one year? Then write down "Time Frame: [number of months, weeks, or days]." I like the idea of even using the Boundaries Health Check when you've just met someone on a dating app or met them for the first time in a business meeting. No time is too soon to start evaluating the health of this relationship. As a matter of fact, the sooner the better; and the more frequently you do a Health Check, the better your data will be.

After you complete the Boundaries Health Check for the first time for this relationship, you will use much shorter time frames for all future Boundaries Health Checks in this relationship; that might be one day, one week, or at the very most, one month.

For the most impactful human relationships in your life, I recommend that you complete a Boundaries Health Check daily (or weekly at the very least) in order to have a solid history to look at and to help you understand what it takes to get lights glowing green on your dashboard; I am developing an app for that, so you can easily look at all your data over time, see average scores calculated for you, and make more powerful and informed decisions based on them. The app is in the works as I type this paragraph.

No matter the time frame you choose, you're likely to not remember every single feeling and every event exactly, unless your memory has an extremely unusual capacity. So, the time frames you choose will only ever represent estimations, not exact calculations.

A doctor doesn't need you to be precise about a pain level of 8.4 or 9.6 to determine that the pain is severe; the doctor only needs an estimate. So, don't worry about faultless precision and perfect accuracy. Your patterns of honest Boundaries Health Check scores will reveal themselves over time and give you the general and reliable information you need.

So, you've written down the time frame? Good. Then let's continue.

For answers to make sense, remember to use the same time frame for each question. In other words, if you wrote down one year, then answer every question according to the past year of your experience with that person. If you just met the person and wrote down one day, then base every answer on the 24 hours of your experience with that person.

The final thing to keep in mind as you answer each of the ten questions is this: in this Boundaries Health Check, you are measuring your own personal sense of health and satisfaction in this relationship. So, when you give a score, base it only on your own thoughts about the relationship, your decisions, your actions, and your feelings in the relationship – not the other person's thoughts, decisions, actions, and feelings about the relationship. Their feelings may impact yours, but your feelings are what we are measuring. You are responsible for reporting your own internal experiences. As long as you remember that, then there are no wrong answers.

I'll guide you through each question with brief examples.

As an extra, I've also included a *"TIP"* with each question to help you understand that each Boundaries Health Check question can also be used to check your relationship with yourself. In other words, at any time, you can return to this same list of questions to check the health of your boundaries in your relationship with you.

Ready to track the health of your boundaries? Let's go.

1. Time

On the page in your Diary where you started your Boundaries Health Check, write the number "1" and the word "Time" next to it.

The Time boundary includes the time you spend together in person, as well as the time you spend interacting in any way, shape, or form.

Part One: Get in the Driver's Seat

There are three aspects to your Time boundary – length of time, the frequency you spend it, and the timing as to when you choose to do or say something. For example, you may spend an hour together (this is the length of time), and you might spend that hour together once a week (this is the frequency), but when you do spend that time, you might choose to do it after or right before another event (this is the "when" or timing).

You might not feel satisfied with the length of time or the frequency; you may want more, or you may want less. Or maybe it's the perfect amount of time and the perfect frequency. You might feel satisfied as to when it happens, or you may need it to happen in a different order on your schedule.

> **Using the 0 to 10 satisfaction scale, how satisfied do you feel about the length of time that you spend, the frequency of that time, and the timing? Come up with one total score that covers your satisfaction with those elements of time.**

So, what's your score?

TIP: When doing a Boundaries Health Check for your relationship with yourself, how satisfied do you feel with how much time you spend working on your personal needs, your wishes, and your personal growth? This question looks at the intentional time you make to take care of yourself in all areas of life. How satisfied do you feel with the time that you dedicate to observing and then taking action on nourishing your own emotional, mental, neurological, physical, biological, and financial health?

2. Topics

Write the number "2" and the word "Topics" next to it. This will be the second score you write down.

Take about one minute or so to think about topics that you feel comfortable bringing up in conversations with the other person.

Did you take some time to think about it? Cool. Now, in contrast, take a minute to think about any topics that you intentionally don't talk about.

You may be satisfied because you freely share topics that matter to both of you. Perhaps your conversation topics are perfect as is.

You may feel unsatisfied because you have the desire to talk about specific subjects but feel as though you can't or shouldn't.

> **Using the 0 to 10 satisfaction scale, how satisfied do you feel about the topics of conversation that you initiate in the relationship and the ones that you refrain from? Write down one total score.**

TIP: When doing a Boundaries Health Check for your relationship with yourself, all the above applies, but the difference is that you're evaluating topics you intentionally think about or topics of inner "conversation" you have with yourself. For example, common internal conversations we have are "Do I like this or not?" or "What do I want?" or "What's the best option for me?" A common phrase people use is "If I'm honest with myself," and this phrase refers directly to the internal dialogue we have with our consciousness, our feelings, our body, and our thoughts. Consider your internal conversation and how satisfied you feel about the topics that you intentionally think about or ignore.

Part One: Get in the Driver's Seat

3. TREASURES

Write the number "3" and the word "Treasures" next to it. This will be the third score you write down.

This boundary includes all forms of investment that you personally put into the relationship – mental, physical, emotional, material, and financial energy. Anything from a small mundane obligation or responsibility to favors, acts of service, trading or swapping things, paying one another for products or services, and anything you do for the other person or for the sake of maintaining the relationship.

In a romantic relationship, this includes things you do for and with the other person on every level including sexual things you do and don't do. In a family relationship, this includes things you do for and with the other person on every level including the money you lend or give. In a professional relationship, this includes things you do for and with the other person on every level including doing what you agreed to do when you signed up for the job.

Let me make a note here that for this score, we're looking at the *energy* you invest, not the time. Time is its own boundary. So, think of every possible form of energy you invest – mental, physical, emotional, material, and financial.

Maybe you're unsatisfied to some degree because you feel you'd like to invest less in some areas and invest more in other areas instead.

Maybe you feel satisfied because you stopped investing where it was not helping.

> **Using the 0 to 10 satisfaction scale, how satisfied do you feel about the things you do (or don't do) for the other person and for the sake of the relationship?**

TIP: When doing a Boundaries Health Check for your relationship with yourself, all the above applies; the kinds of investment you put into your relationship with you include mental, physical, emotional, material, and financial energy to take care of you and to make the relationship with yourself a healthy one. A few examples of investing in yourself include taking yourself out to eat or experimenting with a new recipe at home that you wanted to try, taking yourself outside to sit in the sun, or motivating yourself to do chores. It can be journaling, exercising, or just making that doctor appointment. Or maybe it means keeping track of personal fitness goals, investing your money more wisely, or even taking time to plan out your day's, week's, year's, or lifetime goals in a to-do list.

4. TOOLS

Write the number "4" and the word "Tools" next to it. This will be the fourth score you write down.

Anything and everything that you could use to share thoughts, emotions, and ideas with the other person is a communication tool, and that is what this boundary is about.

There are so many possible communication tools that you can use in this relationship and here I've split them into two types.

First, *sending* tools. Think of anything you can use to say something to the other person. This is a sending tool. Think about phone calls you make, letters you write, social media posts you create, and (the most basic method) the words you speak. In each of these, you are delivering or sending a message to the other person.

The second type of tool is the *receiving* tool. Think of all the ways that the other person communicates with you, and the tools that you use to receive that communication. Think about phone calls you answer, emails you open, social media posts you're tagged in, and the words you hear directly from the other person's mouth. In each of these, you

Part One: Get in the Driver's Seat

are receiving a message from the other person.

Call blocking, airplane mode, accepting a friend request, and any kind of tool, button, or device that controls access to you is also a receiving tool.

Both sending and receiving tools can be broken down again into two types – verbal and nonverbal communication – but I'll talk more about those details later in this book.

So, when it comes to the communication tools you're using, how satisfied do you feel? Maybe you'd prefer more phone calls and more texts, or maybe you'd prefer fewer. Maybe you would be happier if you tried a new way of communicating – new sending or receiving tools.

Maybe your communication tools are working perfectly for you.

It's scoring time!

> **Using the 0 to 10 satisfaction scale, how satisfied do you feel about the communication tools you use with the other person? Come up with one score for both types – sending and receiving.**

TIP: When doing a Boundaries Health Check for your relationship with yourself, all the above applies. Communication tools that you use with yourself can include anything that helps you stop and recognize your own thoughts and feelings, or they can include anything that you use to manage your needs, wishes, and/or promises to yourself.

For example, maybe you use artificial intelligence (AI) technology to help yourself think through or research a problem. Maybe you keep a diary to track to your thoughts, wishes, or ideas. Maybe you keep a photo gallery of screenshots that remind you of your wins. Maybe you use a physical whiteboard, task list, or notebook to help you keep track of the promises you made to yourself. Maybe you use smart phone apps and notifications to track your progress in some area of self-care. Another communication tool may be written or recorded poetry or music that you use to express yourself. Think of any tool that impacts, helps, or hinders your inner "self-talk" throughout the day.

As a personal example, I remember doing my first podcast season because I had discovered that the act of speaking alone into a microphone gave me a great chance to hear myself think out loud, know myself in a deeper way, and have more fun with my own life. The podcast was a communication tool in my relationship with myself.

5. Territories

Write the number "5" and the word "Territories" next to it. This will be the fifth score you write down.

Think about all the physical spaces where you spend time together. And not just the places themselves, but everything about those spaces such as the presence of other people and your overall sensory experience, as well as the four walls and objects within them. This includes even the subtle mood shifters like noise, sounds, music, lighting, air quality, visual elements, design, and smells. Think of everything and everyone that influences the environments you share.

That's the first kind of territory boundary.

The second kind is the physical proximity between you and the other person. Think about the physical distance or physical closeness you place between each other, which I like to call body boundaries. Body boundaries include how physically close you allow yourself to be, how closely you sit or stand, or how you use the material space between you. Your use of this space can impact the relationship in a negative or positive way.

In a professional relationship at the office, maybe you sit too close for comfort and the other person's chewing of potato chips drives you nuts. Or maybe you sit too far away from the people you need, and it slows down your work.

In a personal relationship, maybe you're the partner who stopped snuggling up close to the other person when watching movies; now you watch from a separate couch like a stranger at a movie theater. Maybe you're satisfied with that, and maybe you're not.

So, when you think of your Territories boundary score, think of both kinds of territories – the physical spaces and environments you share as well as body boundaries.

Maybe you'd prefer to add a territory. Maybe you'd prefer to avoid one. Maybe you'd prefer to modify an existing territory. Maybe you're perfectly satisfied.

> **Using the 0 to 10 satisfaction scale, how satisfied do you feel about the kinds of territories you share with the other person in the relationship?**

TIP: When doing a Boundaries Health Check for your relationship with yourself, think about the physical places and spaces you create or manage for yourself (not anyone else). Think about small or large adjustments and permanent or temporary changes to your environment that you make for your own health, desires, and needs. Body boundaries matter in your relationship with yourself, too, because they refer to what physical things you control or allow in the space around your body, such as what surrounds you as you sleep, work, eat, rest, exercise, and play.

6. THIRD PARTIES

Write the number "6" and the words "Third Parties" next to it. This will be the sixth score you write down.

You are reading this book because of the personal or professional relationship you have with the other person. However, other human relationships impact this one.

The Third Parties boundary refers to any human relationships that you believe influence your personal feelings, ideas, thoughts, beliefs, or behaviors about this specific relationship. A third party can be a group or an individual.

A third party's influence might be enlightening, nurturing, neutral, dimming, or worst case, destructive in some way toward your sense of joy, peace, health, and satisfaction about this relationship.

If there are a few influential people or groups, combine all those relationships into one overall score.

> **Using the 0 to 10 satisfaction scale, how satisfied do you feel about how that (or those) human relationship(s) impacts this one?**

TIP: When doing a Boundaries Health Check for your relationship with yourself, all of the above applies. Think of any human relationship in your life that you notice is directly impacting your relationship with yourself. Some third parties can help us have more self-compassion, motivation, or inner peace, while others might leave us feeling empty, unmotivated, or unhappy with ourselves.

Part One: Get in the Driver's Seat

7. SELF-CARE

Write the number "7" and the word "Self-Care" next to it. This will be the seventh score you write down. Using the 0 to 10 satisfaction scale, how true is the following statement for you?

> **"I feel satisfied with the way I take care of myself emotionally, physically, mentally, and financially, and I am happy with the impact that my self-care has on the relationship."**

A score of 0 means it's completely false, and a score of 10 means it's completely true. In one overall score, combine your satisfaction with your level of self-care and your satisfaction with how your self-care impacts your relationship with the other person.

TIP: When doing a Boundaries Health Check for your relationship with yourself, this question is like an umbrella question that covers your satisfaction with how you take care of yourself overall – physically, medically, emotionally, psychologically, financially, sexually, and all possible categories of self-care that matter to you.

8. MOTIVATORS

Your personal values motivate you. They are what keep you moving and looking forward to various things in life. So instead of the word "values," I often call them your "motivators." I use the words "values" and "motivators" interchangeably.

Write the number "8" and the word "Motivators" next to it. This will be the eighth score you write down. Using the 0 to 10 satisfaction scale, how true is the following statement for you?

Chapter 3: Boundaries Health Check

> **"I feel satisfied with how often I make decisions in this relationship that align with my personal values or motivators."**

A score of 0 means it's completely false, and a score of 10 means it's completely true.

TIP: When doing a Boundaries Health Check for your relationship with yourself, think about your satisfaction with how you make decisions for yourself and your life. Consider whether you make decisions based on your own personal motivators and values or whether you based them on someone else's motivators and values. Maybe you base your personal decisions on what someone told you that you "should do" when it's not authentic to you, and you're unsatisfied with that. Maybe you make personal decisions in a way that motivates you regardless of whose values they are and you're happy with that.

9. CONSENT

Write the number "9" and the word "Consent" next to it. This will be the ninth score you write down. Using the 0 to 10 satisfaction scale, how true is the following statement for you?

> **"When it comes to decisions in this relationship, I feel satisfied with how often I seek consent from the other person and how often I express whether or not I consent."**

Give one score that covers both your expression of consent and seeking it from the other person.

TIP: When doing a Boundaries Health Check for your relationship with yourself, think about how often you may or may not make decisions for yourself wholeheartedly. A half-hearted decision is one where you don't fully agree with your

boundariescheck.com | 67

own decision because it conflicts with something you believe, feel, value, or trust. Perhaps you made a decision in your mind, but your heart firmly disagrees. Think about how often you make decisions for yourself with or without your own full consent, then give a score for how satisfied you feel about that.

10. Emotional State

Write the number "10" and the phrase "Emotional State" next to it. This will be the tenth and final score you write down. Using the 0 to 10 satisfaction scale, how true is the following statement for you?

> "Overall, I feel satisfied with the emotions I experience in this relationship."

Think about the period of time that you wrote down at the beginning of this Boundaries Health Check. In that period of time, overall, how satisfied do you feel about your emotional state in this relationship? Maybe it feels mostly volatile. Maybe it feels mostly peaceful. Maybe it feels mostly joyous and fulfilling. Pick a score that measures the truthfulness of the above statement in that time.

TIP: When doing a Boundaries Health Check for your relationship with yourself, remember that you're measuring your emotional state in the context of your relationship with you. Consider the degrees of honesty, confidence, and genuine compassion you feel toward yourself. So, how true is the above statement?

YOUR SCORE

So now, you can add up all ten scores to find out your overall Boundaries Health Check score and status. Remember that the highest overall

Boundaries Health score you can receive for yourself is 100 points.

Now at the bottom of the page, write the words "My Boundaries Health Score," add up all ten numbers, and write your total score beside it.

Remember that each person in a human relationship has their own dashboard, and this score represents your side of the relationship.

If your score falls between 80 and 100, congratulations on maintaining what appears to be a healthy and fully functioning dashboard with steady green lights. A score between 50 and 79 points means your yellow lights are flashing, and this points to various levels of risk, while a score of 49 or below points to what needs immediate attention with flashing red lights.

It's important to keep this number as a record so that you can complete the Boundaries Health Check again to identify patterns over time and track your progress.

If you're unhappy with the Boundaries Health score that you just completed in Part One of this book, that's exactly why you're here right now reading this. It's going to change. However, if your score does look great, good job! This book will make it even better.

If this is your first time doing the Boundaries Health Check, then Part Two and Part Three of this book will give you a deeper understanding of each question you answered so that next time you go through it, you'll have even more precise metrics.

Just as a car mechanic's equipment requires calibration and sensitivity (for example, diagnostic equipment and alignment machines), Parts Two and Three of this book will give you the calibration and sensitivity to come up with a more comprehensive score for each question of the Boundaries Health Check.

Part One: Get in the Driver's Seat

By the end of those two Parts, you'll better understand why lights are flashing green, yellow, or red for you on the dashboard of this relationship.

After you complete this book, download the "Boundaries Health Check" app to your smart phone so that you don't have to do any calculations by hand or in separate notes. The app keeps a historical record of your scores for you, calculates the average, and displays the most current red, yellow, or green status of each relationship that you track. Because the app is so much quicker than doing it manually, this means you can do a Boundaries Health Check far more frequently for your key relationships, including the one you have with yourself.

The more checks, the more awareness, the more accuracy, the better decision-making.

Daily Boundaries Health Checks in the app are a great idea for your relationship with yourself, to get you in top form for all other human relationships. Then, daily or weekly checks for your next most-influential human relationship could be the most powerful thing you do in your life.

For iPhone and iPad users, search for "Boundaries Health Check" in Apple's App Store. And for Android devices, just head over to the Google Play Store and do the same. Then simply tap "Install" to start taking control of your personal boundaries.

If you don't have access to an app store, then come back to this book to do the 10-question Boundaries Health Check on a regular basis – daily, weekly, or monthly. Whether it's through the app or this book, the more often you complete a Boundaries Health Check, the more information you'll have to make better decisions. The more data you collect, the more confidence you will have about the direction you're driving on the road of this relationship.

Note: As a little bit of future-proofing, since who knows what technology we'll all be using in a few years, I'll add here the gentle note to simply search for "Boundaries Health Check" to find the latest ways to track and manage your boundaries.

DEEPER DIAGNOSTICS

If I go to the doctor for a regular medical test and the results come back, but the doctor needs more information to get deeper insights, they'll often do an array of more specific or complex tests to get a more accurate status of my health.

For example, a doctor might do a general "complete blood count," or "CBC" as they call it, to check out my blood cells. Then, based on those results, they may perform a second level of testing to look at the shape and structure of those cells.

That's like the relationship between the 10 questions in the Boundaries Health Check and the exercises that you're about to discover in the next several chapters. The 10-question Boundaries Health Check gives you an overall status, and going through the following chapters and exercises will give you the shape and structure behind your score.

In other words, the rest of this book intends to help you identify more specific causes for the way you feel and think in this relationship and then, most importantly, help you identify new directions to take in the relationship that will shift and move your thoughts and feelings to a new level.

THE BOUNDARY DIALS

Every day, throughout the entire day, you make boundary decisions in your relationship with others and also in your relationship with yourself. The "dials" on the Boundaries Dashboard serve as a metaphor for these decisions you make, and the influence and consequence of those six boundary dials will determine what direction you head and which destinations you reach in your life.

Like a volume dial, you can increase a boundary, as if turning up the volume; you can decrease a boundary, as if turning down the volume; and you can maintain a boundary, as if keeping the volume at its current level.

"Turning down" means to reduce or remove something. Examples of turning down the dial might include cutting out certain places you go, reducing the amount of time invested in something, or removing anything that's hindering you from a more important goal.

"Keeping at the same level" means to support, maintain, or repeat. Examples of keeping the dial set might include maintaining a clean home, keeping technology running smoothly, maintaining a certain income or cashflow, maintaining physical fitness, or repeating a healthy habit of any kind.

"Turning up" means to add, grow, obtain, create, or achieve something. It can also refer to replacing something you stopped doing with something brand new, experimental, or different. On a stereo speaker, you turn up the volume dial to hear more detail, to increase quality, and to feel something you weren't feeling at lower volume levels.

Whether it's your relationship with yourself or someone else, examples of "turning up the dial" might include:

- Experimenting with a new or improved way of investing your energy or your money (Treasures boundary).
- Joining a new organization or community (Third Parties boundary).
- Intentionally aiming for new or different subjects to reflect on,

consider, or think about (Topics boundary).
- Spending a new frequency of time (Time boundary).
- Living in, working in, or visiting a new place (Territories boundary).
- Using new communication tools and technologies to remember things that are important to you or to track your progress on a goal (Tools boundary).

All of these adjustments can make or break your overall sense of peace, joy, happiness, health, and satisfaction in the relationship and can either propel you toward or repel you from the direction you're intending for your life and relationship.

So far, I've given you a picture of each of the six categories of boundaries as a dial, and each dial has an amount or quantity of the boundary it represents; for example, in your relationship with the other person, your Tools dial may include five communication tools that you currently use, but you would like to stop using one (turn down the dial to decrease quantity) and then start using a new one (turn up the dial to increase quantity).

As another example, imagine that you have 10 or 20 topics that you typically talk about with the other person, but you want to add one new topic to deepen the relationship; that's equivalent to turning up the dial to increase the number of Topics.

For those who might think more deeply into the metaphor, I could present you with a more technologically sophisticated version of the six boundaries dials, where each of your dials have an additional feature. This new feature allows you to press the center of each dial like a button, so that you can turn up or turn down the volume for subcategories of each boundary. For example, imagine "pressing in" the center of the Topics dial, and each time you press it in, you can adjust the number of subcategories of topics that you share and don't share in this relationship.

Yes, we can go very deep into this metaphor with sophisticated engineering, but I prefer to keep it more simple than that throughout this book.

ONE DECISION AT A TIME

Did you know that the human brain can only make one decision at a time? This means that you're never going to make more than one boundary decision in the same moment. Never.

The human body runs 11 systems simultaneously, including about 37 trillion moving cells and a heart that pumps roughly 5 liters of blood each minute, and despite all of that happening at the same time, research shows that the human brain works very differently when it comes to decision-making.

Studies show that we humans might be making between 30,000 to 50,000 decisions a day. The rapid switching between thoughts can give the illusion of multiple decisions at once, but in fact, the human brain has been found to only make one decision at a time and in sequential order. Sequential is an important word here.

I share all of this so that you understand that decisions are made sequentially, and when it comes to your boundary dials, you will only ever turn one dial at a time.

And each decision is like a domino, impacting all of the others.

And there is a cumulative effect over time, as they lead you into different places in life.

So how do you prioritize the multitude of decision-making activities in the mind? Here's how: establish one or more end-goals and adjust your boundary dials to make those the priority.

That's how the brain works, and that's how I work with you as your coach throughout this book. You have six dials and multitudes of adjustments you already make throughout the day, but in The Boundaries Health Check, we're focusing on which boundary decisions will make your dashboard lights glow green and will best support you as you drive toward your destinations in the relationship.

There might be thousands of small boundary decisions we make all day every day, but there are also the long-term big visions for our lives that those small decisions either drive us toward or repel us from.

Perhaps you haven't yet taken the reigns of your personal control panel yet. Maybe others are turning your dials for you. When we're born into this world, all of our decisions are made for us by someone else, until, one-by-one, we start making them ourselves.

Throughout this book, you will realize a long list of different decisions you could be making in this relationship, but I am going to bring you through a process that will narrow your boundary decisions into a clear and actionable sequence of decision and action – one at a time – that are all intended to move you toward a specific vision and direction for your life and relationship.

By Part Five of this book, titled "Plan Your Next Stop," you will have put all of your potential boundary decisions into order of priority so that you can take your first and most important next step of action.

You are now almost at the end of Part One. Together over the next five parts of this book, we will walk through the dashboard lights in greater detail (Part Two), take a full inventory of your boundaries (Part Three), identify specific directions you'd like to go in this relationship (Part Four), and lastly, go through the process to identify your very next small step of action along with a repeatable process for you to continue until you reach your intended destinations (Part Five).

Everything is one step at a time and ordered sequentially, because that's how your brain works.

BE LIKE THE MULTIBILLION-DOLLAR BUSINESSES

I've worked in corporate communications for a few multibillion-dollar organizations and multimillion-dollar companies in America and Australia, and I have seen how they make decisions. They are no different than you in two ways.

First, just like you, they have the competing work of managing their relationships with themselves (internal business) and managing their relationships with people outside of themselves (external business).

Second, they have the same six boundary dials that determine whether or not they reach their vision, and they have the same three choices on how to turn each of those dials.

Their three choices for each dial are the same as yours: keeping the current volume, turning down the volume, and turning up the volume. The more corporate way to say it is that companies can:

- Stay on top of "business as usual" tasks such as taxes, complying with labor laws, and maintaining security, all of which are examples of simply keeping the dial set at its current volume.
- Cut back on unprofitable activities through restructuring or budgeting, which is an example of turning down the volume.

- Grow and improve in some area through funding "projects" such as the rolling out of improved technology, replacing old strategies with revised ones, or providing a new service, which are examples of turning up the volume.

If you want to be as fruitful as a multibillion-dollar organization, then continue to follow the process in this book. First, identify where you are now (through the Boundaries Health Check), then get clarity on your vision for the future (through a relationship roadmap, as you will do in future chapters), and finally, take motivated action (a unique coaching process I take you through in the later parts of this book).

I've seen it first-hand; the human relationships that an organization develops are based on the organization's vision – the goals or destinations that they have chosen and documented for themselves. And once they've documented it, they turn the dials in their internal and external human relationships to make it happen.

Yes, they can change if or when circumstances change. Yes, political or economic events sometimes trigger a review or revision. However, the documentation exists for direction, profit, and growth to happen.

Whether you're a multibillion-dollar organization or an individual, you have a direction you're heading, and you have dials to turn up, turn down, or maintain in every human relationship, starting with the relationship with yourself. Those are the three kinds of decisions that bring you to your destinations, whether you're an individual or a multi-national organization.

And those decisions become real once they are written down and you are accountable to them. It's a process, and I'm taking your hand and walking you through it.

PART TWO

CHECK THE LIGHTS

Part Two: Check the Lights

CHAPTER 4

INTRO TO THE FOUR DASHBOARD LIGHTS

(8 minute read)

THEIR PURPOSE

The Boundaries Dashboard™ is a tool that gives you 100% ownership of your health and happiness in this relationship, and it has two basic sections – your dashboard lights that tell you something is working (or isn't working) and six dials to fix what's not working or enhance what's working well.

Just as you keep the car on the road by maintaining continual awareness of a car's dashboard every time you drive, you equally keep your metaphorical car on the road of this relationship by maintaining a continual awareness of the Boundaries Dashboard – it's four lights and six dials.

Your dashboard lights tell you when something's going wrong or right for you. Just as the driver of a physical car has the unconscious habit of glancing at their dashboard, my hope is for it to become an unconscious

boundariescheck.com | 81

habit for you to glance at your dashboard throughout every interaction in this relationship.

Ignoring the four lights on the Boundaries Dashboard is like driving a car while ignoring that the fuel and oil are dangerously low. At some point, you'll have a sudden, unexpected breakdown and possibly an irreversibly tragic accident.

Sometimes it's just easier to turn up the music loudly and ignore the warnings on the dashboard, but maybe that's why you need this book.

Through your nervous system, your brain and body are constantly communicating messages for you to make decisions and take action in this relationship. I'm not a neurologist, but they tell us that there are trillions of nerves in your body. Nerves are sending signals all day long. In my theory of the Boundaries Dashboard, these signals split into four categories that I call the four dashboard lights.

At any moment, any or all four lights can turn one of three colors – healthy signals turn your dashboard light green, unhealthy signals turn it red, and anything in between turns it yellow. In other words, to keep it easy and simple, my theory takes every kind of message that your emotions, thoughts, brain, and nervous system are sending, and puts them into one of three overarching categories.

The concept of dashboard lights is kept simple so that it can make it easier to identify complex physical, mental, and emotional states.

In a car, dashboard lights turn on to tell you the health of the car – when your fuel is low, oil is running out, the battery needs charging, and when temperatures may be too high or too low.

Picture those luminescent symbols on a car's dashboard – a little oil can icon, a fuel spout, a battery, a temperature gauge. Depending on what part of the world you live in, some people refer to this part of a car as dashboard lights, instrument panel, warning lights, or where I grew up in America, we say indicator lights.

Depending on the year, make, and model of car, these lights can flash on and off or they may stay lit. They might light up green for a moment to indicate all is well, yellow to indicate a warning, or flash red to indicate danger.

It's the same on your Boundaries Dashboard, except unlike the complexity of a physical car, you have only four dashboard lights to manage.

Each of your four dashboard lights turns red, yellow, or green to make you aware of what's going on inside of you – something good, a warning, or an emergency. I said it above but it's worth repeating: If a light turns green, it's a sign of health. If a light turns either yellow or red, it's time to adjust any of the six boundaries until the light turns green again.

Your dashboard lights are not adjustable. You don't turn them up or down. They strictly serve as signals from your mind, body, or emotions telling you when to take action on one or more of the six boundaries.

Your Boundaries Dashboard's lights are a measurable way to maintain and track self-awareness in this relationship. You can keep score of how you feel and, over time, observe patterns.

The word "aware" comes from the Old English word "gewær" which means watchful or vigilant. The lights on the dashboard of this relationship empower your watchfulness and vigilance over what's really going on within you.

Part Two: Check the Lights

THEIR NAMES

Please allow me to formally introduce you to the names of your precious dashboard's display lights. They've been flashing the entire time in this relationship, but now's the time to get to know them.

As I said in the introduction of this book, each of you is the driver of your own car on the road of this relationship, and each of you has your own dashboard to manage. The dashboard in your car tells you what you personally need in the relationship, and the dashboard in the other car tells the other person what they need. You both have the same four lights, but they often flash different colors at different times.

Fuel is a metaphor for your unique values, or what I call your "motivators." When we make decisions without knowing our motivators, we can feel empty and powerless with a sense of losing ourselves. Motivators are what fill you up and move you in life and human relationships. To be more specific, the fuel light signals when you're making decisions that are true to you and that align with what uniquely motivates you. You will learn to identify your personal motivators in this book.

We might often make decisions from a place of fear, tradition, from someone else's conflicting values, or even based on assumptions about what others expect from us. However, when we know and name those things that truly motivate us and then intentionally integrate them into our decision-making, we feel more empowered, wholehearted, and sincere with the other person because we are being ourselves.

The battery light is a metaphor for mutual consent and agreement. When a person unwillingly does something in a relationship, it's like a car with a dying battery – difficult to start, interior and exterior lights start to dim, power seats and accessories stop working faithfully, and of course there's stalling. Wholehearted willingness, agreement, or simply "consent", charges up a human relationship with a sense of empowerment and respect.

The battery light tells you how much "charge" there is in the relationship. Without consent, a person can feel like they're being towed along the road of the relationship by the other person, without any say in decisions. This dashboard light helps you know if your voice is heard and whether you hear the voice of the other person in this relationship.

The oil light tells you when to fill or refresh your engine's oil. In the same way that engine oil has to be clean and there must be enough of it to keep the car running, it's the same with self-care in this relationship. Your degree of physical, mental, and emotional self-care keeps you up and running in this relationship. The oil light lets you know how your self-care might be impacting the health, satisfaction, joy, and peace that you experience in your relationship with the other person.

A car's temperature light indicates the engine's temperature range. When the engine is too cold, it doesn't run efficiently, and when it's too hot, there's risk of serious damage. Likewise, in this relationship, the temperature light indicates the range of your emotional state. The phrase "emotional state" refers to everything you feel in your nervous system, your physiological response, and anything else you sense that is associated with the emotion. The temperature light on your Boundaries Dashboard helps you maintain awareness of both your healthy and dangerous emotional "temperature" ranges.

While your Boundaries Health Check gave you an overall score, the next chapters in this book help you dive deeper into each of the ten scores you gave. It's like a 100-point inspection from the mechanic versus a basic 10-point inspection. The basic one gives you a safe overall reading, and the detailed investigation makes you able to name specific causes of concern or celebration.

Part Two: Check the Lights

HOW I FEEL, THINK, AND DECIDE

As you might remember from earlier in this book, I mentioned that there are two sections to your dashboard. They are the four lights that signal when something's going wrong or right, and the other section has the six dials (boundaries) that you turn up and down to make the relationship better.

Those four lights serve two functions.

The first two lights tell you how you feel and think, and those are the temperature light (emotional state) and oil light (self-care). In the metaphorical dashboard of this relationship, picture the words "How I feel and think" above these two lights.

The other two lights tell you how you're making decisions, and those are the fuel light (Motivators) and battery light (Consent). In the metaphorical dashboard of this relationship, picture the words: "How I decide," above these two lights.

So how do I know when a light turns red, yellow, or green? In the exercises over the next few chapters, you'll find out how to convert how you feel, think, and decide into scores, and these scores will let you know the color of your lights.

In the world of professional coaching, we typically use a 10-point scoring system to understand how a client feels, thinks, and decides. We consider scores of 8 and above to signal greatness or optimum health. Scores of 7 through 5 typically signal mediocrity or being at risk, and scores of 4 or below can indicate danger or a generally terrible state. In the coming chapters, I've carried over these same three ranges into the formulas and calculations that determine the color of each of your dashboard lights.

YOUR MENTAL AND EMOTIONAL BANK ACCOUNT BALANCE

Former American Football player and motivational speaker Trent Shelton overcame drug addiction, homelessness, and prison, and then transformed himself into an inspirational influencer to millions of fans on social media. So how did he make such a massive shift in his life? In a personal video he shared on social media, he explained it like this: "My life changed when I stopped being afraid to lose people who did nothing for my life. You got to stop being afraid to lose people who do nothing but bring pain to your life and take your peace."

When Trent refers to people who "did nothing for my life," the implication is that people either add to your life in some way or they subtract from it. The people that only subtracted from his life were holding him back from peace, recovery, and transformation. Some people, intentionally or unintentionally, subtract from your peace. Some leave you bankrupt of peace.

It's as if every human relationship has a net total amount of life and peace that it gives and takes at the end of each day. At the end of each day, we arrive at a mental and emotional bank account balance in each human relationship.

Peace, life, and health are wealth. They make you feel rich, whether you have financial wealth or not. Now that you understand the four dashboard lights, you can keep track and measure how much a relationship adds to or takes away from your mental and emotional wealth.

One way to think of your four lights on the Boundaries Dashboard is to think of them as emotional wealth indicators: yellow and red lights indicate that you've lost emotional wealth to some degree, and the green light indicates you're maintaining or gaining it.

Part Two: Check the Lights

The good news is that to bring your emotional bank account balance back from a negative to positive, it may only require a single boundary adjustment. Yes, just one little adjustment can often have transformative power to put your mental and emotional accounts back in the green.

CHAPTER 5

OIL CHECK (SELF-CARE)

(30 minute read)

THE MOST IMPORTANT HUMAN RELATIONSHIP

Out of all human relationships, what is the one relationship you cannot walk away from?

Hint: You physically cannot walk away from this one.

You get a small break when you sleep, but all waking hours, you're in this relationship with nowhere to run or hide.

The relationship I'm talking about here, of course, is the one with yourself.

The oil light on the Boundaries Dashboard tracks your overall self-care. The oil light keeps self-management in check, and it's one of the four vital lights because your relationship with yourself significantly impacts the health of your relationship with the other person.

You are the only one who lives in your body, constantly negotiating a long list of needs and desires throughout the day, from psychological to biological to medical and of course general safety, all the way to emotional, physical and, yes, sexual.

If you're anything like me, many of those needs combat each other simultaneously, and it can completely drain your brain's processing power. It's like having too many software applications open on the computer, and the computer freezes because it doesn't have the power to execute everything at once.

How much better-quality attention can you give the other person when you are feeling healthy and have your own life and needs in order? How much better do you treat others when you've eaten properly, had a great night's sleep, or finally finished everything on your to-do list? You might be a little more kind to others, more understanding, do much better at your job, be nicer to the postal clerk, and treat your family with a little more patience.

Lack of self-care can quickly drag you into many harmful states like anxiety, depression, financial distress, and disease, and it can equally drag others into the same or more dangers. For example, if I didn't hold my promise to myself to get enough sleep last night, today I might make an expensive mistake at the office. If I didn't keep my thought hygiene in check, then I might believe thoughts that falsely divide me from someone I deeply care about. If I don't pay attention to my own nutrition and exercise, I might lose the energy, immune system support, and health that I need for daily life.

LITTLE NEWBORN YOU

I may not have met you personally just yet, but I know some facts about you. Here are a few things that I can say without any shadow of doubt.

First, you were born. Second, you were once a small helpless baby who couldn't feed yourself or wipe your own behind.

As a baby, someone brought food to your mouth to feed you. Someone changed your dirty diaper for you. Someone eventually responded when your little newborn voice cried loudly. Someone quickly grabbed you before your tiny feet went running out onto the busy street. Someone also probably tried to make your little baby face smile or laugh. A little later in life, someone sent you to school for an education.

Now you carry the spoon to your own mouth. You wipe your own behind when you go to the bathroom. You respond to your own inner cries. You protect yourself from danger. You make yourself smile or giggle. You ensure your own learning.

... Or do you?

How well do you take care of your own needs? Care is the key word here.

Remember your childhood wishes, wins, and desires? Maybe there was someone who heard your wishes as a child. Someone got that candy bar you asked for. Someone celebrated when you said your first word. Someone got that thing you wanted. Someone picked you up and sat you down next to other little children for playtime.

Now you take care of your own wishes. You do fun things for yourself. You celebrate your small wins. If you want something, you get it. You celebrate each little accomplishment. You reward yourself. You decide who you spend your fun times with.

... Or do you?

Needs and wishes don't go away after childhood. Instead, one by one, each life-management responsibility gradually switches over to you from

Part Two: Check the Lights

those who raised you.

Parenting never stopped; you simply learn to parent yourself. You become your own feeder, your own cleaner, your own desire-fulfiller, your own giggle-maker, your own friendship-maker, and your own caretaker.

Self-care is not just a nice thing to do. It's not only a three-day personal development retreat where you walk barefoot on fiery coals (which I admit I have done, and it was a lot of fun!). Self-care includes far more, like paying your bills, listening for and responding to your own internal cries, maintaining hygiene, protecting yourself from danger, and nurturing your own growth, safety, and enjoyment.

Your little newborn crying sounds haven't stopped now that you're an adult. Your cries only changed and take more sophisticated forms. You can use words to name and address them. Now, with this book, it's time to learn the names of the 12 areas of self-care. None of the 12 areas are new to you. Over many years, they've been slowly handed over to you.

And why else does knowing the 12 areas of self-care matter?

In a professional relationship, not knowing how to properly care for yourself directly impacts performance and concentration on the job. You're not fully "there" mentally to solve problems for your manager, your team, or your clients.

In your relationship with your children, not knowing how to identify your needs could result in life-endangering situations like falling asleep at the wheel with the kids in the car because you stayed up too late or accidentally forgetting to turn the oven off because you have too much on your mind.

The need for sleep is one of your inner newborn cries that never goes away, and among the twelve ingredients of self-care, it belongs to the category of physical health and biological needs. I'm bringing it up because I feel it's one of the top areas of self-neglect in our day and age.

Your body will shut down if you don't get enough sleep. At worst, sleep deprivation leads to tremors and hallucinations, and over time lack of sleep has been shown to lead to a weakened immune system, disease, and ultimately a higher mortality risk.

Sleep is only one example of self-care. You can't help others or even enjoy their company when you don't know what areas to manage in your own life.

The adults who raised you were like runners in relay races with you throughout the years, passing batons of care on to you in whatever way they knew. And the batons didn't go away; they are each still in your hands. They may have never named the batons passed to you as you grew up, but here you go; there are twelve batons in total.

But wait, we're using the metaphor of cars and roads in this book, so let's switch from passing batons in a relay race back to that of driving a car and the care that a car needs.

It's great to help the people around you with their car problems, but if yours is about to run out of oil, your engine will stop running in those relationships. So, it's time for your Oil Check, and you'll be doing that in the next exercise.

TWELVE INGREDIENTS

At one time I worked in the corporate office of an international fuel company. I learned that motor oil is made up of a mixture of ingredients – a base oil and several additives that reduce friction, clean engine parts, cool them down, and overall protect the life of the engine.

Part Two: Check the Lights

There is a long list of complicated-sounding motor oil ingredients that you might possibly find annoying to read, such as corrosion inhibitor additives that protect from rust, dispersant additives that help avoid dirt build up, and several other long words I won't share here.[12]

Self-care is just like motor oil in that it's made up of many ingredients. And if the quantity and quality of the ingredients are insufficient, then the engine parts rub up against each other with too much friction, overheat, and suddenly stop working. A proper balance of all the ingredients is required to keep the engine running.

In the same way, self-care is the lubrication in this relationship that keeps you running. If we cannot take care of ourselves, we lose the ability to take care of others, fully enjoy their company, or give them our wholehearted attention.

And it's not enough to just fill the oil tank. The oil needs to have the right thickness (the technical term I learned is "viscosity"), and the right thickness depends on what kind of engine you have. Oil that's too thick or too thin won't protect your engine.

The oil must also be clean.

The right amount, the right ingredients, the right thickness, and cleanliness to keep everything running; it's a lot to keep in mind.

Well, when it comes to self-care, let's make it simple. Please allow me to introduce you to the twelve essential ingredients of self-care that keeps your relationship engine running.

Self-Care Ingredient #1: Your Body Health

Body health encompasses medical health, biological needs, physical health, and fitness. This is about how well you take care of, strengthen, and protect your body and all of its systems, including all forms of hygiene, nutrition, physical safety, and exercise.

About two million species of living organisms in the world have been identified, and as a human, you are the most sophisticated and complex of them all. As a living machine with the most complex systems of all known creatures, you require both regular maintenance and special projects to keep your machine performing.

Can we take a nerdy moment to appreciate your body's twelve general processes? Here's a list of the systems operating in your body right now:

- Reproductive system (sexual health)
- Nervous system (your brain, neurology, and everything it controls)
- Digestive system (what you eat, nutrition, metabolism, excretion)
- Respiratory system (breathing, getting enough oxygen)
- Urinary system (organs that filter waste out of your blood)
- Cardiovascular system (pumping blood to all organs)
- Sensory system (vision, hearing)
- Musculoskeletal system (bones, muscles, and supporting fibers)
- Skin system (hair, sensory regulation, protects organs inside)
- Hematological system (bone marrow forming immune cells to protect body)
- Lymphatic (drainage system, helps immunity)
- Endocrine system (hormones and growth)

I'm not asking you to write down the answers, but here are a few questions for you to reflect on, to help you get a clearer vision of this self-care ingredient in your life:

How often do you take yourself for regular checkups at the doctor's office?

How often do you follow up on what the doctor suggests?

How often do you get the exercise and nutrition your body and brain need?

For your age and weight, how much water does your body need each day?

How much fresh air do your precious lungs get each day?

How well do you take care of your teeth?

How often do you get natural sunlight versus artificial lighting?

Who serves as a model for you of great physical and biological health?

SELF-CARE INGREDIENT #2: YOUR FINANCIAL HEALTH

Think about how well you take care of your income, savings, investments, expenses, cashflow, planning, and spending habits.

Not to write down, but only to think about: How much of your income do you put away into savings? How safe or dangerous are your spending habits? How well do you track your regular living or business expenses? How well do you invest your money? How much advice do you seek for financial decisions? What apps do you use to keep an eye on your inflows and outflows? What information would help you build an even greater financial situation? Who serves as a model for you of great financial health?

SELF-CARE INGREDIENT #3: RESTFUL ACTIVITY

Restful activities reduce stress, boost the immune system, enhance sleep quality, and improve mental health. They include all low-energy activities that you choose to do while you're awake. It could mean sitting in front of a fireplace, reading, meditating, fishing, or any one of hundreds of activities that might help you wind down.

Not to write down, but only to think about: How often do you stop and take a break from your hard work? How often do you lie on a blanket in the sunshine or under the stars? How might you use music or something else to give your mind a rest from the normal grind? How often do you allow a babysitter to give you and your partner a calm evening alone? What hobbies or interests give your body a sense of rest? How many ways do you relax? Who serves as a model for you of a healthy kind of restful activities, downtime, and relaxation?

SELF-CARE INGREDIENT #4: FUN ACTIVITY

Fun activity refers to integrating playfulness, excitement, lightheartedness, and celebration into your life in some way – big or small. The health benefits are proven to be powerful, similar to restful activities. This includes anything you genuinely find fun, uplifting, or amusing, no matter what it is. Think about how well you get your hits of dopamine – in a healthy way, of course.

It could mean adding a joke to a conversation, dancing, attending a concert, or even simply being alone at home watching videos that make you laugh out loud. This also includes the uplifting celebration of your own wins, whether they are big or very small.

Not to write down, but only to think about: How much do you use playful imagination throughout the day? What things do you currently like to do for fun? What fun activities would you like to try for the first time? How often do you celebrate your own successes – big, small, and tiny? What's a new way to celebrate your small wins? How can you integrate more play into each day? Who serves as a model for you of healthy play, excitement, celebration, and having fun?

SELF-CARE INGREDIENT #5: OCCUPATION

Occupation refers to your job, trade, career, or business. Think about how well you take care of whatever it is that you do to earn a living. For most people, this takes up most of your life, and it's typically one of the first things people ask you about: "So, what do you do for a living?" So, think about whatever it is you do for the world that you trade for a roof over your head, food on the table, and maybe some nice things.

Not to write down, but only to think about: What you could you do to make your work more enjoyable? What career change might you desire or need, and when? What business would you like to start? What experience will give you the résumé you need for the career you want? How can you trade your time for money more wisely and profitably? How can you trade your ideas for money more wisely and profitably? What can you change about your business to make it bigger and better or even just more enjoyable? Who serves as a model for you of a great career, trade, or business?

SELF-CARE INGREDIENT #6: EMOTIONS AND THOUGHT HEALTH

This is a big one. On a personal note, I have to say this ingredient is the most important one in this list for me. Everything else in life and relationships depends on this. My entire attitude can change when I simply shift just one thought. My hope is that you see how powerful this self-care ingredient can be for you.

As a child, I felt like emotions and thoughts directed me, and I could not direct them. That changed as an adult. Throughout the years, many personal development authors, speakers, life coaches, therapists, and other experts introduced me to the "I" behind my emotions and thoughts. Eckhart Tolle's *The Power of Now* was the most life-changing among them.[13]

It's a slow and intentional process, but I have become more and more capable of directing my emotions and thoughts as opposed to them directing me. For me, the power to move through emotions and thoughts works exactly like the power to move weights and build muscle: you start weak and lift light, then build up strength over a very long time and with patience.

You can do it, too.

Psychiatrist Daniel G. Amen, M.D., says, "As a psychiatrist now for over 40 years, I would never believe every stupid thing I think. You need to learn how to direct and control your thoughts."[14]

Dr. Amen has been in business for over 40 years, guys. If he thinks you can do it, maybe you actually can direct and control your thoughts.

Trying to take control of your thoughts might feel like trying to stop a river with your bare hands. However, it's a wiser, more gradual, and powerful process if you build a dam one stone (or one thought) at a time – one by one – eventually creating a complete wall to control where the river flows. Then once you complete the dam, you maintain it regularly.

Awareness and directing of thoughts are what I call "thought hygiene," and other people use this phrase too. It's just like learning, as a child, to become aware of the need for things like brushing your teeth, showering, and wearing clean clothes. At first, you may not like doing it, like a child might hate brushing their teeth or showering, but with practice over time, thought hygiene becomes an unconscious habit.

Little by little, you can eventually achieve a stable awareness of your thoughts to the point that you can identify and reject the ones that bring you down or at least withstand them until they pass.

Think about how well you give attention to and take care of your own feelings, thoughts, and attitudes throughout the day. For example, being single and living alone, one day I was able to observe myself feeling lonely, as opposed to being controlled by the feeling. I recognized the space between myself and the thought, and I sat with it.

I realized that in order to feel lonely, I had to believe that my own presence is not enough. As a personal coach, I know too much about human potential to believe that I am not enough. I took the time to sit down, put space between me and the thought, check if it was true, and then fix it.

A broken thought is as important to correct as a broken bone. My willingness to challenge this kind of thought – that I'm not enough – created enough space for self-compassion and a sense of warmth to flow in me. That warmth replaced the loneliness; it felt a bit magical. And the more I practice this kind of thought hygiene, the stronger, mentally, I become.

I took the time to observe my inner world. The human brain provides us with the extraordinary ability to have what feels like a third-person view of our internal feelings, thoughts, and attitudes.

Have you ever heard the saying: "Be honest with yourself?" Just as you have the choice to be honest (or not) in your dialogue with other people, you also have the choice to be honest with yourself in your inner dialogue. Just as you have the choice to ignore what other people say, you also have the choice to ignore what you think.

In my own mind, I can intentionally ignore what part of me is saying or

I can engage with it, and perhaps one of the best examples is how I've ignored red flags on a date. For a long time, I would hear a part of me say, "Hey, watch out for this!" while on a date, but I'd choose to not engage with that voice in me. I refused to observe it or validate it at all.

Being honest with yourself requires a third-person experience of yourself. It requires you to step back from your own inner thoughts, feelings, and attitudes, and make some observations about all of them. It requires you to stop what you're doing, look, identify, and engage with all the parts of you that disagree or agree.

However, I want to emphasize that being honest with yourself isn't about being honest in a condescending way, but it is about being honest with compassion. If you only face a feeling, thought, or attitude with honesty but you do it in a hostile way, then it can turn dangerous for your mental health.

For a long time, I felt afraid of being honest with myself about what I desired in life because, at that time, I had an unhealthy form of religious belief that my desire for my life doesn't matter and that most human desire is "evil" in some way. Thank God, however, that I read the book *Love Wins* by Rob Bell,[15] which corrected my worldview and self-view, and most of those toxic fears melted away. I was far more able to observe myself, my desires, and my thoughts with genuine compassion.

Self-honesty can only empower you if it's driven with genuine love, patience, kindness, and gentleness toward yourself. Creating moments of honesty with self-compassion and unconditional positive regard for ourselves serves as the best training sessions for creating that same honesty, compassion, and positive regard toward anyone else.

I've also heard and read these phrases: "Building trust with yourself," and "How to rebuild trust with yourself." They have to do with the inner conversation that we either neglect completely or act on too quickly

Part Two: Check the Lights

without genuine desire or reflection.

How do we get to that point where we have lost trust in ourselves?

By breaking our own internal promises – internally saying to ourselves, "I'll do that later," then not doing it.

Ignoring the messages our instinct says to us, like ignoring red flags in an interview or on a date.

Watching a TV show or video on social media instead of sitting with a journal and thinking through a problem.

Making decisions too hastily or making decisions that do not genuinely align with our values.

We have a deep and complex emotional and thought life that is almost as fragile and needs as much attention as a newborn baby.

There seems to always be that newborn inside of us that never stops needing our attention, needing us to lovingly find what our body and nervous system are crying out for.

It's time to turn your ear inward.

I love the quote I've seen around the internet: "It's time to start being loyal to your own peace of mind." So far, this has been my favorite quote when it comes to self-care.

Self-care of my feelings, thoughts, and attitudes is about first creating a sense of loyalty to my own peace of mind, and that is the only genuine way to have peace of mind and model it for others.

Now for some questions for reflection – not for you to write down, but only to think about: How aware are you of the inner dialogue taking place in your heart and/or mind? How well do you manage your thought hygiene? How often do you stop to consider the truthfulness of your thoughts and beliefs? What new thought habits would help you the most? How often do you keep yourself in check and make attitude adjustments? Who serves as a model for you of a great emotion and thought life?

How well can you witness your own feelings and identify them, such as the ability to say, "I feel sad," when you feel sad; and when you don't know what you feel or think, how well can you witness that state and say, "I don't know how I feel, think, or believe"?

Self-Care Ingredient #7: Self-View

Think about how you view yourself. This includes your ideas and beliefs about your specific role or value in this world as an individual, as well as your unique strengths and weaknesses as a person.

Not to write down, but only to think about: Do you see yourself worthy of respect, the same as everyone else? How often do you see yourself better than, the same as, or not as good as someone else in some way? How do you see yourself fitting into or not fitting into the culture around you? What lifestyle changes would make you feel more comfortable to be yourself? What clothing and hair styles empower you? Who do you want to be in a difficult situation? Who do you want to be in general? How would you tell the story of your life? What degree of control do you have over your own decisions and actions? What degree of control do you have over what happens in your life? Who serves as a model for you of a great self-view?

Self-Care Ingredient #8: Worldview

Worldview includes your spiritual, religious, intellectual, moral, and/or philosophical life. Think about how you view the world around you – everything and everyone else in it. Self-view is about yourself, and worldview is about everyone and everything else. One is sort of like a microscope looking inward, and the other a telescope looking outward. Yes, the two are related and one can directly impact the other.

Not to write down, but only to think about: How do you believe the world began, and who or what governs it? Does God or a god exist? What ideas and principles do you believe guide people's decisions? What do you believe is right or wrong in the world? What does an ethical life look like? What kind of laws should be passed and what existing laws should be changed? What role does humanity play in the history of the world? How can we make the world a better place? What degree of control does society have? How much personality, feeling, knowledge, awareness, presence, and intelligence does the source of our universe have, if any? Who serves as a model for you of a great worldview?

Self-Care Ingredient #9: Discovery

Discovery refers to all forms of learning, novelty, and exploration. Think about how you seek new experiences, adventures, experiments, or knowledge in any area of life – big or small.

Not to write down, but only to think about: What new subjects would you like to learn about? What new experiences might improve life for you? What experiments would help you figure things out? Where have you always wanted to go? What would you like to discover about yourself? Who serves as a model for you of great learning, novelty, exploration, and discovery?

Self-Care Ingredient #10: Time Management

Think about how well you prioritize, plan, and manage your calendar and schedule.

Not to write down, but only to think about: How often would you like to set time apart for planning and prioritizing? How well do you manage your plans? What kinds of tools would help you make better use of your time? What can you do in the morning to conquer your day? What can you do at night to better prepare for the next day? How do you choose what to say yes to and what to say no to? How often do you use a task list or any system of prioritizing your time? Who serves as a model for you of great time management, prioritizing, and scheduling?

Self-Care Ingredient #11: Environments

Think about how well you manage everything and everyone in your physical and digital spaces. I split this into a few general categories – work, home, and other environments.

Consider physical sensory environments inside and out, such as lighting, furniture, space, sounds and noise, proximity to other people and things, weather or temperature, local culture, national or political environment, and the digital or virtual environments and devices you use.

Work Environment
Not to write down, but only to think about: How do fluorescent lights in an office impact you versus natural sunlight? How does proximity of your desk to other people impact your concentration? How much do you enjoy or not enjoy the office culture? What apps at work might make your job easier? How can you better organize your workflow, files, and documents? How positive or negative is the impact of the conversations people are having around you? Who serves as a model for you of maintaining a great work environment?

Home Environment
Not to write down, but only to think about: What lighting changes can you make to improve your mood or sleep? What can you do to make your home more comfortable? What apps can you use to make home life more enjoyable – for example cooking, life management, screentime controls, television usage, food delivery, security systems, music, or thermostat controls? If you live with others, how well do you organize your own personal space? How well do you organize your digital belongings like photos, other media, and important personal documents? If the television is on, how does that impact your mental health and peace? Who serves as a model for you of maintaining a great home environment?

Other Environments
How healthy are the places you choose to go outside of home and work? Where would you like to visit or not visit? What forms of transportation work for you better than others? What kind of traveling would you like to do more or less of? How would it help you (or not help you) to change the places you regularly go? When it comes to people who inspire you the most, how might their places of inspiration also inspire you?

SELF-CARE INGREDIENT #12: HUMAN RELATIONSHIPS

Think about how well you manage your boundaries in all human relationships and how each relationship impacts your self-care or, in other words, how each impacts your relationship with yourself:

- Friendships
- Acquaintanceships
- Family relationships
- Romantic, intimate, or sexual relationships
- Professional and business relationships
- Local community groups, organizations, and neighbors

- Political or national relationships (citizenship, relationship with your government or nation, etc.)

Not to write down, but only to think about: How can you adjust boundaries in any of the above relationships to improve your sense of health, happiness, peace, and satisfaction? Who serves as a model for you of maintaining great human relationships?

CHAPTER 5 EXERCISE, PART 1

SELF-CARE SCORES

This chapter's exercise is meant to simplify self-care into something you can easily measure. You're also about to reveal if the oil light on your Boundaries Dashboard is flashing green, yellow, or red.

Open your Dashboard Diary, find a completely blank page, and write the title "Oil Check" with today's date on top. Then, draw three columns from the top to the bottom of the page.

You're going to enter a list into the first column, enter numbers into the second, and symbols in the third column. Make the first column wide enough for up to four words. However, the second and third columns can be narrow since you will only write one or two numbers or symbols in them.

At the top of each of the columns, give them these titles: "Ingredient" (first column), "Self-Care" (second column), and "Impact" (third column).

Part Two: Check the Lights

FIRST COLUMN: INGREDIENT

In the first column, write the below names for each of the 12 ingredients. Each one gets its own row.

1. Body Health

2. Financial Health

3. Restful Activity

4. Fun Activity

5. Occupation

6. Emotions and Thought Health

7. Self-View

8. Worldview

9. Discovery

10. Time Management

11. Environments

12. Human Relationships

SECOND COLUMN: SELF-CARE

Did you write down all twelve ingredients in the first column? OK, let's move on.

This middle (second) column focuses only on your relationship with you. In this column, you evaluate how you take care of yourself.

Next to each one of the twelve ingredients you listed, answer this question on a scale of 0 to 10: **How well do you take care of your own personal needs and wishes in this area?** A score of 10 means that "it couldn't get any better" and a 0 means that "it couldn't get any worse."

This score is about your self-parenting. It's not about the other person.

If you feel it's necessary, go back to the section of this chapter titled "Twelve Ingredients" to remember what each ingredient means so that you can give a more accurate score.

When thinking about a period of time for evaluating your self-care, use the same time frame that you wrote down in your Diary when you completed the Boundaries Health Check in Chapter 3.

THIRD COLUMN: IMPACT

In this third column, you will measure the impact that your self-care score has on this relationship. In other words, the degree to which you take care of yourself can directly impact how much you show up in other human relationships emotionally, physically, financially, mentally, or any other way. In short, self-care impacts your relationships with others. On the next page or two, you'll read several examples.

Part Two: Check the Lights

The overall impact that your self-care has on you in this relationship might be positive or negative, even if it's only slightly one way or the other.

In the third column for each ingredient, here's the question to ask yourself: **Does my self-care in this area impact me in this relationship more in a negative way or in a positive way?** Pick only one option – more negative or more positive, overall.

If you feel that the self-care score is impacting you in this relationship more negatively than positively, write down a negative symbol "–" in the third column.

If you feel that your self-care score is impacting you in this relationship more in a positive way, write down a plus symbol "+" in the third column.

If you feel unable to identify a more positive or negative impact, then write down the letter "n" for "neutral."

When thinking about what period of time to evaluate, use the same time frame that you wrote down in your Diary when you completed the Boundaries Health Check in Chapter 3. As a matter of fact, for all exercises contained in Part Two of this book, use that same time frame so that your scoring is consistent.

If you feel stuck in this column, here's some help.

FEELING STUCK IN THE IMPACT COLUMN?

If you had no problem completing your impact scores on your own, feel free to skip this section and go straight to the next.

However, if you are like me and prefer thorough explanations, I'll run through detailed examples.

Let's say that for the self-care ingredient "Body Health," I gave myself a score of "6" in the second column ("Self-Care" column).

I gave myself a score of 6 for a few reasons. I lift heavy weights at the gym (safely, thanks to personal trainers), and I take great care of my fitness overall. As for nutrition and diet, I eat well, and I protect myself from my dietary allergies and intolerances. I also try to get fresh air and sun.

However, when it comes to taking care of my medical health, I have an issue with my iron level. I've been putting off a blood test that I know will help me make progress with that issue. Because of low iron, I often feel very tired and unable to concentrate.

So, those are my reasons that I gave myself a score of 6 in the second column (the "Self-Care" column).

In the third column, I asked myself: "Does this score of 6 impact me in my relationship with this person more positively or more negatively?"

My iron levels directly impact my physical energy, and because my energy levels are terribly low and unpredictable, I'm not doing all the activities that I want to do with this person, I don't have the energy for the relationship that I want, and I'm rejecting several of their activity ideas because of it.

If I got the bloodwork, then I could make progress to treat my low iron issue. Treating it properly would mean I get to share more fun activities with them. We would bond more. We would enjoy each other more often. Our quality of life and depth of relationship would improve.

This medical issue is not an overwhelmingly negative impact, but it's certainly significant enough that it impacts this relationship more negatively than positively.

Part Two: Check the Lights

So, in the third column, I'll write a negative symbol.

When you're not satisfied in some area of your own self-care, it can often impact your emotional or mental state in any or all of your other relationships, and it may impair the activities you share with them; and this applies to all human relationships of course – professional and personal.

For each of the 12 self-care ingredients, here are several short examples of how they can impact a human relationship both positively and negatively.

Body Health

Negative self-care impact: I don't exercise regularly at all and would rather watch TV or just sit and scroll social media, but this all makes me feel insecure about how unfit I've become, making me less confident and less energetic in the relationship.

Positive self-care impact: I go to the gym regularly and this gives me the physical strength, self-discipline, and confidence that the other person admires in me.

Financial Health

Negative self-care impact: I don't manage my money well, and the stress from this seeps into the way I talk with the other person, making our conversations irritating for both of us.

Positive self-care impact: I hired a bookkeeper, so now I don't have to think about where my money's going, and now I can easily decide when, where, and how often I can pay for special events for us.

Restful Activity

Negative self-care impact: I don't ever just chill out and truly relax, and since this non-stop lifestyle wears me out, it makes me grumpy when I'm around the other person.

Positive self-care impact: I finally get enough downtime, and we both share that downtime together.

Fun Activity

Negative self-care impact: I have become so dull and boring lately, not doing anything that makes me laugh or even remembering how to, so now everything I do and say with this person is a bit too serious.

Positive self-care impact: I found a comedy channel that puts me in a great mood, and I think it's made me lighthearted enough to joke around and make the other person laugh a bit more.

Occupation

Negative self-care impact: I hate my job, and it shows in my interactions with the clients who call our office.

Positive self-care impact: I found a niche service that I do naturally and love, and clients love talking with me.

Emotions and Thought Health

Negative self-care impact: I don't stop to check if my own negative thoughts are true or not, so I end up making tons of assumptions in the relationship and messing things up.

Positive self-care impact: I made a daily habit of using various coaching techniques to get my thought habits healthier and more uplifting, and the other person sees this and appreciates it.

Self-View

Negative self-care impact: I don't like most things about myself, so I withdraw in many situations in this relationship.

Positive self-care impact: I learned to be compassionate with myself about the things I don't like about myself, and this makes me kinder to the other person, too.

Worldview

Negative self-care impact: I admit that sometimes I feel like my worldview is fully correct and flawless, and when the other person disagrees with me, I feel defensive.

Positive self-care impact: I'm eager to learn how the other person understands the world and what experiences made them believe that way.

Discovery (learning, novelty, exploration)

Negative self-care impact: I sit in front of computer screens for work and entertainment, but I don't watch much of anything that will help me learn more about myself, or the other person, or the world in general.

Positive self-care impact: I regularly go looking for new things to understand, discover, and explore about myself and the world around me, and the other person loves that about me.

Time Management (prioritizing, scheduling, calendaring)

Negative self-care impact: I don't keep any kind of prioritizing system, task management software, calendaring software, or even a paper calendar, so I'm forgetting my plans a lot in this relationship.

Positive self-care impact: I started using a reminders app on my phone, so I remember all my commitments each week, and it's helping me keep my word in this relationship.

Environments

Negative self-care impact: The lighting situation at work strains my eyes and makes me feel miserable and exhausted by the end of the day, putting me in a bad mood when it's time to talk with the other person.

Positive self-care impact: I changed some elements in the room to make me feel better, and now when the other person approaches me for a chat, I'm a bit more calm and collected.

Human Relationships

Negative self-care impact: I haven't really thought much about what boundaries to adjust with my ex-partner so that my current partner feels more respected.

Positive self-care impact: I removed my ex's access to me on social media. Now I can see more updates from my friends and my new partner, and I see news sources that move me forward in life.

CHAPTER 5 EXERCISE, PART 2

THE COLOR OF YOUR DASHBOARD LIGHT

Motor oil minimizes friction between an engine's moving parts. It's like this in relationships, too.

In the "Impact" column of (Chapter 5) Exercise Part 1, the ingredients with negative symbols create friction, and those with positive symbols make the relationship run more smoothly like engine oil.

So, let's look at your total number of positives and negatives. Neutral responses are not counted.

In the third column, count your total number of negatives.

If you have no negatives in the third column, then that means the oil light on your dashboard in this relationship is green.

If you have between one and three negative scores, then the oil light in your dashboard is yellow.

Part Two: Check the Lights

If you have four or more negative scores, your light is red.

Even with only one negative, it means that your self-care is having a negative impact on this relationship, and it is either something to monitor or something to act on.

Why can't the oil light be green if I have only one or two negatives? Because just one negative can potentially have the power to degrade or "damage the engine" of this relationship at some point. One to three negatives trigger a yellow light, signaling you to look into it and see what risks you face if you do nothing about it.

If your light is yellow, the relationship might still work well for you, if you can carefully manage those areas.

So what color is your oil light?

In your Diary, at the bottom of the page or anywhere you find room, write down the color of your dashboard light and circle it boldly so you can easily spot it when you return to this section later in this book. If using a digital device, you can bold, underline, or perhaps use an emoji so you can quickly find it later on.

Did you give it a big circle or make it stand out in some way? OK, cool. You're ready to continue reading.

CHAPTER 6

FUEL CHECK (MOTIVATORS)

(10 minute read)

DECISION FUEL

Roy E. Disney, partner and co-founder of The Walt Disney Company, said, "It's not hard to make decisions, once you know what your values are."

When you don't know what's most important to you when faced with a decision, it can feel like painting a portrait on a canvas in the pitch-black darkness. When you don't know what's important to you, it can also make people around you feel unsettled, annoyed, or confused.

Knowing what you value most helps you make clear decisions, yes, and it helps you be true to yourself. It pumps you up with extra motivation in life, giving you that edge that others don't have because they're still flopping around.

Part Two: Check the Lights

WHAT ENERGIZES YOU?

On the Boundaries Dashboard, remember that two out of the four dashboard lights signal how you make decisions in this relationship; the fuel light is one of those two.

Specifically, the fuel light lets you know how much your decisions align with your personal motivators.

Integrating your unique values into your decisions makes it easier to get out of bed in the morning. These values also give you a sense of life and a sense of who you are in the relationship.

Through my personal coach, I discovered my number one value is beauty – inside and out, physical and emotional. I discovered that my personal value of beauty gets me through negativity, fear, and discouragement.

The fact that I have identified and can name my value is life-changing; it not only fuels my decision-making, but it helps me realize what to look for in a person to make the relationship stronger. Because I know internal and external beauty motivates me, that's what I look for: what beautiful thing have they done that I can appreciate? What beautiful personality traits do they have? What beautiful physical traits do they have?

It's much easier to feel forgiveness and compassion for a person when I can spot beauty –in any form – in them; in a sense, for me, finding beauty is like finding God.

I once had a boss who was gorgeous both in character and in looks; she was physically beautiful and her character was an incredible mix of intelligence, kindness, humility, and positivity. When she asked me to do something, I wanted to do it with more energy than I had with any other boss. Why?

Chapter 6: Fuel Check (Motivator)

It was because beauty motivates me. I saw tons of it in her in both ways – appearance and character, inside and out.

In my relationship with myself, I feel an incredible boost of energy when I do my hair and makeup first thing in the morning versus waiting until after breakfast. Putting beauty first triggers a positive momentum of thoughts and mental energy for the morning. If I wait to take care of these things until late in the morning, I feel low and ugly inside, and that "ugly" feeling can somehow snowball into the day.

Self-discipline is beautiful to me. I find it genuinely attractive in others and myself; it's like an intricately designed piece of art. So, when I push through the pain of completing a chore such as my own laundry, dishes, or a gym workout, it makes me feel an incredible surge of energy and satisfaction afterwards. I feel like I can conquer the day and feel motivated, and that's because I made a decision that aligns with my values.

Your values, or what I synonymously call "motivators," give you the mental energy to get stuff done in life and relationships. They also allow you to live with psychological integrity about who you are and what you want in every part of life, including this relationship.

It's frustrating when people don't know what motivates them in life or relationships, and it often causes life-sucking boredom, laziness, or an irritating amount of friction, which often eventually leads to the end of the relationship itself. So, to prevent that situation, it's essential that your unique reason for getting out of bed in the morning is something that is integrated into the decisions you make and actions you take in this relationship.

Thinking through your past up until this moment: what values have made you feel most energized, joyful, or deeply grateful in life?

The answer to that question marks the beginning of understanding your

Part Two: Check the Lights

Fuel light in this relationship.

Remember, each person in a relationship needs fuel to run their own car, and it's likely you don't run on the same fuel. Their engine may require 91 octane, while yours may require diesel. Unless you both share the same motivators – the same fuel type – filling up on someone else's fuel will only break down your engine.

You each have your own motivators. The good news is that you are about to identify yours in the next exercise.

THE RESEARCH BEHIND YOUR MOTIVATORS

The idea of "motivators" is inspired by psychological theory and research. Most notably, I am inspired by a reputable research project called the *VIA Classification of Strengths* conducted by the University of Pennsylvania and the VIA Institute on Character.[16] A team of 55 social scientists, led by Christopher Peterson PhD, came up with a list of what they call character strengths and virtues.[17] This list is used by coaches around the world to help their clients align decisions with what uniquely and truly motivates them.

There are several more inspiring studies that demonstrate the importance of identifying what truly motivates you and how important it is for your well-being to consciously make decisions that align with that.

A psychologist and researcher named Shalom H. Schwartz developed the Theory of Basic Human Values, showing that people experience greater well-being when they act in ways that align with their core values. Another work from psychologist Edward Deci and Richard Ryan shows that when people make decisions based on their intrinsic motivations, they will have greater psychological well-being.

A disconnect between your decisions and your motivators can negatively impact everything.

Your motivators are life-giving. Motivators keep you committed to a project or person when it becomes hard work, and motivators are an essential tool for whole-hearted decision-making.

Using all of the above as a basis, here below is a full list of motivators with descriptions next to each one.

Drum roll please!

A. **Courage**
bravery, facing external or internal opposition, provocation, or challenge

B. **Creativity**
ingenuity, change, open-mindedness, innovation, invention, novelty

C. **Beauty**
the visual, audible, emotional, artistic, or spiritual attractiveness of people or things

D. **Health**
wholeness, energy, vitality, physical and mental wellbeing, self-care

E. **Wisdom and Knowledge**
curiosity, learning, making sense of how the world works

F. **Community**
society as a whole, empathy, love of people, teamwork

G. **Justice**
   individual or community rights, fairness, equality, citizenship, integrity

H. **Order**
   organization, control, prioritization, structure, self-regulation

I. **Transcendence**
   gratitude, laughter, hope, optimism, humor, humility, spirituality

J. **Freedom**
   lightheartedness, unrestraint, flexibility, liberation, opportunity

I also discovered a quick and easy way – a hack of sorts – to identify the motivator that is most meaningful to you so that you can start using it in your decision-making. I'll be using a fun coaching technique in this chapter's exercise to help you get clear on which one or two are most fundamental to creating a more motivated life and more fulfilling human relationships.

CHAPTER 6 EXERCISE, PART 1

MAKE BELIEVE

In your Dashboard Diary, write today's date at the top of the page and the title "My Motivator."

This Exercise is in two parts. For Part 1, we're going to play "make-believe." Remember as a child when you pretended to be someone you weren't or pretended to do something you couldn't really do, like being an astronaut floating in outer space or a mermaid out in the ocean? Well, get ready for some grown-up make-believe.

Here we go!

Take a moment right now to imagine yourself leaving this world and starting a whole new world that is 100% your own. Yes, it's a brand-new world where you make all the rules.

Out of the ten motivators listed below, you can *only take one* with you to create your brand-new world. Which one would you take to start your new world?

A. **Courage**
bravery, facing external or internal opposition, provocation, or challenge

B. **Creativity**
ingenuity, change, open-mindedness, innovation, invention, novelty

C. **Beauty**
the visual, audible, emotional, artistic, or spiritual attractiveness of people or things

D. **Health**
wholeness, energy, vitality, physical and mental wellbeing, self-care

E. **Wisdom and Knowledge**
curiosity, learning, making sense of how the world works

F. **Community**
society as a whole, empathy, love of people, teamwork

G. **Justice**
individual or community rights, fairness, equality, citizenship, integrity

H. **Order**
organization, control, prioritization, structure, self-regulation

I. **Transcendence**
gratitude, laughter, hope, optimism, humor, humility, spirituality

J. **Freedom**
lightheartedness, unrestraint, flexibility, liberation, opportunity

Take time to really feel out your answer. Pick only one, even if there is second one that comes very close.

Feeling stuck between two options? Then imagine a spaceship with the two in the cockpit. Imagine that one of the two takes the passenger seat, and the other one is the driver. For your answer, write down the one that you placed in the driver's seat.

In your Dashboard Diary, under "My Motivator," write down "#1" together with the full name and description of the motivator that you chose.

If you've written it down, please continue reading. If not, then take a little more time.

You've written #1 down! Great. Now, we're still in the land of make-believe. Imagine one whole year after starting your brand-new world with your first motivator, you're suddenly able to invite a second motivator!

From the same ten options listed above, you can add a second one to your new world. Which would you take?

In your Dashboard Diary, under your first motivator, write "#2" and then write the full name and description of your second motivator.

Congratulations! In a fun way and with a child-like spirit, you have discovered something fundamental about what motivates you the most in the decisions you make. Consciously name your Motivator #1 when making decisions, and when you're stuck, bring in Motivator #2 to make your answer clear.

When deciding on something important to you, simply ask yourself, "What option aligns best with [insert the name of your motivator]?"

When it comes to this relationship, how often are you asking yourself this? We're about to see.

CHAPTER 6 EXERCISE, PART 2

COLOR OF YOUR DASHBOARD LIGHT

The metaphor of a full tank of fuel represents how often you make decisions in the relationship that align with your personal motivator.

Remember that this book is concerned with your own dashboard, and we let the other person be responsible for theirs. It is up to them to identify and integrate their motivators into relationship decisions and actions in a way that they believe works for them, and it is up to you to do the same with yours.

In a human relationship, two people integrating their motivators together in decisions is like ingredients coming together for a mouth-watering recipe.

The fuel light lets you know if you're making decisions that agree with your motivator, and it's what makes you feel "the authentic you" with the other person. When your fuel is low in the decisions and actions made in this relationship, your dashboard light turns yellow, and when dangerously low, it turns red.

Part Two: Check the Lights

So what color is your fuel light? For this exercise, write the title "My Fuel Light" in your Dashboard Diary with today's date.

Underneath the title and date, write down the list below of all six boundaries, exactly as you see them here, and write out the full sentence that goes with each one.

For each boundary, there are two blanks – one blank is for a score and the other blank is for your motivator.

You already know your motivator from the last exercise, so when you write each sentence, write your Motivator #1 in the blank space.

After you finish writing out this list, read the instructions that follow for how complete the "score" blanks.

_____
BOUNDARY #1 – TERRITORIES SCORE: _____
_____

My decisions about the environments and places that I share with the other person (as well as everything within those spaces) align well with my motivator, (insert Motivator #1 here) .

_____
BOUNDARY #2 – TREASURE SCORE: _____
_____

My decisions about the things I do or don't do for the sake of this relationship align well with my motivator, (insert Motivator #1 here) .

BOUNDARY #3 – TOOLS SCORE: _____

My decisions about the communication tools that I use with the other person (sending, receiving, and access) align well with my motivator, (insert Motivator #1 here) .

BOUNDARY #4 – TOPICS SCORE: _____

The topics that I decide to talk about and don't talk about with the other person align well with my motivator, (insert Motivator #1 here) .

BOUNDARY #5 – THIRD PARTIES SCORE: _____

When it comes to other relationships I choose to keep in my life that impact this one, they are well-aligned with my motivator, (insert Motivator #1 here) .

BOUNDARY #6 – TIME SCORE: _____

My decisions about the amount of time I spend interacting with the other person align well with my motivator, (insert Motivator #1 here) .

Great job writing those out! Now, here's how to enter each score.

For each of the six boundary statements you wrote, think about how true the statement is for you, and pick a number on a scale of 0 to 10. A score of 0 means the statement is not true at all, and a score of 10 means it's completely true.

Remember to use the same time frame that you've used in all of the previous exercises.

Ok, now that you have written down your scores, you can convert those numbers to discover the color of your fuel light.

Add up all six scores. What is the total?

If your total score is between 0 and 29 then your dashboard's fuel light is red.

A score between 30 and 47 means your dashboard's fuel light is yellow.

It's a beautiful bright green, if your score falls between 48 and 60.

Write down your total score and the dashboard light color that it converts to, then draw a big obvious circle around both of them in your Diary before you move on to the next chapter. This way you can spot it easily when you look back at it later. If using a digital device, you can bold, underline, or perhaps use an emoji so you can quickly spot it later.

CHAPTER 7

BATTERY CHECK (CONSENT)

(8 minute read)

STRIPPED OF YOUR WILL

Picture an obsessed-looking girl with a suspicious smile and eyes opened frantically wide as she says to her partner, "We are in a committed relationship. I don't think you should be making your own decisions."

What I just described is a meme about romantic relationships, and the face of this particular girl in the meme is especially great at looking "crazy."

This kind of meme spreads fast across the internet most likely because the majority of people have either acted in a controlling way to some degree, like her, or have known someone who has acted that way.

It's common in human relationships for someone, at some point, to force their decisions on the relationship and disregard the other person's will, needs, autonomy, and desires. Her slightly sinister face emphasizes just how unhealthy it is to do that.

It's a look and behavior of domination. It happens subtly or overtly in intimate relationships, family relationships, and social relationships, as well as political and professional relationships.

Not involving consent in decisions and actions in any kind of human relationship leads to domination, which strips you of your own will and humanity. It reduces us to a sense of slavery and steals autonomy. It doesn't make for a happy relationship of any kind – personal or professional or political.

In some contexts, people do want someone else to make decisions and take action on their behalf within certain areas of life; but in that case, it is consent and no longer domination.

On the Boundaries Dashboard, remember that two of the four display lights show you how you make decisions in the relationship; they are the fuel light, as introduced in the last chapter, and the battery light as you're reading about in this chapter. Fuel is the metaphor for how much your motivators align with your decisions, and the battery is a measure of how much consent is involved in your decisions.

How much of your will is involved in your decisions and actions? And how much do you involve the will of the other person? Who might be stripping whose will in this relationship?

How much are you like the crazy-faced meme girl? How much is the other person like her?

And how does this consent and agreement apply to your relationship with yourself? You can force yourself to do or say things without your own full consent. In your mind, you might make a decision and take action based on someone else's values or what you think they want or what you heard from someone else, even though you don't fully agree with those values or know how they align with your direction in life.

Failing to check in with your own internal sense of consent in your decisions can create feelings of failure, self-betrayal, distrust, and guilt.

If a part of you is waving a red flag but you go ahead anyway, then you can easily become the crazy-faced meme girl in your own relationship with yourself.

YOUR PERSONAL VOLTAGE

When a car battery starts dying, the engine becomes slow to crank like it's gasping for air before it kicks in. It becomes harder and harder to start the car, and eventually the battery loses charge. The car goes nowhere without power.

Likewise, when your metaphorical battery finally dies in a relationship, you feel as if you're just towed along by the decisions and actions of the other person like a car hanging off the back of a tow truck. The other person has full control.

In a vehicle, the technical name for the device that measures battery power is a "voltmeter." The voltmeter indicates the state of charge in a battery. Keeping an eye on the charge levels gives you the cue to plug in and recharge the power.

The Boundaries Dashboard "battery" light is like a voltmeter, and consent is the voltage that powers your battery in this relationship. Consent means to agree on the decisions and actions that impact one or both of you. It means that each voice in the relationship matters. It honors everyone's autonomy.

Part Two: Check the Lights

Car batteries have two terminals – positive and negative, and a circuit of power is formed when they connect. That connection and the power formed is like the giving and receiving of consent. It isn't an empowering relationship if only one of the terminals is connected.

There's a problem with the circuitry when your consent doesn't play much of a part of the decisions in the relationship. Equally, there's a circuitry problem when the other person's consent doesn't play much of a part in the decisions.

Remember that you can consent to the other person making certain decisions and actions on your behalf. If you consent to letting someone else decide or handle something on your behalf, then whatever they decide or do under that authority is done with your consent.

For example, in politics, someone who refuses to vote is someone who consents to having no say in the election process; they hand over those decisions to their fellow citizens.

Someone who prefers to give their romantic partner all the decision-making power in a specific area of life, such as finance, is someone who willingly consents to having no direct say in financial decisions.

Someone who signs up for the defense force joins with the understanding that they are consenting to military leaders deciding on their behalf where they live, how long they sleep, and their hours of work. Those who sign up for the defense force consent to a large degree of someone else making much of their daily life decisions.

The non-voting citizen, the romantic partner who doesn't want anything to do with finances, and the new recruit to the military – they are each consenting to their decisions being made by someone else on their behalf.

Sometimes you lack knowledge or experience to make an informed decision, and in those specific areas, you might let the other person completely make decisions for you. Other times, you might agree with the other person making decisions and taking action on your behalf because you have not yet identified what you want, need, desire, or value at the time.

All of those scenarios respect your autonomy. However, a relationship begins to look like a dictatorship when a person's consent is not sought in the decisions and actions of the relationship. It looks more like a slave and master, when either person's autonomy is not acknowledged properly in the process.

When you provide and seek consent in the choices and decisions of a relationship, it's like a democracy where the voice of each individual can be counted.

Your free will, your needs, and your desires matter.

It also goes both ways; without consent, either of you can be the dictator, slave owner, or a democratic leader.

Part Two: Check the Lights

CHAPTER 7 EXERCISE, PART 1

YOUR CONSENT SCORE

Now it's time to look into your battery power in this relationship.

In your Dashboard Diary, write the title "Battery Light" and today's date at the top of the page.

Underneath the title, write a numbered list down the page from 1 through 12, and leave space for a score next to each.

For each of the six boundaries, you'll write down a score for two forms of consent – giving and receiving. So, by the end of your scoring, you'll have a total of 12 scores.

At the end, you'll add those 12 scores together for a total number, and that total number will equate to either a red, yellow, or green battery light.

Take time to reflect on each score before you write it down. Check in with your memory, your body, and your nervous system for each question; that will give you the best answer.

Part Two: Check the Lights

So, let's get started.

When thinking about your own decisions and actions in this relationship, how true is each statement for you on a 0–10 scale? A score of 10 means "it's completely true" for you, and a score of 0 means "it's not true at all" for you.

Write down a number for each of the following 12 statements, and at the end, we will add them all together for one total score.

_____

TIME
_____

1. When it comes to deciding the hours and minutes I share with the other person and the frequency of those blocks of time, I clearly express my consent or lack thereof.

2. When it comes to deciding the hours and minutes I share with the other person and the frequency of those blocks of time, I clearly seek consent from the other person.

_____

TERRITORIES
_____

3. When it comes to decisions about the environments and spaces that I share with the other person (including body boundaries or personal space), I clearly express my consent or lack thereof.

4. When it comes to decisions about the environments and spaces that I share with the other person (including body boundaries or personal space), I clearly seek consent from the other person.

TREASURES

5. When it comes to decisions about the investment of my energy (my mental, physical, emotional, material, and financial resources), I clearly express my consent or lack thereof.

6. When it comes to decisions about the investment of my energy (my mental, physical, emotional, material, and financial resources), I clearly seek consent from the other person.

TOOLS

7. When it comes to decisions about communication tools I use with the other person, I clearly express my consent or lack thereof.

8. When it comes to decisions about communication tools I use with the other person, I clearly seek consent from the other person.

TOPICS

9. When it comes to decisions about the topics I bring up and don't bring up with the other person, I clearly express my consent or lack thereof.

10. When it comes to decisions about the topics I bring up and don't bring up with the other person, I clearly seek consent from the other person.

THIRD PARTIES

Besides the relationship I have with this person, there are other human relationships that I believe, to a noticeable degree, influence my ideas, feelings, thoughts, and behaviors toward this relationship. I share the planet Earth with billions of other humans, so technically, the entire planet is a third party, but realistically, only one or two relationships most directly impact this relationship on a day-to-day basis.

Any human relationship outside of this one that I believe currently impacts this relationship (as just described) is a third party to this relationship because of their influence, whether positive or negative.

11. When it comes to decisions about any human relationship that impact this one, I clearly express my consent or lack thereof.

12. When it comes to decisions about any human relationship that impact this one, I clearly seek consent from the other person.

You did it! Good job. That was a lot of work. Now, if you add together all 12 of your scores, what is the total number? Write down the total in your Diary and circle it so that it stands out. If using a digital device, you can bold, underline, or perhaps use an emoji so you can quickly spot this later.

CHAPTER 7 EXERCISE, PART 2

COLOR OF YOUR DASHBOARD LIGHT

Now it's time to convert your total score to the color of your battery light. In Part 1, the highest possible total was 120 (12 questions with a maximum of 10 points each).

If your total score equals a number between 0 and 59, then your indicator is red.

A total score between 60 and 95 gives you a yellow light.

It's a beautiful bright green if your score falls between 96 and 120.

In your Diary, write down your total score and which of the three colors that it converts to. Draw a big obvious circle around both the score and the color – or highlight it in some other way if your Diary is digital – so that you can spot it easily whenever you look back to this exercise.

CHAPTER 8

TEMPERATURE CHECK (EMOTIONAL STATE)

(38 minute read)

REPRIORITIZING FEELINGS

In the past, emotions were often dismissed or belittled. The concept of "feelings" was given far less respect in life and business. For example, at work, a "sick day" had to be physical or visible or else it wasn't valid or respected. And workers experiencing "burnout" were dismissed as lacking resilience or dedication. But as science has advanced its understanding of emotions, society is recognizing the growing significance of feelings.

Now, in the UK, there is no legal difference between taking a sick day for mental health or physical health reasons. In a growing number of developed countries, companies now provide well-being checks and mental health support to workers, which is increasingly becoming an activity mandated by law.

There are many more examples of the growing importance of feelings, such as "emotional distress" being legally recognized in many jurisdictions as a just cause for compensation, and schools switching from writing off certain children as "troublemakers" who require disciplinary action to seeing the need for those children to participate in social and emotional learning programs for healthy development.

Many women who may have been once brushed off as "overly emotional" at a certain time of the month are now properly diagnosed with premenstrual dysphoric disorder (PMDD), a serious hormonal condition with distinct emotional and physical symptoms.

Brain scan technology now shows that both emotional and physical pain activate the same areas in the brain. Both physical injury and emotional pain, such as the painful feelings of a breakup, can cause a part of the brain called the "hippocampus" to shrink. Also, both kinds of pain can cause changes in certain chemicals related to inflammation and affect how immune cells work.

As medical technology continues to advance, the equal significance of emotional and physical pain are becoming increasingly evident and trackable. We are continually learning about the direct relationship between emotional state and physical health, and we are, for the first time in history, seeing the dire medical consequences of belittling or ignoring them.

WHAT "EMOTIONAL STATE" MEANS

OK, it's a serious subject but what does the phrase mean? When I use the words "emotional state," or "emotions" for short, I am referring to neurological and physiological states throughout the body as well as the name or label that I give to that experience.

Emotional states can involve several bodily systems such as breathing patterns (fast or relaxed), feelings in the tummy (like indigestion if nervous or butterflies if in love, etc.), heartbeat (fast or calm), muscular tension (relaxed or tense), and sensory perception.

An emotional state can be felt anywhere from head to toe, such as from deep in the abdomen – that "pit in the stomach" feeling that something's wrong – all the way to the skin when you "get chills" from something spooky or sweaty palms from anxiousness. Even a subtle twitch can be part of the experience of an emotional state.

Since the term "emotional state" is a well-established phrase, I'll stick to that language in this book. But because emotional states can encompass and integrate both neurological and physiological states, I would rather use a phrase that covers all of those biological elements of emotion – an idea called "biomotional state."

"Biomotional state" combines the words "biological" with "emotional" and it refers to the biological state produced by emotions in the body, how they express themselves through the body's neurological and physiological systems.

Biomotional state encompasses a more complete representation of the biological impact of emotions – what's felt neurologically, physiologically, and in any other way by the person experiencing feelings anywhere from head to toe.

However, I've introduced enough new terms in this book, so I'll leave "biomotional state" here in this chapter as a passing reflection, and I'll continue to use the more popular "emotional state" or "emotions" for short.

And now that you know what an emotional state encompasses, the next time you check your boundaries, you can give a more wholistic and accurate score.

Part Two: Check the Lights

EMOTIONS VS. THOUGHTS

What role do thoughts play in an "emotional state"? Thoughts trigger my emotional states, and emotional states trigger my thoughts. So, I like to think of emotions and thoughts as a kind of brother and sister, separate but part of the same family. They argue often, and it's beautiful when they find peace.

It might be hard to pinpoint a clear distinction between them, but perhaps the easiest way to think of the difference is that thoughts are words or images in the brain, and emotions are experienced anywhere throughout the body. Both emotions and thoughts belong to the umbrella topics of mental health, philosophy of mind, neurology, and psychology, but thoughts and emotions are not synonymous. Perhaps the place where emotion and thought first overlap is when you give the emotion a name.

Another overlap of emotion and thought, as I see it, is *attitude*. An attitude adjustment is a shift of your emotional state triggered by an intentional change in your thoughts. For example, I might feel bitter and ungrateful about a situation in life, but then I can decide to change my thoughts to "I am owed nothing, and I am grateful for everything I have." And my emotional state suddenly shifts.

By turning the Topics boundary dial of my inner thoughts, I improve my emotional state. Some days I need to make adjustments 95 times to get my internal conversation right; other days my healthy thought momentum is strong, and I only need a few adjustments.

Chapter 8: Temperature Check (Emotional State)

EMOTIONS MEAN SURVIVAL

As we know from the studies at the beginning of this book, negative or positive emotions repeated over time can make or break your physical health and longevity.

Emotions also have the power to send people into life-threatening situations like dangerous levels of recklessness or severe depression leading to suicide.

If you drive while intensely emotional, for example, you might find yourself so distracted by those emotions that you run off the road into a tree, as I've nearly done before. You also can feel so emotional that you momentarily lose track of where you're walking and step out in front of a bus, which I've also done before (thank God the bus was moving slowly enough for me to jump out of the way!).

Awareness of your temperature light means survival.

Emotions also have the power to save your life. They have a way of giving you a nudge when something doesn't seem right, and your brain does not know the words yet, but you do know something needs your action or attention.

Emotional state awareness is powerful, even when you cannot name the emotion. The truth is, you simply will not always know the right or best word to describe what you're feeling. With roughly 700,000 words in an English dictionary, an adult knows on average only 4% of those words, and language is constantly evolving.

Whether we know the right words or not, signals from the brain matter. If an emotional state can risk your life or save it, then maintaining awareness daily, regardless of labelling it, is just as important as making sure

Part Two: Check the Lights

the knobs on your gas stove are turned off or remembering to fasten your seatbelt on a roller coaster ride.

The temperature light is the most important of the four lights on the Boundaries Dashboard in every kind of relationship because it tracks the health of your emotional state, whether or not you have the words.

The temperature light is also important because of the power of consequences. In a real car, when one part breaks down, it can impact other parts soon after like a domino effect. Likewise, the temperature light will often turn yellow or red before other parts of your life break down, too.

Catch the breakdown before it happens. Keep an eye on the temperature light. You'll learn how in this chapter.

SELF-OBSERVATION
INSIDE HUMAN RELATIONSHIPS

"The right people feel different to your nervous system." That's a quote I saw on my Facebook newsfeed today before I started writing.

Not long before seeing that quote, I encountered a similar theme on TV. I was watching one of those reality dating shows where people dress overly sexy and compete for their love interest's attention – a genre which I happen to love, and please don't hate me for that! On the show, a single girl named Julia spoke to the camera, thinking out loud and comparing her two potential partners.

Julia said, "John and Stephen are completely different. John's very explosive. Stephen is very explosive in happiness. John drains me. And Stephen kind of refuels me."

In this show, it was up to each contestant to find their best match, and Julia felt conflicted because she felt sexually attracted to both John and Stephen, but emotionally she felt different. In front of the camera, she stopped to observe how differently each man impacted her nervous system and physiology.

That's self-observation.

When Julia reads this book, she'll be able to recognize that what she was doing was checking the temperature light on her dashboard; in other words, she was observing how her body – nervous system and all – responds when interacting with each of the two guys. While feeling sexually attracted to both, one of them drained her emotionally and the other energized her. She was doing this to help her figure out what's healthy for her and who to choose.

While you might not have a reality show producer prompting you to do it in front of a camera, we all do have the same kind of need for a self-observation process to analyze our nervous system and physiological response in human relationships.

You can think of your observation of your emotional state as simply the gathering of neurological and physiological data. Data simply gives you information, and it's up to you to sort out what that data means as well as what it does and doesn't point to.

In your interactions with other people, the temperature light gives you data about the interaction. It categorizes your emotional state. This dashboard light gathers data about how you feel inside of your body about this relationship. You'll take a look at your data in this chapter's exercise.

Part Two: Check the Lights

SELF-OBSERVATION
IN MY RELATIONSHIP WITH ME

The temperature light is also how you measure your emotional state in your relationship with yourself. For example, I have been learning to observe my own tone of voice and the speed at which I speak, because these two things help me realize when I feel anxious or too excited.

Doing a solo podcast – where I talk for an hour straight alone into a microphone – turned out to be excellent training in self-observation. In my headphones during the recording, when I hear my own voice talking too quickly, or I notice it going too high for too long or too low for too long, these are yellow flags to myself to pause and ask myself what I need and what's behind this shift of energy.

Listening closely to the speed and pitch of my own speaking voice is a skill that I learned from a communications expert and keynote speaker from Australia named Vinh Quang Giang.

When I catch myself speaking too fast or my energy seems a bit too hyper for too long, I stop and observe. I pause because I know that when I speak with certain kinds of energy, it can wipe me out suddenly – I can drain my own energy if I don't slow down. And in other situations, I can bring my energy down if I don't look for ways to perk myself up.

In addition to my voice, I also have been learning to observe my thoughts.

I remember how, for a large part of my life, I could not sit alone in silence with my own thoughts or else I'd feel like crawling out of my skin. Even in my car, I could not drive in silence. Something had to be playing on the car stereo to drown out what was in my mind. My thoughts ran through my head unchecked, unfiltered, unobserved, and had me afraid and disgusted at the idea of hearing what those thoughts were saying. But all of that changed when I read the book *The Power of Now* by Eckhart Tolle.

Through that book, I learned forms of meditation that I could understand. I had heard of other forms of meditation prior to reading that book, but they seemed too weird or too impractical for me. The imagine-yourself-floating-above-the-universe kind of meditation just left me feeling helpless and scared in outer space – hah!

However, with Tolle's practical form of meditation, I learned how to practice sitting with my own thoughts and observing them for long periods of time rather than letting my thoughts rule me and my emotional state. I call it "thought observation." At first, I'd set the alarm and do it for any amount of time that I could fit into my day – from 30 seconds up to an hour. Then, for a long time, I did only one minute a day.

Now, thought observation practice is something I just naturally do throughout the day. Sometimes I do return to timed meditations, though. When I feel myself slipping emotionally, I go back to the dedicated practice of setting a timer, and I observe my thoughts until the alarm rings.

It only involves sitting and observing – not trying to stop my natural flood of thoughts as some meditation practices hopelessly urge you to do. It's as if I become a third party to my own thoughts and feelings in a purely sane and peaceful way.

These days, when I sit in silence, instead of feeling like a scary stranger to myself, I often feel entertained by my own thoughts and a warm sense of being "with myself."

With every Boundaries Health Check score that you complete, you are practicing the sanity-saving skill of thought observation. More than that, when you witness both your thoughts and your body's sensations and reactions to them, then it becomes "self-observation." Observing thoughts is step one, and observing how you feel in your body is step two. Together, they are the act of self-observation. Each of the four dashboard lights require you to step back and observe how you think and feel.

If you ignore the temperature light – in other words, if you ignore your emotional state – or if you suppress it or even gaslight yourself about how you feel, then it ends up spilling messily into unwanted areas of life and often in embarrassing or even devastating ways.

FROM CRAWLING TO WALKING, FROM WEAK TO STRONG

If you're new to the act of paying attention to the inner world of your thoughts, feelings, and nervous system, then self-observation can sound exhausting.

If self-observation is new to you, think of it in terms of baby steps. You might feel like a baby learning first to crawl, then to get yourself up off the ground, and then to balance on your two little feet for the first time. At first you're very wobbly and constantly falling over. But each day you wobble a little less, until one day you don't wobble anymore.

Learning how to observe your thoughts and feelings will happen slowly and gradually, one small win at a time.

And, just as everyone celebrates a child's first step, each tiny bit of evidence of progress deserves your acknowledgement and celebration. Every attempt and each step are momentum-building victories.

You can also think of self-observation like lifting weights. At the gym, it can take a few years of consistent nutrition and training to lift two times your body weight. Endurance and strength build over time. The good news is that this book is like your personal trainer for self-observation;

I prepared exercises at the end of each chapter to help you build the endurance and strength it takes.

INTRODUCING "YOU"

There's a distinction between you and your emotional state.

I am the *observer* of my thoughts and feelings; I *am not* my thoughts and feelings.

At any given moment, I can choose to either face or ignore the thoughts and feelings that pass through me. And in every one of those moments, there is the "I," there are the thoughts, and there are the feelings.

Thoughts, beliefs, and feelings all matter, but they also change throughout life; yet through all of them, something remains constant in me. What remains constant behind all thoughts, beliefs, and feelings?

When I reached one of the lowest emotional points in a relationship, my therapist at the time handed me a book that made me aware of that question and the answer. At any other time of my life, I would have felt confused and even bored by it, but the book *The Power of Now* spoke loudly and straight to my soul because of the timing. "When the student is ready, the teacher will appear," as they say.

It felt as though the author introduced me to the real "me." For the first time in my life, I experienced the liberating sensation of stepping back to notice the distinction between myself as the observer of my thoughts vs. the thoughts themselves. The "I" of my life is the one who observes my thoughts, and the same goes for feelings. The "I" is the one that observes thoughts and feelings.

"I" remains constant as an observer, while thoughts and feelings form, move, and change over me like clouds in the sky, creating sensations as they pass through. I feel the rain from those clouds, but I am not the rain. I feel the cold from the wind, but I am not the wind.

Here's a key excerpt, where the author describes his own mental struggle and breakthrough moment:

> *"I cannot live with myself any longer." This was the thought that kept repeating itself in my mind. Then suddenly I became aware of what a peculiar thought it was. "Am I one or two? If I cannot live with myself, there must be two of me: the 'I' and the 'self' that 'I' cannot live with." "Maybe," I thought, "only one of them is real."*[18]

Unlike that author, I do believe both my thoughts and I are "real." However, the recognition of the space between the two is as lifesaving as recognizing the space between my feet and the edge of a steep cliff. It is utterly emotionally lifesaving.

By checking the lights on your Boundaries Dashboard, I believe that you will begin to learn the liberating distinction between "you" and the "feelings and thoughts" that pass through you.

BODY VOCABULARY

The temperature light is about stopping to observe changes in your nervous system and recognizing bodily signals and symptoms. Without words, it's mind-blowing how the body screams out a message that something's wrong or about to go wrong.

Many years ago, I had a job where, on the outside, things looked outstanding for me. I had a good title, and I nailed my role. My manager expressed appreciation for my work on a regular basis. But at the same time that I was doing well on the outside, little did my manager know that my body was constantly sending me very different signals.

I felt new and strange pains in my chest throughout the day. I also felt extreme fatigue that had me doing whatever I could to not fall asleep during meetings or fall into a deep dreamlike state at my desk.

At the same time that I was fighting chest pains and experiencing what seemed like a kind of narcolepsy, I also started to lose my 20/20 vision and found it hard to see straight.

I went through multiple tests with several medical specialists to figure out the root of these problems, and the results all pointed to one thing. I remember sitting in the hospital while the sleep doctor was reviewing my test results. I vividly remember how he rolled his chair over to me, looked me in the eyes and said, "You need to quit your job."

The big shock in this story was when my cardiologist gave me the same exact message: "Quit your job."

And if that wasn't enough confirmation of my body screaming something was wrong... I had never needed eyeglasses before, but while working that job, my eyesight changed and the eye doctor prescribed me glasses.

Ending my relationship (on great terms) with that employer resulted in my eyesight returning, my chest pains leaving, and the sudden narcoleptic episodes ending. After quitting, I returned to the same eye doctor for an exam, and he discovered my vision had returned to 20/20.

Your body speaks. It has its own vocabulary that requires you to acknowledge, listen, and translate. It took three doctors for me to decode the message, but I eventually learned my body's way of saying: "Quit your job."

And I must add here that the next job I took was the most exciting position I ever had. So, the reward for quitting the wrong job to find the right one was extraordinary.

I have also "read" the message in my body in my dating life many times. In one relationship, I unintentionally caught myself on my security camera walking around with what looked like tensely raised shoulders. I became fixated on this discovery and thought about it deeply over several days. What was my body saying?

I checked old security camera footage to see how often I was doing this. I seemed to always have that tightness in my shoulders around my boyfriend at the time. After a few weeks of figuring out what my body was saying to me, I was able to recognize that the relationship was doing it to me.

We were sexually attracted to each other, but I also felt tense around him. I needed more transparency, and this left me feeling unsafe in the relationship.

In another intimate relationship, I found myself feeling increasingly irritable all the time. Most people knew me as cheery, but I felt my normal facial expressions changing. I took this to a therapist to help me translate it all and realized that the cause was extreme dissatisfaction in the romantic department and an overall mismatch on many levels.

Another example. In phone calls with a particular family member, I noticed a distinct pattern at the 30-minute mark of every call – my face would start to sadden, my energy would suddenly drop like a rock off a cliff, and I would just feel like I was dragging myself through mud. But after recognizing that clear pattern, I decided that from then on, at the 25-minute mark I would say, "Alright, it's time for me to go now."

The body speaks. Like a newborn baby cries without words and its parents have to decode its needs, I believe that as adults all parts of our body still cry out when something within us needs our attention.

It is not only the unpleasant or painful feelings that require interpreting; it's the pleasant ones, too. It's interpreting what feels good that has helped me make healthier decisions about what to keep or add more of in my life as well.

I once accepted a contract with an employer, even though the pay wasn't as high as my skills could earn elsewhere, simply because I was convinced ahead of time that the people I'd be working with would make me feel relaxed and happy each day.

And that's what happened.

I found myself cracking up laughing whenever I worked with that team. I genuinely looked forward to going to the office just to experience the surprise of what a particular coworker would say that would be a hilariously unintentional TMI ("too much information") moment or an innocent but hilariously awkward observation about someone else.

I enjoyed my life a bit more while working that lesser-paid role, and a few of those memories were priceless. That "TMI" co-worker's influence on me was also profound. I learned how to lighten up in the workplace, something that the corporate soldier in me desperately needed.

ORIGINAL OWNERSHIP

"You don't get to choose how I feel."

When I first heard that saying, it hit me straight in the gut.

Another person may observe and assume how I feel, but no one else can enter my nervous system to feel my feelings for me.

You are the world's leading expert on what you feel because you own and live inside of your nervous system – and no one else in this universe does. That's why you are the only authority on how you feel, and you are the only one who can confirm the temperature of your internal emotional state.

Others may observe you from the outside and offer descriptions or labels for how you feel, and that might help you come up with the right language, but only you can verify and confirm what best matches your emotional state.

So where do you begin in that identification process? The temperature light helps you quickly identify which of three general ranges of emotion you feel at any given moment, and this chapter introduces you to how it all works.

If I get sick with what feels like a fever, I don't put the thermometer into someone else's mouth to check my temperature. Likewise, each of us is responsible for checking in on what we feel inside our bodies and nervous systems.

While it can be helpful for others to assist in finding the words for how you feel, they cannot see or feel the complexity of images and sensations running through your brain and body. While there is technology being developed to help us identify emotions, the job is ultimately up to us as the owners of our bodies to confirm or deny what's really happening.

THE SCIENTIFIC TOOLS INSIDE OF YOU

There is a device developed by researchers at MIT's Computer Science and Artificial Intelligence Laboratory called "EQ-Radio" that uses wireless signals to detect a person's emotions through their breathing and heart rhythms.[19] With 87% accuracy, EQ-Radio can identify a person's emotion as joy, pleasure, anger, or sadness.

While EQ-Radio may be useful in the marketing industry to help businesses understand customers' responses, it's not yet a technology that's available to the public to help figure yourself out after a bad day at work.

Even if you don't yet have your own EQ-Radio to help sort out what your nervous system is saying to you, you do have the Boundaries Dashboard. The temperature light reading, as you will see in this chapter's exercise, allows you to identify which one of three "temperature ranges" your emotions fall into – healthy, dangerous, or somewhere in between.

While it's sometimes hard to say how we feel, placing a feeling into one of these three ranges can clearly separate what's life-giving from what's life-taking.

It can be hard to find the right name or emotion-label for a feeling. So, more important than labeling a feeling with a word such as "pleasure" or "sadness," I find that it's far more important and fundamental to identify how healthy a feeling might be; and this is what the temperature light does for you.

Part Two: Check the Lights

THREE DEGREES

We know with certainty that temperatures outside a certain range will simply kill us, while temperatures within a certain range keep us healthy.

If you spend enough time outdoors in the range of 90°F to 105°F (32°C to 40°C), you'll end up with heat cramps and heat exhaustion. Spend enough time in temperatures over 130°F (54°C), and you'll get heatstroke.[20]

Monitoring outside temperatures keeps you alive. Monitoring the internal temperature of your body also keeps you alive.

For human organs to function normally, we need an internal temperature somewhere in the range of 96.8°F to 100.4°F (36°C to 38°C).[21] A core body temperature of around 108°F (42.22°C) results in convulsions or death. If it's too cold or too hot inside the human body, it becomes a life-or-death situation.

In human relationships, there's another temperature range to monitor – your emotional temperature.

Human relationships can push your emotional temperature into dangerous ranges, too, like a sense of emotional frostbite or heatstroke.

There is a temperature range where the relationship remains healthy for you, there is a temperature range that puts you at risk, and there's a range that's outright unhealthy.

On the Boundaries Dashboard, the temperature light lets you observe and measure your emotional state at any moment, allowing you to identify which of those three broad temperature ranges that it falls into. If it's a risky or dangerous temperature, you know it's time to adjust boundaries to get you back into a safe range.

Chapter 8: Temperature Check (Emotional State)

At any given moment in your interactions with the other person, your emotional state falls into any one of three broad ranges. I call them: first-degree (healthy), second-degree (a mix of healthy and unhealthy, or uncertainty about it), and third-degree (unhealthy).

There are many visuals I can use to illustrate the three temperature ranges, but my favorite way is to imagine a single circle divided into three concentric rings, like a target board. The inside of each of the three rings symbolizes a wide range of emotional states that you can find yourself in at any moment.

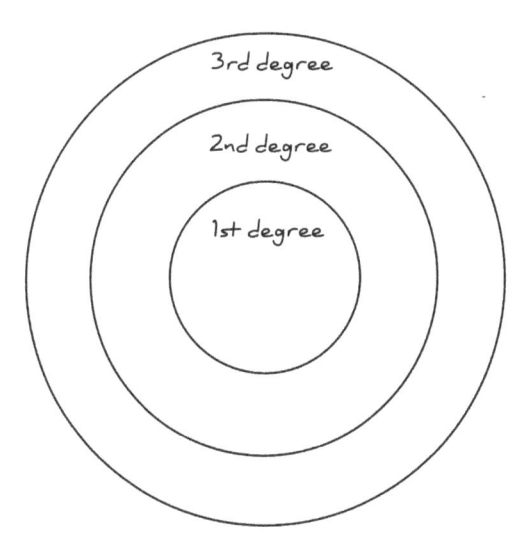

The ring in the center of the circle represents first-degree emotions (healthy), the middle ring represents second-degree emotions (uncertain or a mix of healthy and unhealthy), and the outer ring represents third-degree emotions (unhealthy).

Think of the center ring as your focal point and aim, like the bullseye on a dartboard.

Finding and maintaining the center creates and maintains power. In technology, when a satellite dish is pointed toward the center point of a satellite, it maximizes the sending and receiving of signals. In performing arts, dancers often focus on a central point to maintain balance and orientation during complex movements.

Aim for the center.

First-degree is the aim.

WHEN NAMES DON'T MATTER

When thinking of your emotional state and trying to place it into one of the three temperature ranges, it's important to remember that the feeling of the emotion – the pleasure, peace, or pain that it triggers in your body, the power with which it controls your behavior, the impact it has on your day to day function, the degree to which it distracts you or empowers you – is more important than the name of the emotion itself.

Emotional states can have multiple levels of complexity, so picking only one label can feel inaccurate. On top of that, we may each have very different experiences associated with the same name of an emotion. So, communicating the word can prove confusing.

One person thinks of the emotion "excitement" as a positive force for healthy growth and fulfillment, while another person thinks of "excitement" as a risky thrill to escape problems.

One person thinks of "hope" as a strong emotional state for overcoming adversity and being a creative problem solver, while another person sees it as naïve, unrealistic, and leading to disappointment.

One person may think of "compassion" as a source of empathy and connection that strengthens human connection, while another person may see it as a weakness that leaves you open for exploitation.

Different people can have very different meanings and stories attached to the same name for an emotion, and so in the Boundaries Health Check, you simply pick from three general ranges of feelings.

You can check in with the state of your mind and body to identify whether it belongs in the first-degree, second-degree, or third-degree range of emotional states, which I will define for you in about a minute.

As I found out while listening to one of my current favorite podcasts hosted by Andrew Huberman, PhD, I'm not alone in splitting emotions into three basic categories. There is a famous neuroscientist, Markus D. Meister, PhD, who identified three basic emotional responses: "Yum, I like it," "Yuck, I hate it," or "Meh, whatever." It's referred to as a "trinary response."[22]

To make it even easier, in the Boundaries Health Check app, which I'm building as I write the first edition of this book, you can fully bypass the complexity of assigning names and words by picking either a facial expression or a color on a scale from red to yellow to bright green. A score is then calculated from the colors or faces you choose, and that score automatically falls into one of the three temperature ranges.

For each of the temperature ranges that I am about to describe, I've also shared their corresponding colors from the Boundaries Health Check App. So, here is my theory on the three temperature ranges, the essential rule for each one, a visual metaphor to help illustrate their differences, and a list of examples of emotions that fit into each one.

First-Degree Emotions (Green Range)

The rule of first-degree emotions is this: an emotional state falls into this range if, and only if, your mind and body agree that it feels nourishing, life-giving, or healthy for you.

Examples for me include gratitude, joy, peace, adventure, thrill, healthy excitement, liveliness, confidence, laughter, contentment, feeling grounded, comfort, sanity, a sense of safety, compassion, stability, respect, productivity, innocence, teamwork, balance, ownership (i.e., ownership of my feelings), an overall sense of health or goodness, or just a simple uneventful state of calm. These emotions can range from an intense and healthy thrill that makes my senses come alive all the way to a quiet and neutral state of calm.

These emotions are like fresh fruit that is ripe, bright colored, and healthy.

Second-Degree Emotions (Yellow Range)

The rule of second-degree emotions is this: feelings fall in this range when they give you any degree of doubt as to whether or not they're healthy.

In other words, if your mind and body do not fully agree whether an emotional state falls into the category of first-degree (healthy) or third-degree (unhealthy), then it belongs here in the range of second-degree emotions.

These emotions feel less than good to any degree. For me, examples include feeling bored, confused, lost, lonely, imbalanced, slightly agitated, subtle discomfort, rushed, complacent, or just a general less-than-good feeling at some level.

Second-degree feelings have a range of intensity, but they will never feel extreme or severe. These emotions can range from feelings of "something's just not right" all the way to feelings of bodily discomfort.

These emotions are like fruit that's edible but small parts of it taste "off" – even just a little.

As an example, the modern concept of "good stress" falls into the second-degree range for me. This is when I feel stressed but there's a mix of good feelings woven into it, like my very first shaky day working under a new contract at a new organization, or like the slightly terrified feeling of going to meet someone for the first time from a dating app.

It's exciting to experience a new office, but there's an emotional weight of feeling buried under too much new information on day one. The possibility of meeting a potential partner is exciting, but it's a horrible feeling to worry whether or not the guy will look like his profile photo, or if he is secretly married.

"Good stress" doesn't feel nourishing, but it doesn't feel dangerous either; so, it's second-degree for me.

If at any given moment you feel unsure about which of the three ranges an emotion fits into, then it belongs to the second-degree range. Questionable feelings are just that – questionable! And even if they give a stronger positive sense than a negative one, then they still contain uncertainty and so belong in the second-degree range.

Third-Degree Emotions (Red Range)

The rule of third-degree emotions is this: your mind and body agree that the emotional state feels unhealthy for you.

To varying degrees of intensity, these feel heavy, unhealthy, sickening, or at worst, violating. They may last only a moment or a very long time.

Third-degree emotions can start subtly with a passing moment of rage and they can grow into what feels like emotional frostbite or the scorching heat of the Sahara Desert. Third-degree emotions can also feel like you're slowly losing your sense of stability and peace, or it can feel as though you have lost control.

For me, third-degree emotions include feeling obsessed, anxious, arrogant, unsafe, guilty, angry, shamed or desiring to shame others, manipulative or feeling manipulated, feeling threatened or being threatening, scapegoating or being scapegoated, and obvious negativity in any form.

These emotions are like overripe or decaying fruit; it doesn't taste good. It makes you want to spit it out of your mouth.

A second-degree emotion can often repeat so often or last so long that it eventually intensifies into third-degree. It's like a fire that you sit beside for so long that it starts to burn your clothes or like a cold hard breeze that blows so often and so long that you don't realize you've been frostbitten.

A feeling of uncertainty about the health of an emotion usually means there is a mix of healthy and unhealthy, but if this kind of uncertainty continues or repeats for a significant amount of time, most likely it will cross over to a third-degree emotion.

The three ranges of emotions consist of broad spectrums of feelings, sensations, physiological, or neurological states. Since you have your own personal and cultural meaning to the names of each emotion, it's ultimately up to you to decide in which range they belong.

OUT OF RANGE

Out of the three ranges of emotions, where does it fit when you feel "nothing"? Does feeling nothing fall outside of all three ranges? In other words, where do the emotional states of callousness and neutrality belong? They're almost hollow emotions.

First, let's talk about callousness.

Many people who do manual labor get calloused hands because of the friction and weight of tools rubbing against their skin. Their skin thickens and loses sensation. It seems no different in human relationships: too much emotional friction causes the loss of emotional sensation.

Callousness can mean depression or the loss of hope after several repeated experiences of disappointment or anger. So, for that reason, I'd put callousness into third-degree emotions since it's long-term and severe.

Next, let's talk about feeling neutral.

A sense of "feeling nothing" does not always mean callousness; it can also refer to a very healthy sense that you haven't formed an opinion yet. It's a feeling of calm like a still lake – no winds or activity to move the water, just flat and motionless.

Neutrality is an emotional state where there is no strong charge either for or against someone or something. Neutrality easily moves into a passionate or obvious emotional state after you are given enough information or evidence to form an opinion.

Until you have enough information to form an emotional opinion, neutrality is an emotional state of calmness. It's simply a state of no data, so there's no "for or against." Neutrality is like an impartial judge in a courtroom before they are given all the evidence.

I would place neutrality, in that case, in the range of first-degree emotions.

Diagnosing your "nothing" feeling as callousness or neutrality is up to you. Just as your body temperature can only be read with the thermometer in your own mouth, not in the mouth of other person, it is the same with your emotional state.

Someone might look at you and believe you are experiencing a certain emotional temperature range, but only you inwardly feel its truth or falseness.

PATTERNS DETERMINE YOUR TEMPERATURE FORECAST

Because of studies like those mentioned earlier in this book, we know that prolonged positive emotions in your relationships, such as peace, encouragement, joy, and laughter, elongate life. The opposite is also true regarding prolonged negative emotions like stress, discouragement, and anger; they shorten life.

Short-lived negative emotions can happen in healthy relationships, as many of us would agree, but not many of us realize the dangers of long-term patterns of negative emotions. Relationship interactions with long-term negative patterns aren't only metaphorically toxic; they can lead to mental and physical illness.

So, observing and keeping record of your temperature light over time isn't just a nice exercise or even an interesting thing to do – recognizing patterns in your relationship could be lifesaving.

Over time, the temperature light will give you patterns. It will give you a more honest impression of your emotional state in this relationship, and those patterns can serve as a general forecast of what to expect. However, the more data you collect over time, the more patterns will show up. This means that the longer you observe your emotional state over time, the more honest and the more reliable your forecast will be.

Recognizing patterns isn't fail-proof, but it gives us a rough idea of what we're likely to keep experiencing. Even though a typical weather forecast on the local news might only be about 70% or 80% reliable, it does give enough information to know about major weather risks.

I know photographers who look at the cloud forecast for their outdoor shoots. Surfers and hang gliders check the forecast for wind conditions. Farmers need weather forecasts to plan their planting and harvesting. Pilots need to know about potential storms to ensure safe flight routes. Tour operators and resort managers use weather forecasts to plan activities and ensure the safety of their guests.

In human relationships, I look at my emotional state weather forecast to see how much my career, health, and other human relationships might be at risk or headed toward reward.

Sometimes the big storm that the weatherman forecasted never comes, but at least with a forecast, you know when you are putting a whole day's plans and your safety at risk.

After you complete your first Boundaries Health Check, repeat it regularly – daily, weekly, or at minimum monthly – so that you can identify a history of patterns. In the Boundaries Health Check app, which I'm building as I write this book, you will easily be able to build a history of quick Boundaries Health Checks so that you can clearly see a forecast.

For those human relationships in which you've known the person a long time, the very first time you do the Boundaries Health Check, your time frame may be one year. The second time and every time you do your Boundaries Health Check afterward, your time frame would be the amount of time from the last date you completed it to the present date, which hopefully is only one day or one week.

The more data you collect over time, the more reliable the forecast. However, you can learn a lot in a short time, too. If you just met someone new and red lights flash right away, it immediately increases the risk for more frequent and dangerous patterns ahead – not a guarantee, just a high risk.

First impressions are not everything, but they do matter and give us decision-making data. For example, a job interview lasts only 20 to 40 minutes, and a company makes a forecast about the candidate after that very short meeting and with limited information.

As a more fun example, consider first or second dates. I know how I want to feel with a guy, so I evaluate how I feel on a first or second date, and it gives me a sense of what the relationship climate might be for me. That information helps me decide whether I agree to another date. Yes, feelings could potentially change, but in my experience, they usually don't.

Occasionally on a first date, a man will walk in the room and I immediately feel comfort. Other times a man will walk in the room and I immediately feel like running. While it's logically possible for me to feel differently on date two or three, I don't invest time in a second date if my body tells me to run on date number one. I'm not willing to endure that kind of emotional climate so early.

Now, let's get your forecast. Part 1 of this exercise takes an estimated temperature light reading and gives you a forecast of what patterns you can expect if nothing changes.

CHAPTER 8 EXERCISE, PART 1

TEMPERATURE FORECAST

Open your Dashboard Diary and write today's date with the title "Temperature Forecast." Beneath the date and title in the blank space, draw an empty circle.

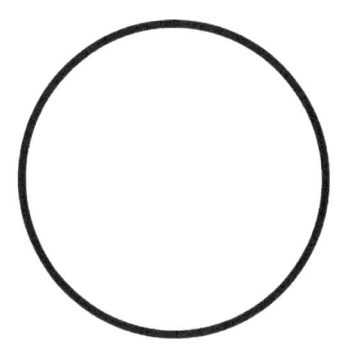

○

This circle represents the entire time frame that you have been using in previous exercises. Write "Time Frame" under the circle and the amount of time that your time frame represents.

We're about to estimate how much of the time you felt first-degree

Part Two: Check the Lights

emotions, how much you felt second-degree, and how much you felt third-degree.

I am about to explain how to put all of that into the circle.

I had a hard time figuring out how to draw a circle freehand with 10 evenly spaced slices, but then I realized it's easy if you think of the circle as a pizza pie. This pizza represents your time frame in this relationship.

I used Photoshop to cut the pizza up into ten triangles. These lines are not perfect, but it will help you draw your slices.

Chapter 8: Exercise, Part 1

The first time I tried drawing these lines it was a mess. So, for everyone who is like me, here are step-by-step instructions.

After you draw one big empty circle, draw one long line that cuts the entire "pizza pie" into two halves.

Next, focus on one half of your pizza. In this illustration, we focus on the left side of the circle.

Are you looking at just one half? Good. Now your mission is to turn the left half into five equally sized slices. To do that, draw one modest pizza slice in the center of the left side, as you see in the image below.

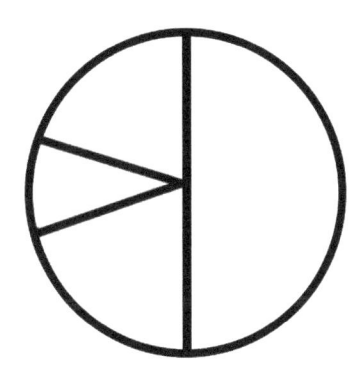

boundariescheck.com | 177

Part Two: Check the Lights

Make sure you leave two large slices on each side of it.

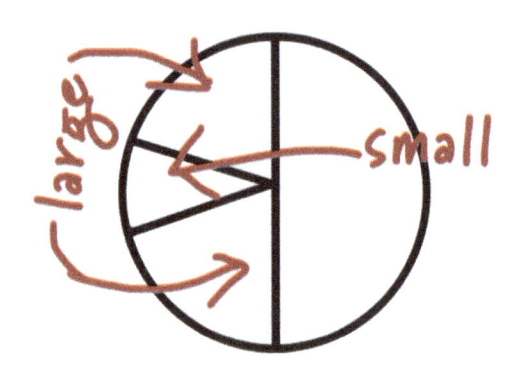

After that, you now have three slices on the left side of the pie – two large slices and one small one in the middle. Next, draw a line in the middle of each of the two large slices. This will give you five slices on the left side of the pie.

Chapter 8: Exercise, Part 1

Repeat all the same steps with the other half of the pizza pie.

Voila! Now you have ten equal sized slices.

This pizza pie and all ten slices represent the time frame that you wrote down for this relationship. Those ten slices represent that entire time frame, whether it's one year or one week.

In the next three questions, you're going to roughly determine what percentage of the pie – in other words, what percentage of the time frame – you felt each of the three temperature ranges.

For each of these three questions below, think about your own emotional state in the presence of the other person, when communicating with them, thinking about them, interacting with them, and simply when sharing space and time with the other person in any way.

Part Two: Check the Lights

QUESTION #1:

The pie and all ten of its slices represent your time frame in this relationship. Roughly, how many slices of that time represent how often you felt first-degree emotions? Pick a number of slices out of 10, and then write the word "green" on that number of slices in your pie.

For example, if you felt first-degree emotions in this relationship for a large portion of the time frame, you might decide to write "green" in 8 slices.

If you felt first-degree emotions half of the time, you might write "green" in 5 of the slices.

In order for this to work, the rule is: only one color per slice!

QUESTION #2:

Now you probably have some slices remaining. How many of the remaining slices represent how often you felt second-degree emotions? Pick a number of slices, and then write the word "yellow" on that number of slices in your pie.

Remember, the rule is only one color per slice.

For example, if you felt second-degree emotions half of the time frame, then you might write "yellow" in five of the slices.

QUESTION #3:

Roughly, how many slices of your time frame represent how often you felt third-degree emotions? Write the word "red" on the number of slices that represent third-degree emotions for that period of time.

For example, if you felt third-degree emotions a small amount of the time, you might write "red" in only one of the slices.

Remember: for the math to work, only one color per slice, and there must be only 10 slices in total.

When you're done labeling all ten pie slices with either red, yellow, or green, continue reading.

CHAPTER 8 EXERCISE, PART 2

COLOR OF YOUR DASHBOARD LIGHT

Your emotional state in this relationship is like the climate in a region of the world – there's the temperature right now as you read these words, but then there's the overall range of temperatures in the region over all seasons of the year.

You might find that your feelings in this relationship are as varied as the climate in Melbourne, Australia where the temperature can drop by 20 degrees between morning and afternoon. In the morning you wore a bathing suit out by the pool, and in the afternoon, you cuddle up next to a fire in a big fluffy sweater.

All the patterns throughout the year add up to one overall climate.

When it comes to weather and temperature on our planet, there are five general categories of climate – tropical, dry, mild, continental, and polar. When it comes to the Boundaries Dashboard, there are three categories of climate – red, yellow, and green, which are the three temperature light colors.

Part Two: Check the Lights

In Part 1 of this exercise, you looked back at the general history of emotional temperatures you've felt in this relationship. In Part 2, we will convert your answers from Part 1 into a green, yellow, or red light on the dashboard.

Open your Dashboard Diary, and either underneath the pie you already drew or on a new blank page, write today's date, the words "Time Frame," the length of your time frame, and beneath that, write the title "Temperature Light Color."

Beneath the title "Temperature Light Color," you can do a calculation to find out your score. Once you have the score, you'll be able to find out the color of your temperature light and write down your color beneath the title.

So that I can carry mathematical integrity of scores across these exercises, I consulted with a mathematician, Dave Best, who is based in Melbourne, Australia (Hi, Dave!), and he helped me put together the Temperature Light formula and chart.

Now, here's how to get your temperature light reading and forecast.

1. Add up your total number of green slices, then write the word "green" and the number of green slices next to it.

2. Add up your total number of yellow slices, then write the word "yellow" and the number of yellow slices next to it.

3. No need to count red slices! No matter how many there are, each red slice counts as zero value. You only need to count the number of green slices and the number of yellow slices.

4. Using the chart below, find your number of green slices along the top ("Number of Green Slices"), and then find your number of yellow

Chapter 8: Exercise, Part 2

slices along the left side ("Number of Yellow Slices"). Where those two numbers intersect on the chart, you'll find your temperature light color and your total score.

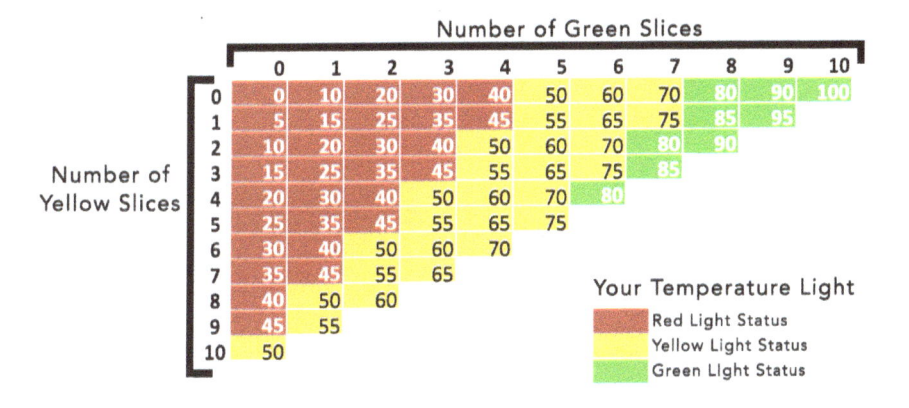

Here's an example below. If there are six green slices and four yellow slices, the score is 80 and the temperature light status is green.

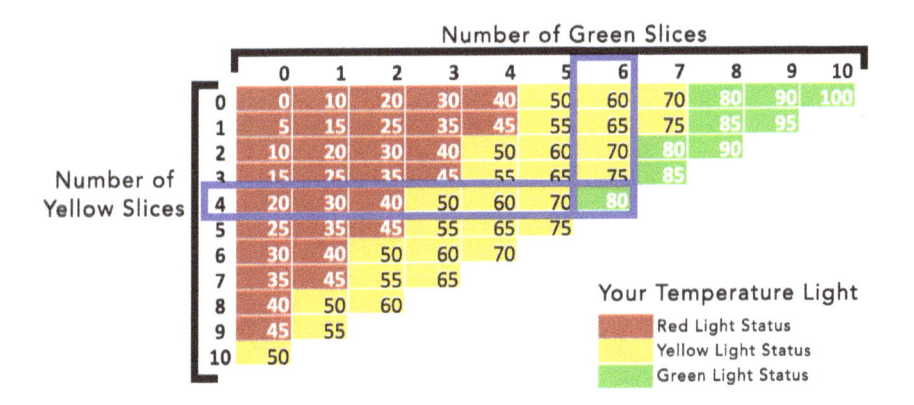

boundariescheck.com | 185

Part Two: Check the Lights

THE MATH FORMULA

Here is a simple explanation of the formula behind the above chart.

In this math formula, red slices do not count; they have no value.

The value of each green slice is 10 points.

The value of each yellow slice is 5 points.

So, first multiply the number of green slices by 10.

Then, multiply the number of yellow slices by 5.

Finally, add up those two totals for one grand total and identify which of the three colors your score fits into.

If your total score is 45 or below, your light is red. If your total score adds up to a number between 50 and 75, it's a yellow light. If your total score is between 80 and 100, it's a green light.

Remember that we are only talking about forecasts, which are by nature general. So, for this exercise, the scores are only in multiples of 5 and 10.

YOUR TEMPERATURE FORECAST

In your Dashboard Diary, write down the color of your light (red, yellow, or green) based on the above exercise, and then circle the word boldly so you can easily spot it when you return to your notes later. If you're using a digital diary, then of course you can add an emoji or use bold or other digital options to make it stand out, as you may have done in previous exercises.

This color now represents your "Temperature Forecast" in this relationship. This, in other words, is the current pattern of emotions or the emotional "climate" of this relationship for you personally. If nothing changes, you can reasonably predict similar emotional patterns will continue over the period of time until your next Boundaries Health Check. The key here is "if nothing changes."

The past does not always predict the future; that's for sure. However, if nothing changes and your boundaries remain the same, then, like the weather, you now have a general emotional forecast you can reasonably expect to continue in this relationship.

The more often you do the Boundaries Health Check, the more clearly you will see your patterns. I would encourage you to do the Boundaries Health Check as regularly as possible – even daily – so you can establish a clear history of what you're experiencing within yourself in this relationship. This way you can also track real progress over time!

Through this book, you have the tools to decide what needs to happen to improve your forecast.

PART THREE

GET ROADWORTHY

CHAPTER 9

INTRO TO YOUR VEHICLE INSPECTION

(3 minute read)

ARE YOU ROADWORTHY?

On the road of this relationship, how "roadworthy" are you?

In Australia where I now live, we call your car "roadworthy" if it passes a legally required vehicle inspection in which they check if everything's in working condition and if there are any safety issues. They do this because your car can cause you and/or other people damage, serious injury, or even death on the road if it's not working properly.

The last time I took my car for its mandatory inspection, the mechanic said it would cost over $1,500 to get it up to the legal standard. Keeping a car roadworthy carries a cost!

When it comes to a human relationship, what does it cost to keep your (metaphorical) car up and running? Part Three of this book answers that question.

Part Three: Get Roadworthy

An inspection identifies what's causing issues. If you don't pass inspection, then when you go back on the road, it puts you and anyone else on the road at risk. Your (metaphorical) car could suddenly come to a halt or a tire might fly off and hit the other person.

So, allow me to introduce you to your own personal safety inspection, where you inspect the six dials on your dashboard to see what's triggering the red, yellow, and green lights in this relationship.

The exercises in each of the next six chapters, which I call "inspections," will look at your Boundaries Dashboard to see exactly what's working and what's not working with the other person. The inspection will show you the cost of keeping your vehicle roadworthy on the road of your relationship.

And just like regularly scheduled vehicle inspections, it is important that this be a formal and regular event – quarterly, monthly, weekly, or more. That's because as you drive on the road of the relationship, natural wear and tear happens, and things stop working or they need fixing. You may need some new spark plugs to reestablish your roadworthiness.

Here's what to expect. A Safety Inspection exercise will appear in every subsequent chapter here in Part Three. The inspection is an audit of your six boundaries to identify what triggers your red, yellow, and green dashboard lights.

It's not only going to look at what could be wrong, but it will also look at what's going right. By the end of the next several chapter exercises, you'll also have identified the boundaries that enable you to bring your best into this relationship.

GREEN LIGHT STATUS

A simple red, yellow, or green light status is used across the world and in multiple contexts. It is used by financial organizations to indicate financial health. It's used by meteorological organizations to communicate weather hazards. Medical professionals use it in a variety of contexts including mental health assessments, rehabilitation metrics, health risk assessments, medication management, communicating life-threatening conditions, and more.

Businesses and organizations use the same simple three-color system to make decisions. Having worked with executives and senior managers in several multimillion- and multibillion-dollar organizations, I have seen those three simple lights used to trigger the movement of millions of dollars.

Whether it's day-to-day tracking of key performance indicators, budget management, or a big project, decision-makers hope to see the highly desired green light status in their reports. If anything has happened that presents a level of risk, they'll see a yellow light. When a risk threatens the health or continuation of business or of a project, they'll see red.

When millions or billions of dollars are at stake, decisions and actions often come down to looking at how many green, yellow, and red lights appear on the page.

By now, you have become familiar with how the Boundaries Dashboard uses the same simple three-color system. It's used effectively around the world to signify urgency, risk, and achievements, but now it's time to use it just as effectively in your relationship. In the next several chapters, we're going to look at the details behind your red, yellow, and green lights.

CHAPTER 10

TERRITORIES DIAL

(19 minute read)

SPACES MATTER

The exact same plastic bottle of water can cost 50 cents at a supermarket, $2.50 at the local gym, $4 at a movie theater, and $6 on an airplane. The same bottle of water changes value depending on its environment.

That's because a multitude of factors change from one physical space to another such as laws, policies, availability, accessibility, human capability, and natural or other material resources.

And since any of those factors can change with each physical space, so can health and quality of life – mentally, emotionally, and physically.

So, spaces matter. Environments can change anything or everything.

In the next few sections, I'll run through some examples.

ENVIRONMENTS CHANGE PEOPLE

I once saw a post on social media that said, "I can literally go from introvert to extrovert in 0.0330 seconds according to the people and situation."

I deeply relate to that. However, the opposite also applies. I've seen people go from extrovert to introvert in the same amount of time.

An environment consists of both things and people, and so just as lighting and music can impact your emotional state in a room, so can people. People in a room can energize us out of the blue, making us feel like social powerhouses or they can completely deflate us, making us feel like a shriveled-up worm.

I've noticed that when I stand next to someone I love, I somehow grow an incredible amount of courage to entertain and make jokes. Once they leave, that courage goes into stubborn hibernation.

Environment impacts our personality. The people and the things in any environment can change who you are – and that change can be temporarily, or it can impact who you decide to become in the future.

Consider the sounds, scents, and sights that come with the presence of other people. Sharing a space with additional people might mean continual interruptions to the connection you are trying to build with the other person. Interruptions can hinder the depth or speed of communication and growth.

Consider the difference it can make for romance in a married couple's life when they stop sharing their bed with their young child.

ENVIRONMENTS CHANGE COWORKERS

In a professional context, think of how a newly built coffee hub with the best-tasting coffee, fun games, and great food located inside the office can bring people together to network who have never networked before. Just one new room with different things and experiences can change life at work.

It's strange how environments define professional relationships. For some reason, it feels weird and new to unexpectedly see a coworker outside of the four walls of the office. It's like meeting them for the first time or meeting a different version of them. What are the new rules between me and that person now that Human Resources aren't in the next room directly regulating our behavior?

In the US, I kept a poker face inside and outside of the office. However, in Australia, people aren't as stiff or formal, and this more laid-back Aussie corporate culture rubbed off on me. I would have never touched alcohol at a corporate office event in the States, but my first work office party in Australia was out in a bar and was probably the wildest party I can remember.

Environments Change Dating

It's tragically a "norm" for many, but these days people are meeting strangers from dating apps and inviting them to their homes for a first date. After trying it myself, I know it's a terrible idea.

As much as I tried to ignore it, I felt an unusually high degree of anxiety whenever I've had a first date with a guy at either my apartment or his. There's something about the two of us alone with no people around for accountability makes me feel inwardly terrified and stuck, like a deer in the headlights, despite the fact that I appear confident and calm on the outside.

Environment impacts the health of a date and my own mental health; so, when it comes to men on dating apps, it's a rule to keep the first

Part Three: Get Roadworthy

meetup short and public, and there are very few exceptions.

When it comes to first dates, there are also, of course, other factors that make your home a dreadful idea, such as having a near stranger know where you live so that they can show up drunk in the middle of the night knocking on your door, which also happened to me. I thought it only happened on TV shows, but no.

Unspoken dating rules and expectations are shockingly different in private vs. public environments.

Environments Change How We Feel

There's something incredibly satisfying about getting off an airplane and stepping out into a brand-new environment – new smells, new sites, new accents, new ways of moving and socializing, and everything touching your senses for the first time. It's like Madonna's song: *Like a virgin, touched for the very first time.*

Even the air running through your lungs is different.

However, as I write this paragraph, I am sitting on a jam-packed train and an old woman sitting next to me is wearing a cheap perfume that's making me feel lightheaded and nauseated.

I usually love the train because it gives me a space for focused writing, but right now it feels like this woman is drowning us all in a noxious pool of sour milk and acid. I desperately need fresh air and can't wait for the next stop to empty the train so that a different seat becomes available.

I can't concentrate.

...

(Moments later)

Ok, I found a new seat and can comfortably take a deep breath now.

Environments impact all five senses: sight, hearing, taste, smell, and touch. By environment, I mean the physical space around you – everything and every substance in the air and everyone in it.

Even the quality of air makes up an environment. A gas leak or carbon monoxide can literally kill you; that's how important awareness of this boundary can be.

On your dashboard, the Territories dial controls the physical spaces that you choose to share with the other person. Let's talk about the impact of those physical environments.

Consider the four walls you might share with the other person, as well as every object, every pet, every unwanted insect that flies in through the window, and every person in the room. Think of the impact of the sensory dimensions of the space – sights, sounds, aesthetics, textures, the cleanliness of the environment, the design, weather or temperature, furniture, noise, local culture, animals, and the proximity to people and things that are in the space with you both as well.

And if there's food around, that's environment, too. To some degree, it's all impacting your connection whether it's a corporate office you share, a home, your local town, or the country where you live.

Ok, question. Would you take a romantic partner for a romantic picnic at the local sewage plant?

If your answer was no, then why not? What elements about the space would impact the relationship?

The sewage plant smells. The sights. The sounds. The textures. And forget about eating anything near a sewage plant since the smell of the air enters your mouth as you eat. The mood would probably be significantly unhappy. Your date would also probably not feel like a very special person in your life, if that's where you decide to take them for a special evening.

Clearly, certain environments nourish the relationship and other environments can do the opposite.

Now imagine being a business owner and taking a potential client to an important lunch at a fancy restaurant, but in the middle of the business conversation, you need to use the bathroom. Would you invite your client to follow you into your bathroom stall to continue the conversation?

Most likely your answer was "no." You'd set a boundary and step away for a few minutes.

Every bathroom door affirms the power of the Territories boundary.

Environments, spaces, and places of all kinds – they are all managed by the Territories dial on your Boundaries Dashboard.

The word territory is from Latin terra which translates to "land." The Territories dial is about your decisions and actions around the grounds that you share, the physical spaces where you interact with the other person, as well as everything and everyone that exists within those spaces.

That's the first kind of territory.

Your Territories boundary also includes how you use the space between your body and the other person's body, the physical space between and around the both of you, or what I call body boundaries. This is about physical proximity, not the things you do for each other in that space.

Body boundaries are strictly about the amount of distance or closeness. Think of the differences between sitting, standing, or walking very closely or far apart.

My point in sharing the earlier examples of a restaurant bathroom door and romantic dinner at a sewage plant is this: Territories – both physical environments and body boundaries – impact your human relationships. They often leave lifelong and lasting impressions.

Territories can make or break a connection.

Environments Change Culture

Environments change your way of life, from the immediate space surrounding you, to the local neighborhood, to the borders of the country where you live. Your environment consists of local laws, the local economy, social norms, food and drink options, plant and animal life, natural resources, and so much more.

Your clothing choices are also often the product of many environmental factors – not only the weather – that impact your personal culture. I saw a quote somewhere that said, "Regular me and dressed up me are two different people." Yes, clothes can change personality dynamics in a person, in a room of people, and in a relationship. What a person wears (or doesn't wear) has the power to shift the human experience.

Living plants, vegetation, and water are part of your environment. To eat food is to literally eat an environment, since food comes from the land. If you're a carnivore, food also includes the animals that live off the land.

Consider what you eat together in the relationship (or don't eat), what kind of drinks you share (or don't share), and how those decisions impact your closeness in the relationship.

After a hard day's work, imagine coming home to the scent of freshly cooked dinner and how that can deepen the bond and history between two people. As they say, "The way to a man's heart is through his stomach."

I've read that when a house is for sale, the smell of fresh-baked cookies during the home viewing has an impact on converting an uncertain prospect into an actual buyer; that's powerful stuff for a real estate agent's relationship with prospective buyers. The right food can turn prospects to clients.

Sharing traditional cuisines can deepen cultural understanding and increase respect between people who grew up quite differently.

And consider the cultural impact of lighting. Poor lighting in a professional relationship can impact the efficiency and effectiveness of your work – a culture of dissatisfied workers.

For me, the blue light emissions in fluorescent lighting and digital screens make me lose concentration and get ocular migraines. So, I often wear blue light eyeglasses, which help to block the blue light and significantly reduce headaches.

So, I started wearing those handy glasses every day. They became habit and a part of me. They started showing up in my selfies and social media, so that now it's become a part of my current personal identity. And it all traces back to the lights and computers at the office – my environment.

TERRITORIES AND YOUR RELATIONSHIP WITH YOU

In your relationship with yourself, you also have the same considerations – how you manage the lighting, atmosphere, people, sounds, design, the energizing or draining foods you keep in the cabinets, the television or internet and what it's feeding your mind, and everything in your environment whenever you spend time with yourself.

As I write this paragraph, I'm feeling distracted and antsy, sitting alone in my apartment. I know that I can cure this feeling by changing my environment and going down to the gym on the 6th floor of the building where I live. Even just showing up in the gym environment changes energy levels for me. It somehow revives vision and ambition in me.

Or I can keep my butt here on the couch and just turn on a great playlist. Sometimes just the right music gets my hips moving and gives me an energy surge, too.

One of the many life-changing environment boundaries I made in my relationship with me was to buy a weighted blanket and 100% organic bamboo sheet set. Just about every single day I look forward to jumping into bed and nestling my head into that silky bamboo pillowcase while throwing the weight of the blanket over my shoulders to feel snuggled. The blanket wraps around me, pressing lightly down on me, reminding me of a human cuddle every time.

BODY BOUNDARIES

The most warm-hearted and surprising experiences I've had in the corporate world were on two separate occasions when fully suited professional work colleagues – whom I did not know well and did not know outside the confines of the office – greeted me with a warm hug instead of a handshake. These were two very different and unrelated people. Most interesting is that both happened to be from Melbourne, Australia.

My corporate poker face was melted by a human touch. Hugs just don't happen amongst business professionals in multimillion dollar organizations.

Hugs are not normal in a corporate environment because of the mostly unspoken rule of physical personal space, but the hugs from those two made me feel so special and warm. For fear of legal policies around sexual misconduct, 99% of the time it's safer to stick to physical distance and handshakes. In the office, keep space between torsos!

Those hugs and my associated shock were just a great example of body boundaries in this way: the boundaries of physical proximity between coworkers in a corporation run by executives and shareholders is very different from the proximity between family, friends, or lovers.

Except in that case with those two wonderful people from Melbourne.

When it comes to the Territories boundary, your body boundaries refer to the physical distance you keep or don't keep between your body and the other person – the physical proximity. This area immediately surrounds your physical body, otherwise commonly called your personal space. You regard it as psychologically yours; it's intimate territory.

Everyone's different, no matter the relationship. Someone from a rural part of the country gives people a different amount of personal space than someone from a congested city. The rural person is used to giving strangers wide open spaces, and so standing close is more like suggestive behavior.

Wide open spaces between people are the norm in rural cultures, whereas a city person to some degree isn't too surprised when they are pressed up against a stranger on a peak hour subway train or being suspended by sweaty strangers in a crowded city concert stadium.

In general, a city person has a smaller circumference of body boundaries.

Body boundaries are the amount and quality of physical closeness that you allow in your personal space, whether it be handshakes or hugs, lip kisses or cheek kisses, standing far apart or close together, and so on.

In an intimate relationship, the topic of body boundaries extends into romantic life, such as how closely you sit, stand, or sleep with the other person. Body boundaries are important in both non-intimate and intimate relationships, and they help to distinguish between a professional relationship versus close friend versus romantic interest.

You also manage body boundaries in your relationship with yourself. It's just me and you right now as you read this book, so I hope it's safe to bring up the fact that you have your own rules around how closely you interact with your own body.

I clearly remember feeling a sense of being a complete alien to my body as I became a teenager. I remember seeing myself naked right after a shower, horrified at what I saw in the mirror and not wanting to look. That alienness continued for a few decades. Only later in life did I start to want to stand close to the mirror and get to know this human being in front of me. After years of working on myself, I don't dread the thought of standing close to my own body reflected in the mirror.

That is an example of body boundaries in my relationship with me, and that has significantly impacted my decisions, actions, and other human relationships.

Part Three: Get Roadworthy

So, what are healthy physical spaces and body boundaries for you in this relationship? You'll look into that question in the following exercise.

CHAPTER 10 EXERCISE

TERRITORIES DIAL INSPECTION

TITLES AND DATE

So now it's time to take out your Dashboard Diary.

Put today's date on top and write the title "Territories Dial."

Underneath the title, write "My Top Motivator: _____" and in the blank space, write your motivator that you discovered in Chapter 6: Fuel Check. Underneath that, write "My Second Motivator: _____" and in the blank space, write your second motivator from that same chapter.

After that, split the page into three columns. Title the first column "Green," the second column "Yellow," and the third column "Red."

Part Three: Get Roadworthy

FIRST COLUMN: GREEN LIGHT TERRITORIES

This is the column to identify physical spaces and body boundaries that trigger green lights for you in this relationship.

What does it mean for a territory boundary to trigger green lights?

A green fuel light means the territory aligns with your motivators in some way.

A green oil light means the territory agrees with (doesn't conflict with) your self-care.

A green battery light means the territory involves consent (expressed and sought).

A green temperature light means the territory shifts your own emotional state into the first-degree range of emotion.

In this column, think about territories that currently trigger green lights for you in this relationship that you would like to maintain and continue at this time. Also in this column, think about new territories that you believe have a good chance of triggering green and that you'd like to experiment with.

I suggest you aim to write down a minimum of five Territories if you can, but write as many as you'd like.

Think of ideas, very big or very small. Be as ornately detailed or broadly generic as you wish. If you feel stuck, use the Brainstorming section toward the end of this Exercise to generate ideas.

Here are some general examples of what someone might write in the first column:

1. The cozy café down the street

2. Our bed with organic bamboo sheets

3. The living room with my favorite playlist

4. Sitting on the same couch, close together while watching movies

5. Keeping our computer desks in separate rooms to give us space while we work

6. Our annual trip up North

SECOND COLUMN: YELLOW LIGHT TERRITORIES

This is the column to identify physical spaces and body boundaries that trigger yellow dashboard lights for you in this relationship.

What does it mean for a territory boundary to trigger yellow lights?

A yellow fuel light means you feel unsure whether the territory aligns with your motivators.

A yellow oil light means you feel unsure whether the territory agrees with (doesn't conflict with) your self-care.

A yellow battery light means you feel unsure whether the territory involves consent (expressed and sought).

A yellow temperature light means that the territory triggers an emotional state that you're unsure is healthy or unhealthy for you.

I suggest you aim to write at least a couple of territories in this column, but write as few or as many as you'd like. If you feel stuck, use the Brainstorming section toward the end of this exercise to generate ideas.

Here are some examples of what someone might write in this column:

1. The restaurant where that incident happened

2. The local nightclub "Frankie's"

3. Our disorganized, messy balcony

4. Where I sit when we eat dinner together at our big dinner table

5. Our small bed on a hot day

THIRD COLUMN: RED LIGHT TERRITORIES

This is the column to identify physical spaces and body boundaries that trigger red dashboard lights for you in this relationship.

What does it mean for a territory boundary to trigger red lights?

A red fuel light means the territory does not align with your motivators in any way.

A red oil light means the territory clearly conflicts with your self-care.

A red battery light means the territory does not respect consent

Chapter 10: Exercise

(expressed or sought).

A red temperature light means the territory shifts you into an unhealthy emotional state.

In this column, think about territories that currently trigger red lights for you in this relationship and that you would like to adjust, discontinue, or replace with something healthier or better.

I suggest you aim to write at least a couple of territories in this column, but write as few or as many as you'd like. If you feel stuck, use the Brainstorming section toward the end of this exercise to generate ideas.

Here are some examples of what someone might write in this column:

1. His ex's property

2. The restaurant where we always get tempted to eat crap food

3. The pictures in the drawer that bring back bad memories

4. The junk food stored in the cabinet

5. The broken carbon monoxide tester in our room

BRAINSTORMING

To help stir up more ideas for your three columns, here are some brainstorming questions to think about, depending on the type of relationship this is. Read the questions, see if they generate any ideas, and then return to your three columns of the above exercise if you feel inspired to add to or update your answers.

Part Three: Get Roadworthy

- What towns, cities, suburbs do you share that work well for you (or not) in this relationship?

- What outdoor areas do you share (or not)?

- What environments have particular sensory elements like weather or room temperature that contribute to your closeness or distance in this relationship?

- What rooms or physical spaces in those rooms have been working well or not (too much stuff or not enough, impact of furniture and interior design, organization or disorganization of the contents in that space, size of room and objects in it, accessibility, etc.)?

- What sights and visual elements work well or not (interior design, lighting, artwork, view, position of furniture, organization of the room, etc.)?

- What smells work well or not (cologne or perfume, food smells, maybe an ocean smell nearby, etc.)?

- What spaces or arrangement of spaces offer comfortable (or uncomfortable) proximity to the other person?

- What spaces or arrangement of spaces offer comfortable (or uncomfortable) proximity to other people who share the space with the two of you?

- What degree of physical closeness or distance works and doesn't work between the two of you?

- What sounds work well or not (music, quietness or background noise, people talking or distracting you with conversation, etc.)?

- What about the national environment (laws, politics, geographical boundaries, etc.) contributes to your sense of health in this relationship?

- What local cultural spaces do you share or not share (historic landmarks, entertainment venues, local markets, etc.)?

- What commercial locations do you share, such as restaurants or shopping centers, that seem to feel good in this relationship (or not)?

HIGH FIVE TIME

I'm going to repeat this "High Five Time" section in the next several chapters as a ceremonious ending to each exercise, like a mini graduation ceremony.

So, how will you celebrate your win of completing this exercise?

If you can't think of a small way to celebrate your work, here's a challenge. I dare you to do something that sounds awkward at first, but I can assure you it's a technique that's been used by lots of well-educated and successful professionals to give themselves a psychological boost.

I learned the brain hack of high-fiving yourself from two prestigious and successful people: first, Kara Loewentheil, a graduate of Yale College and Harvard Law School and now a podcaster and coach; and, second, Mel Robbins, recognized as one of the top 50 business thinkers in the world by Thinkers50, a prestigious ranking of global management thinkers.

Now's the best time to go find a mirror and give yourself a high five. If you don't like to risk a handprint, just bring it as close as possible without touching; move your hand as if you were high-fiving someone else.

Part Three: Get Roadworthy

I also understand that not everyone is the type to "high five" at all, even if other successful people endorse it. If that's you, be assured that it's only a simple symbol of winning. Whether it's a high-five or something else you choose to do, it's powerful to have at least a little celebration ritual after the smallest of successes because of the undeniable momentum that it builds and sustains over time.

If you'd like to step up your game or simply do this as your little celebration ceremony for this chapter, I challenge you to take a selfie of your high five, or any other celebration, and share it to my Facebook, @boundariescheck, or share it on your own social media and tag me @boundariescheck with the hashtag #chapter10.

Of course, if you're reading a printed copy of this book five years after it's written, then there's probably some totally new platform for you to share it on and tag me, or maybe there will be a way we can high five in the metaverse or in a hologram by that point.

You've finished the Safety Inspection for the Territories boundary! When it comes to this boundary, you have metaphorically taken apart the electronics connected to this dial and inspected it. Now, you've identified which wires are working well for you and which need your attention or replacing.

If you close this book and suddenly come up with more ideas when you're in the shower, cooking, or when your head hits the pillow, just come back and write them into your Diary anytime.

Part Three: Get Roadworthy

CHAPTER 11

TREASURES DIAL

(10 minute read)

INVESTING

On the Boundaries Dashboard, the Treasures dial controls the amount of energy or effort that you invest in this relationship or in the other person. So, one way to understand "treasures" is to simply think of them as investments you make.

Your energy or effort – physical, material, financial, emotional, and mental – is your form of investment and you might think of it like a currency. What types of transactions do you make with this currency? Lending, trading, bartering, buying, selling, or freely giving or receiving without anything in return.

The amount of time that it takes you to invest your energy or effort is a different unit of measurement than the energy or effort itself. So, for that reason, time itself is its own boundary in an upcoming chapter. Here in this chapter, we are focusing on the investment, not of your time, but of your energy and effort – physically, materially, financially, emotionally, and mentally.

Some examples of your treasures include trading your physical labor for something in return, trading your mental or intellectual labor, doing favors of any kind, giving gifts, lending or giving money, giving or trading something material, acts of kindness, or giving assistance of any kind, including training or knowledge.

Even when we don't "get anything in return," we're still investing. When we do something selfless without any expectation of a specific return on investment, it is often the emotional pleasure of doing something for the other person that is our return on investment. For example, I volunteered my energy and effort in a local African refugee center, and although it looked "charitable," I genuinely did it because it brought me joy.

Investing into healthy human relationships brings each person a return on investment emotionally, physically, materially, financially, and/or mentally.

A mother invests her energy in her child because it brings her joy and satisfaction, and it would bring her emotional pain and distress if she didn't. A gym-goer finds a "gym buddy" so that they both can lift weights together, challenge each other, and grow physically. A client invests money with a stockbroker because they trust the stockbroker can create a profit for them. A gardener joins a local gardening club where members share knowledge and tools with each other, growing and expanding their range of fruits and vegetables.

Currency is only one metaphor. Calories are another way to represent the effort and energy you "burn" in the name of this relationship.

CALORIES BURNED IN THEIR NAME

Did you know that you burn calories every day by simply thinking, moving, walking, and even sitting? It's true. Well, think of all the ways you're burning calories for the sake of this relationship. This is your literal energy burned for the other person.

You're burning calories if you go shopping for them, teach them how to manage their money, perform a chore to keep your shared space organized, use your own two hands to fix something, do a favor for them, or even enjoy a fun or relaxing time with them. Those are examples of your energy spent and invested, even when sitting and doing "nothing."

The giving of your physical presence is also a treasure, and you burn calories doing that too. It matters to simply sit there in the room to keep them company. Not everyone in the world can experience your physical presence right now and not everyone can access you, and that's because you're only one physical body. You can broadcast yourself to a worldwide audience online, but your shared physical presence is a rare treasure that can only be experienced in one physical place at a time.

Throughout this entire book, you're investing a commendable amount of your brain's energy simply thinking about this relationship. Thinking requires biological energy. I've read a study showing that the brain's thinking power alone consumes 20% of our calories burned every day![23]

So, consider what percentage of your brain energy you invest in this relationship. In other words, how many calories do you burn in their name, just thinking about them? How much energy do you burn simply thinking about activities that you perform for and with them? How much of your brain's computing power goes toward planning ahead and how much goes into reflecting on the past in this relationship?

The Brainstorming section near the end of this exercise may stir even more vivid images of what the Treasures boundary includes in this relationship.

Treasures change throughout different seasons of life as you grow older,

Part Three: Get Roadworthy

as you experience more of the world, and as your physical needs change. But right now in this book, we're focusing on your investments in this current season of your life in this relationship.

CHAPTER 11 EXERCISE

TREASURES DIAL INSPECTION

Your currencies of investment in this relationship are physical, material, financial, emotional, and/or mental energy, and your body literally burns its resources in the name of the relationship. In this exercise, we'll take a look at the health of your investments and, in a sense, the health of your metaphorical "metabolism" in this relationship.

TITLES AND DATE

So now it's time to take out your Dashboard Diary.

Put today's date on top and write the title "Treasures Dial."

Underneath the title, write "My Top Motivator: _____" and in the blank space, write your motivator that you discovered in Chapter 6: Fuel Check. Underneath that, write "My Second Motivator: _____" and in the blank space, write your second motivator from that same chapter.

Part Three: Get Roadworthy

After that, split the page into three columns. Title the first column "Green," the second column "Yellow," and the third column "Red."

FIRST COLUMN: GREEN LIGHT TREASURES

This is the column to identify treasures that trigger green dashboard lights for you in this relationship.

What does it mean for your Treasures boundary to trigger green lights?

A green fuel light means the treasure aligns with your motivators in some way.

A green oil light means the treasure agrees with (doesn't conflict with) your self-care.

A green battery light means the treasure involves consent (expressed and sought).

A green temperature light means the treasure shifts your own emotional state into the first-degree range of emotion.

In this column, think about treasures that currently trigger green lights for you in this relationship that you would like to maintain and continue at this time. Also in this column, think about new treasures that you believe have a good chance of triggering green and that you'd like to experiment with.

I suggest you aim to write down a minimum of five treasures if you can, but write as many as you'd like. If you feel stuck, use the Brainstorming section toward the end of this exercise to generate ideas.

Here are some examples of what someone might write in this first column:

1. Finding ways to make her laugh

2. Looking up a recipe that she was trying to find

3. Teaching her how to use apps that make her life better

4. Taking her to dinner once every few months

5. Sharing the inspiring videos that I love, which I think she might like

SECOND COLUMN: YELLOW LIGHT TREASURES

This is the column to identify treasures that trigger yellow dashboard lights for you in this relationship.

What does it mean for your Treasures boundary to trigger yellow lights?

A yellow fuel light means you feel unsure whether the treasure aligns with your motivators.

A yellow oil light means you feel unsure whether the treasure agrees with (doesn't conflict with) your self-care.

A yellow battery light means you feel unsure whether the treasure involves consent (expressed and sought).

A yellow temperature light means that the treasure triggers an emotional state that you're unsure is healthy or unhealthy for you.

I suggest you aim to write at least a couple of treasures in this column, but write as few or as many as you'd like. If you feel stuck, use the Brainstorming section toward the end of this exercise to generate ideas.

Here are general examples of what someone might write in this second column:

1. Our weekly meeting where we catch up on task status

2. Receiving compliments on your appearance, given that this is a professional relationship

3. Attending lunches that you feel peer pressured to attend

4. Putting money into the office lotto pool

THIRD COLUMN: RED LIGHT TREASURES

This is the column to identify treasures that trigger red dashboard lights for you in this relationship.

What does it mean for your Treasures boundary to trigger red lights?

A red fuel light means the treasure does not align with your motivators in any way.

A red oil light means the treasure clearly conflicts with your self-care.

A red battery light means the treasure does not respect consent (expressed or sought).

A red temperature light means the treasure shifts you into an unhealthy emotional state.

In this column, think about treasures that currently trigger red lights for you in this relationship and that you would like to adjust, discontinue, or replace with something healthier or better.

I suggest you aim to write at least a couple of treasures in this column, but write as few or as many as you'd like. If you feel stuck, use the Brainstorming section toward the end of this exercise to generate ideas.

Here are some examples of what someone might write in this third column:

1. Lending money, because it keeps disappearing

2. Continuing to speak when her tone makes me feel terrible

3. Investing intellectual energy trying to understand why she's this way

4. Doing anything that constitutes me trying to fix her

5. Scheduling a call when doing so doesn't sit right with me

BRAINSTORMING ALL THREE COLUMNS

To help stir up ideas for all three of your columns, here are some brainstorming questions you may want to think about, depending on the type of relationship this is. Read the questions, see if they generate any ideas, and then return to your three columns of the above exercise if you feel inspired to add to or update what you wrote in your three columns.

When you read through these questions, remember that treasures are what you do or don't do with your own energy or effort, whether it's lending, trading, bartering, buying, selling, or freely giving or receiving.

Part Three: Get Roadworthy

- ○ What energy or effort do you invest (or not) into general medical health in this relationship?

- ○ What energy or effort do you invest (or not) into mental health in this relationship?

- ○ What energy or effort do you invest (or not) into basic biological needs like drinking enough water, nutrition, hygiene, safety, and fresh air?

- ○ What ways do you share (or not share) food or share food preparation?

- ○ What ways do you share (or not share) exercise or physical activity together?

- ○ What ways do you check in (or not) if they're alright?

- ○ What energy or effort do you invest (or not) into cleaning or organizing the spaces you share?

- ○ What ways do you share (or not share) your financial health or financial knowledge (income, savings, investments, expenses, cashflow, planning, spending habits)?

- ○ What ways do you share (or not share) restful activity, relaxation, or low energy downtime together?

- ○ What ways do you share (or not share) times of playfulness together or share (or not share) experiences of uplifting excitement, celebration, or having fun? This includes treating or rewarding yourself or the other person, celebrating wins –big or small.

- ○ What ways do you share (or not share) activities that involve learning or novelty? This is about learning and adventuring into something new with the other person, whether it's something you do sitting

Chapter 11: Exercise

down together or performing a physical activity.

○ In professional relationships, what ways do you share (or not share) activities related to your expertise, curiosity, and/or excitement about the business goals that one or both of you are working on? Some examples include creating or going to professional events, conferences, or small group activities that are related to the business goal or task.

○ In personal relationships, what ways do you share (or not share) activities related to your career, trade, or business with the other person? This includes anything from deciding to do a business together or helping with career plans and decisions, being a joint party for contracted services, or a change of career activities. This can also include sharing or trading skills, studying together, researching together, and anything of the sort.

HIGH FIVE TIME

It's ceremony time! Remember that there is power when celebrating even the smallest of successes because of the momentum it creates over time. So, how will you celebrate your win of completing this exercise?

Now's the best time to go find a mirror and give yourself a high five. Or avoid a handprint and just bring it as close as possible without touching.

If you're up for it, I also challenge you to take a selfie of your high five, or take a pic of a different celebration that you might choose to do instead, and then share it to my Facebook, @boundariescheck, or share it on your own social media and tag me @boundariescheck with the hashtag #chapter11.

You've finished the Safety Inspection for the Treasures boundary! When

Part Three: Get Roadworthy

it comes to this boundary, you have metaphorically taken apart the electronics connected to this dial, and you inspected it. Now you have identified which wires are working well for you and which need your attention or replacing.

If you close this book and suddenly come up with more ideas, come back and write them into your Diary.

Part Three: Get Roadworthy

CHAPTER 12

TOOLS DIAL

(21 minute read)

ACCESS TO JOY

I had a girl-crush on Joy Ofodu as soon as I found her comedy videos on social media. Not in a romantic way, but a how-can-I-be-her-friend kind of way. From listening to her style of motivational pep talks to watching the kinds of awkward sounds and movements she makes just to get a laugh, I thought Joy was the kind of person with whom I could easily see myself sharing many hours of laughing and deep conversations. I wished from the bottom of my heart we could hang out.

There are only a small handful of people I follow religiously on social media, and they are often the voices that get me through very dark times. Joy seemed like my latest and greatest light in the dark.

So, I looked for a way I could communicate with her directly, one-on-one. But, at that point, it appeared she had a setting on her account that didn't allow direct messages. I don't know if it was a software glitch or an intentional and temporary setting, but I kept seeing that the only way to keep in touch with her was by signing up for an email newsletter.

That's when I suddenly realized the limits of my love for her. I loved Joy, but not enough to get her bulk email newsletters that are written for the masses; my inbox already overflows with those, and I can't keep up.

I wanted a two-way connection, not a newsletter fanship. Even an acquaintanceship would have been cool, but I didn't see a channel where she accepted incoming one-on-one messages.

At other points in life, I've been surprised and humbled that I've somehow been able to establish a genuine human relationship with people I admire through a direct message on social media. I was able to have one-on-one conversations with authors, speakers, and musical artists who deeply impacted me. I used social media to set up a photoshoot with the platinum album-selling band Flyleaf, and got a one-on-one phone call with singer Kim Walker-Smith.

Social media is a communication tool. The settings and levels of access that these people provide within those tools can and do change lives.

The secret potion of dating apps is that they allow you access so that you can send a message to an attractive stranger. When two people "match," what is really happening is that communication access is being granted to each person.

Communication tools are one of the six boundaries that define relationships. Whether it's a social media fangirl relationship with someone like Joy, or a friendship, or a relationship between lovers, or a relationship with your business partner, the access you provide through communication tools can start, enhance, break down, or shut down any human connection.

Access control within those tools impact whether a relationship starts between two people, how long a relationship lasts, and how deeply people connect.

Access depends on the relationship. For example, when I am committed and in an intimate partnership, I'll give my partner access to me through email, text, voice messages, videos, phone calls, and in-person access of course, but if I allowed everyone else that same amount of access to me, I'd feel emotionally and mentally trampled to death.

Whether it's a romantic partner, a friend, a family member, a client, or a work colleague, giving that person access does not mean giving unconditional and unrestricted access. Varying your levels of access for each relationship gives you sanity and respects that there's a place and time for each relationship in your life.

As said by one of my talented personal coaches named Martha, "Unconditional love does not mean unconditional access." Access at the wrong times or in the wrong ways can be disrespectful or cause harm, even from those we love.

My nervous system can only manage certain amounts of communication, and everyone has varying limits on what healthy communication access looks like, depending on your schedule and communication tools available. People who have the attention of hundreds of thousands of followers and fans have an even more complex task of managing their access tools.

As much as I respect someone else, for my own health's sake I have an obligation to first respect my capacity.

Access to my own inner joy depends on how much access I give others.

Let's dig a little deeper into all of that in the next section.

Part Three: Get Roadworthy

WHAT ARE COMMUNICATION TOOLS?

I named this boundary "Tools" so that it fits into the "T" theme of all six boundaries – Territories, Time, Treasures, etc. but when I refer to the Tools boundary, I really mean communication tools or communication technologies. The Tools boundary is about communication tools.

Anything in the world that you and the other person could possibly use to share messages is a communication tool, whether it's your own mouth or a satellite dish. There are thousands of tools, both natural human tools like hands that can point at something to man-made tools like a pen and paper to software tools.

Tools include anything in the world that you can use to send or receive messages – physical mail or digital mail, a video chat, a song, a poem, a change in vocal tone – anything.

A "message" refers to anything you want to say, whether it's a question or a statement. Sometimes our message is: "I have nothing particular to say, but I feel like thinking out loud." That's still a message.

Our messages can use words (verbal communication) or we can use nonverbal communication (facial gestures, voice quality, and body language). There are tools for both verbal and nonverbal communication.

I remember seeing a funny video one day where a guy said something like this: "I'm done talking on the phone and texting with people for today, even the people I love. I love you, but I can only manage you speaking to me in meme, GIF, or emoji for the rest of the day."

What makes it funny is the hard truth behind the joke, and the truth in that funny video is that writing and speaking words demands effort and energy. Words are work. Certainly not all the time, but nonverbal communication, such as a meme, GIF, or emoji, is often far less work and can communicate in one image what 10,000 words can't.

When I think of how communication tools impact relationships, I often think back to a woman I worked with years ago who was like a ray of sunshine when she walked into the room – fully disarming and incredibly encouraging with a radiant smile. I felt sunshine in her eye contact.

However, in her emails, somehow this woman communicated like a cold, heartless, and inconsiderate army commander, and I felt like a peon soldier. I would read her emails and wonder, "Who is this?!" To this day, I remember my repeated sense of shock over the difference between her personality talking to me in person versus her personality in emails.

The fact is that email and text cannot properly communicate a person's vocal inflections like pitch, tone, rhythm, emphasis, and other vocal qualities that communicate gentleness or force, hesitation or confidence, anxiety or calmness. Email and text are devoid of the vocal melody of a joke or sarcasm. They hide the sigh of a wish or desperation, and they leave you to your own imagination about the other person's intention.

Use of emojis might have helped my colleague at that time, but it wasn't cool to use them back then.

Our relationships change depending on the communication tools we use. This chapter is about identifying those tools in your relationship.

SENDING TOOLS

Your mouth only *sends* words and messages; it doesn't receive them. Receiving words and messages is the role of our ears. Your mouth is the basic sending tool that you were born with.

Anytime you use something to send a message, it becomes a sending tool. Sending tools include anything from phone calls you make, letters you write, social media posts you create, a bumper sticker, a sticky note, any smart phone app designed to send messages, and – the most basic method – the words you speak. In each of those, you are delivering or sending a message to the other person.

Receiving Tools

You know those two strangely shaped things on the side of your head? They are receiving tools. They don't communicate words and messages; they only receive them.

For those with hearing impairment, electronic hearing aids serve as receiving tools.

Receiving tools include both natural and technological ways that you receive communication from the other person. Think about phone calls you answer, emails you open, letters you read, social media posts you're tagged in, and the words you hear directly from the other person's mouth. In each of these, you are receiving a message from the other person.

And what about tools that stop the sending or receiving of messages, like ear plugs? Anything that can manage the amount of communication is an "access tool," as I'm about to explain.

Access Tools and Levels

I signed up for an online course, provided my email address and phone number, and the company that sold it to me thought that they could spam me with text messages and phone calls for more upsells afterwards. After paying for the course and signing up, I received several irritating text messages from different people from their organization.

After blocking one number, another would call from the same company!

They assumed that this was OK. I'm not sure of this, but it's possible that there was very fine print I'd agreed to in the overwhelmingly long list of terms and conditions, but I never read it.

I paid them for the course that I believed could be valuable, and I wanted knowledge in return. I did not realize that they were going to shove upsells at me via text messages and phone calls at every opportunity.

However, I take total responsibility for not reading their fine print. It was up to me to manage the level of access that I gave them. I should have given them a fake phone number and junk email address, or at least I should not have given my primary phone and email.

Communication tools give people access to you, but communication tools also allow you to set different levels of access through what I call "access tools." Think of call blocking features, airplane mode, the tools on social media that allow you to ignore or accept a friend request, tools that allow you to mute a notification so the person cannot access you during meetings, and so many more.

I don't have only one inbox on Instagram anymore. Instagram now gives me three! One inbox gives my existing contacts access to me, one allows access to me for people Instagram thinks I may know, and then a third inbox is hidden for spammers and strangers to access me. The number of tools, buttons, features, and devices that let us create multiple levels of access are evolving constantly.

Access tools aren't only digital. You have ears but you can stop sound with a great set of foam ear plugs. The ear plugs are an example of an access tool. Whether it's your front door or bedroom door, if it has a lock and key, that's an access tool.

You may have a phone, but you can turn the ringer on or off. The ringer is an access tool. You can use certain ringtones to prioritize a particular person's call. The ring tone creates an access level to you, since that one priority ring tone gets access to you above others.

You can also get separate phones for your business and personal lives, where business relationships are not given access to your personal phone and your personal relationships are not given access to your business phone. The two phones create two access levels.

Thank God for the various access tools of blocking and restriction settings in phones, email, and social media. They give us many access levels to choose from.

Think of how you can now allow only certain hours of availability, visibility of only certain content, and access only to certain inboxes. On Facebook, for example, you might have a Facebook friend whose inbox messages you "restrict" at times because of their tendency to send overwhelming messages, but whose timeline updates remain visible for you to keep up to date with their life.

Access level settings, such as blocking and restrictions, are like dams. An actual dam is a physical barrier in bodies of water that stops or restrict flooding of the area. That's what access levels do in human relationships, too.

Dams restrict flow in order to allow people to have enough water for life-giving activities like navigation, irrigation, human consumption, aquaculture, and industrial use. Likewise, communication access levels allow you enough time for life-giving activities, like taking care of your basic needs, goals, and other human relationships.

So, you can think of access tools as metaphorical dams that regulate communication levels.

And in a funny way, when you "dam" certain people by restricting their

Chapter 12: Tools Dial

access to you, some of them may want to "damn" you (with an "n") in return. Those people, of course, don't respect your needs. If someone is flooding your life, respectfully and kindly "dam" them with a healthier access level.

NONVERBAL COMMUNICATION

When selecting a tool to communicate, keep in mind that some tools more often result in disaster than others: tools that are plain text can be understood in drastically different ways than intended, including the *opposite* way. That is because vocal elements like intonation and emphasis, along with visual cues like facial expressions and gestures, can radically change the meaning of a message.

Most of my career has been in communications, and so I've heard it said many times throughout the years that 70% of our communication is nonverbal, and some sources report that up to 93% of communication is nonverbal.

In other words, in this and every human relationship, a minimum of 70% of what you and the other person communicate will come from your facial expressions, vocal sounds, bodily cues, actions, and behaviors. Only a small part of what you communicate is expressed in words.

Your audible cues communicate messages to the other person more than your words themselves. As a matter of fact, the same exact sentence can be understood or misunderstood in a shocking number of unintended ways, depending on which word you emphasize with your voice.

All seven of the following sentences have exactly the same words, but when you use your voice to emphasis different words, the one sentence can tell seven very different and even conflicting stories.[24] The bold font and underline of each word below indicates a vocal emphasis.

boundariescheck.com | 235

1. "**I** did not tell Chris you were late." (*Someone else* told Chris you were late.)

2. "I did **not** tell Chris you were late." (This did not happen.)

3. "I did not **tell** Chris you were late." (I may have *implied* it, but I didn't say this directly.)

4. "I did not tell **Chris** you were late." (I told *someone else* you were late, but not Chris.)

5. "I did not tell Chris **you** were late." (I told Chris *someone else* was late, but it wasn't you.)

6. "I did not tell Chris you **were** late." (I told him you are running late *now*, not in the past.)

7. "I did not tell Chris you were **late**." (I told him something else about you, but not that you were late.)

Nonverbal communication changes the meaning of words. It sends strong messages to the other person that can either bring you closer or drive you apart.

Nonverbal vocal characteristics include at least eight qualities: speed, breathing pattern, volume, articulation, emphasis, tone (emotional quality), rhythm, and vocal pitch (the rise and fall of voice or the musicality).

The same exact words in a sentence can mean a multitude of different things to different people, all depending on the voice. In addition to words, you also use body language, facial gestures, and your behavior to communicate your intentions, confidence, kindness or anger, interest or disinterest, strength or weakness, calmness or excitement.

UNSCHEDULED PHONE CALLS

Please allow me a moment to rant, in order to illustrate the importance of the Tools boundary when it comes to phone calls.

Apart from the two or three closest people in my life, I don't do phone calls unless they are scheduled ahead of time and the purposes are clear and meaningful, and here's why.

Communication on a phone these days is not the same as communication back when phones were only telephones. Telephones used to just be only for voice conversations, and nothing else. Today, a phone isn't only where you talk; it's where you conduct high-level business activities and live video meetings. It's also where you create files, edit videos, record audio, and hundreds of other uses.

When someone calls on a smartphone, it's startling because now a call can interrupt one of several high-concentration activities. I could be in the middle of hosting a recorded business video meeting with five other people through an app on my smartphone, and if a phone call unexpectedly comes through, it suddenly cuts us all off. I can lose all my work, and it becomes an utter mess to try to recreate and reorganize.

When a phone call comes through on a smartphone, it cuts of the screen that I'm in the middle of working on. Unexpected phone calls cut off my work on other time-intensive media projects that I may be recording like a podcast, audio notes, or a video.

For those of us who use our phones' multiple and complex functionalities, an unscheduled phone call can feel like someone unexpectedly opening the front door of your home without permission and banging a loud drum.

Part Three: Get Roadworthy

THE ONLY THING TEXT IS GOOD FOR

I say the "wrong thing" quite often. But whenever that happens, eight out of ten times it happens over a text message or email. By "saying the wrong thing," I mean the other person interpreted my words as something negative when, at least consciously, I didn't mean it in the way they understood.

At work I'm slower and more careful with communications, but in non-work relationships, I'm more spontaneous and casual, which comes with a cost. All too often, I realize immediately after pressing the send button that my text could easily be misunderstood. Sending any follow up texts to explain myself somehow seems to make it worse, too. This has indeed been a consistent weakness for me in my personal life. I'm working on it.

Anyone who knows me well has heard me say how much I hate text messages; that's because texting utterly strips the majority – yes, majority – of the meaning, tone, and intention from me and the other person. My latest conclusion on texting is that it is good for one thing – facts, not feelings! It works for sharing facts like dates, times, street addresses, account numbers, arrival times, names of places, and any other non-emotional name or number-oriented information.

However, if anything with emotional content has to be shared, then there's a high likelihood that, to some degree, the message will be read in a way I never intended. Anything that may be slightly negative can be taken as extremely negative. Anything slightly positive can be taken as extremely positive. The opposite also happens, where I send something with a feeling of great positivity, but it's read as negative, and vice versa.

So, instead of text, I stick to sending voice notes back and forth whenever possible. Problem solved. The ability to send voice notes in a smart phone app, with real-time back and forth communication, first became possible in the 2010s. So, in the context of human history, it's brand new. Let's use it!

CHAPTER 12 EXERCISE

TOOLS DIAL INSPECTION

TITLES AND DATE

So now it's time to take out your Dashboard Diary.

Put today's date on top and write the title "Tools Dial."

Underneath the title, write "My Top Motivator: _____ and in the blank space, write your motivator that you discovered in Chapter 6: Fuel Check. Underneath that, write "My Second Motivator: _____" and in the blank space, write your second motivator from that same chapter.

After that, split the page into three columns. Title the first column "Green," the second column "Yellow," and the third column "Red."

Part Three: Get Roadworthy

FIRST COLUMN: GREEN LIGHT TOOLS

This is the column to identify tools that trigger green dashboard lights for you in this relationship.

What does it mean for your Tools boundary to trigger green lights?

A green fuel light means the tool aligns with your motivators in some way.

A green oil light means the tool agrees with (doesn't conflict with) your self-care.

A green battery light means the tool involves consent (expressed and sought).

A green temperature light means the tool shifts your own emotional state into the first-degree range of emotion.

In this column, think about tools that currently trigger green lights for you in this relationship that you would like to maintain and continue at this time. Also in this column, think about new tools that you believe have a good chance of triggering a green light and that you'd like to experiment with.

I suggest you aim to write down a minimum of five tools if you can, but write as many as you'd like. Think of ideas, very big or very small. If you feel stuck, use the Brainstorming section toward the end of this exercise to generate ideas.

Below are some examples of what someone might write in the first column, but in brackets next to each one, I also indicated the type of communication tool (sending, receiving, or access). You don't have to put the part in brackets into the column. I only added it here in order to help you better understand the types of communication tools.

Chapter 12: Exercise

1. The voice-to-voice app Voxer (sending and receiving tool)

2. A self-written poem (sending tool)

3. A handwritten letter (sending tool)

4. Video chat (sending and receiving tool)

5. My podcast, talking about the other person or even bringing them in for a recorded conversation (sending tool)

SECOND COLUMN: YELLOW LIGHT TOOLS

This is the column to identify tools that trigger yellow dashboard lights for you in this relationship.

What does it mean for your Tools boundary to trigger yellow lights?

A yellow fuel light means you feel unsure whether the tool aligns with your motivators.

A yellow oil light means you feel unsure whether the tool agrees with (doesn't conflict with) your self-care.

A yellow battery light means you feel unsure whether the tool involves consent (expressed and sought).

A yellow temperature light means that the tool triggers an emotional state that you're unsure is healthy or unhealthy for you.

I suggest you aim to write at least a couple of tools in this column, but write as few or as many as you'd like. If you feel stuck, use the Brainstorming

Part Three: Get Roadworthy

section toward the end of this exercise to generate ideas.

Below are some examples of what someone might write in the second column, but in brackets next to each one, I also indicated the type of communication tool (sending, receiving, or access). You don't have to put the part in brackets into the column. I only added it here in order to help you better understand the types of communication tools.

1. WhatsApp (sending and receiving tool)

2. Temporary restriction settings in Messenger (access tool)

3. Call blocking feature/using it temporarily (access tool)

4. Airplane mode on my phone (access tool)

THIRD COLUMN: RED LIGHT TOOLS

This is the column to identify tools that trigger red dashboard lights for you in this relationship.

What does it mean for your Tools boundary to trigger red lights?

A red fuel light means the tool does not align with your motivators in any way.

A red oil light means the tool clearly conflicts with your self-care.

A red battery light means the tool does not respect consent (expressed or sought).

A red temperature light means the tool shifts you into an unhealthy emotional state.

In this column, think about tools that currently trigger red lights for you in this relationship and that you would like to adjust, discontinue, or replace with something healthier or better.

I suggest you aim to write at least a couple of tools in this column, but write as few or as many as you'd like. If you feel stuck, use the Brainstorming section toward the end of this exercise to generate ideas.

Below are some examples of what someone might write in this third column, but in brackets next to each one, I also indicated the type of communication tool (sending, receiving, or access). You don't have to put the part in brackets into the column. I only added it here in order to help you better understand the types of communication tools.

1. Live telephone calls (sending and receiving tools)

2. Being Facebook friends (sending, receiving, and access tool)

3. Text messaging (sending and receiving tool)

BRAINSTORMING FOR ALL THREE COLUMNS (FOR REFLECTION ONLY)

To help stir up more ideas for your three columns, here are a couple brainstorming questions you may want to think about, depending on the type of relationship this is. Read the questions, see if they generate any ideas, and then return to your three columns of the above exercise if you feel inspired to add to or update what you wrote in your three columns.

When looking at this list of communication tools (for both business and personal use), what ideas does it bring to mind? What works well for you in this relationship, what might work well for you to try, and what doesn't?

Part Three: Get Roadworthy

This is not a comprehensive or ordered list; it's just to help you realize that there are many options.

- Face-to-face conversations
- Email
- Instant Messaging
- Voice over Internet Protocol (VoIP) services (e.g., Skype, Google Meet)
- Video conferencing tools
- Social media platforms
- Document collaboration platforms (e.g., Microsoft SharePoint, Google Docs)
- Project management collaboration tools
- Team communication apps
- Webinars and web conferencing tools
- Teleconferencing services
- Customer communication management (CRM) systems
- Intranet for internal communication
- Video messaging apps
- Live chat software in websites
- Online communication forums
- Multimedia messaging apps
- Podcasting
- Postal mail
- Telephone
- Handwritten letters
- Bulletin boards
- Flyers and posters
- Public announcement systems
- Digital signage
- Language translation apps
- Pen and paper
- Chalkboard/Blackboard
- Whiteboard
- Flip chart
- Sticky notes
- Postcards
- Public speaking
- Debates
- Intercom systems
- Oral storytelling
- Conferences
- Voice

Finally, a note about the last one – voice. Yes, your voice is a communication tool, and these days you can even use artificial intelligence technology to deliver a message in someone else's voice, too. But when it comes to your voice, I'd like to point out that, like many advanced technologies, you have several "settings" you can modify to adjust its power and impact, some of which are:

- Vocal pitch, the highness or lowness of voice (higher pitch can indicate excitement, surprise, or anxiety, while lower pitch can convey seriousness, authority, or sadness).
- Voice intonation, the rise and fall of pitch that can indicate different emotions (like a rising intonation for questioning or uncertainty and a falling intonation for certainty or finality).
- Voice volume, which can communicate anger, enthusiasm, or assertiveness (louder), or sadness, hesitation, or confidentiality (softer).
- Voice tempo, i.e., the speed or pace at which someone speaks, which can indicate excitement, urgency, or nervousness (fast speech), or calmness, thoughtfulness, or sadness (slow speech).
- Voice rhythm, i.e., the pattern of stressed and unstressed syllables.
- Pronunciation, which can communicate cultural, regional, or individual identity.
- Vocal tone, which is made up of the quality or character of the voice like warmth, friendliness, sarcasm, or irritation.

Each adjustment of your "settings" can deliver a whole new message, even with the same exact words.

HIGH FIVE TIME

Remember the power of momentum, which increases with each little celebration, however small it may be.

Part Three: Get Roadworthy

So, how will you celebrate your win of completing this exercise?

You may want to find a mirror and give yourself a high five or come up with another small but uplifting action to acknowledge your effort.

To step up the game, I challenge you to take a selfie of your high five, or a pic of the other celebration you choose (if any), and share it to my Facebook, @boundariescheck, or share it on your own social media and tag me @boundariescheck with the hashtag #chapter12.

You've finished the Safety Inspection for the Tools boundary! When it comes to this boundary, you have metaphorically taken apart the electronics connected to this dial, and you have inspected it. Now you've identified which wires are working well for you and which need your attention or replacing.

If you close this book and suddenly come up with more ideas, remember you can come back and write them into your Diary anytime.

CHAPTER 13

TOPICS DIAL

(18 minute read)

TOPICS CREATE OR CUT TENSION

If you want to understand the power of the Topics dial on the Boundaries Dashboard, tell someone who you care about that you are going to give them 30 minutes of conversation that is 100% focused on discussing them and their happiness. The topic will not include you or your thoughts or your happiness or any other topic in the world.

Very powerful. Life-changing if you stick to it as promised.

Conversation topics have all sorts of power in human relationships, both life-giving and life-taking. Some conversation topics create tension, and others cut it out like a perfectly sharpened knife.

In some countries, sharing certain topics is considered an anti-state crime, punishable by imprisonment, and in some cases, even death.

On a smaller scale, in "free" countries people still punish each other verbally for sharing certain topics, which you can clearly see in contexts like Facebook's comment threads and offline, too, inside many social groups.

I remember one of my most relevant personal examples of tension-creating topics is from an experience I had at a church in the States. At that time, I had looked into the first-century context of the words "Hell" and "forever" in original biblical texts and discovered life-changing and worldview-altering facts. These discoveries cleared away a thick fog from questions I had throughout my life about the Bible and the nature of God.

Thinking that a church Bible study was the perfect place to share my excitement, I brought up those topics. However, the pastor pulled me aside privately afterward, and with his office door closed and in a gentle tone, he asked me not to discuss those topics further, saying that he was worried it would confuse others.

His tone was so soft that I had no heart to argue. I cared about him and didn't want to go against his wishes, but at the same time, asking me to avoid such a pivotal topic – a topic that is fundamental to our faith – caught me completely off guard and genuinely left me feeling muzzled. I lost the feeling of being comfortable and free around him.

Soon after, I found different friends locally and around the world who weren't afraid of the difficult topics that I wanted to explore. We were able to chat freely about those major linguistic, theological, and philosophical questions with intellectual rigor and open-hearted honesty, without judgment, shame, or censorship. They were the most intellectually and spiritually liberating group of friends I've had in my life so far.

I know first-hand how topics can cut down or cut out tension completely.

They say that the second most feared thing in the world next to death is public speaking. I've even heard about studies showing that people fear public speaking more than death itself. So, when I signed up for the public speaking organization "Toastmasters" in order to overcome this fear, I came face-to-face with a feeling stronger than the fear of death itself.

And through that experience I somehow discovered that there is one liberating topic that was able to magically cut through the tension.

I felt that tension radically cut by at least 50% when I brought up the topic of how I felt in the very moment that I was speaking. That's right – the magical tension-cutting topic is my emotional state in the moment I'm speaking. It's a lot of work because it requires that I pay attention to my own physiological and neurological response while I stand in front of the audience. However, the power is solid.

Not only does this topic create a potent authenticity to whatever subject I present, but it turns out that instead of running away from my emotions during public speaking, I can actually feel good calling them out while I feel those feelings in front of the audience.

No matter what the surface topic might be, the most important tension-cutting topic while I'm speaking is the topic of how I feel while I am doing the speaking. I realize that it's something I've always looked up to in others at work and social situations; I've loved when people confess how they really feel in the moment with a sense of vulnerability and transparency.

In corporate meetings when everyone is gathered around talking corporate jargon, it makes my tight shoulders suddenly relax when someone politely interrupts with, "I'm hungry and finding it hard to concentrate," or, "I'm really tired and need a break."

Simply saying, "I feel nervous," when I feel nervous or, "I feel so frustrated," when I feel frustrated has the power to shave a huge layer off of my anxiety. When I'm witnessing and confessing how I feel right now, it's like taking the other person behind-the-scenes.

What you feel right now, in any given moment, is a topic of conversation, and topics are boundaries. In your relationship, how often do you transparently share the topic of your emotional state while in conversation? How often do you take them "behind the scenes" of what you're communicating?

When we feel scared in the moment while we're speaking, instead of vulnerably sharing what we feel behind our words, we often start bringing up topics that redirect attention to some other topic or the other person. In some cases, that may be the right thing to do, but more times than not, it's a richer human experience to pull back the curtains and go behind the scenes.

I heard a beautiful saying: "Be kind. Everyone is still healing from things they don't talk about." For some people, it's too traumatic to say what they feel. So, there are exceptions.

It does not always feel safe to bring up the topic of our emotional state with the other person, and sometimes it's good to say exactly that.

When a feeling is too much or you don't know what to say or how to identify feelings, it can be incredibly powerful to say, "The feeling I have right now is too much to talk about," or "I don't know what to say or how to identify my feelings right now," or "I don't know what I feel about that yet," or "I need to process that one."

Topics change the dynamics in any human relationship for better or worse. All depending on the topic, they can cause people to open up or shut down. Topics are a boundary because they have the power to draw us apart or bring us closer.

TOPICS ARE RELATIONSHIP-SPECIFIC

From the six rules of every human relationship that are described in Chapter 2, Rule #5 says that all boundaries are relationship-specific. In other words, your boundary settings change depending on the kind of human relationship. Conversation topics are one of the great examples of how boundaries change with each relationship.

Do you share your darkest secrets with the person who is interviewing you for a new job? Most likely not. Rather, you stick with conversation topics that are only relevant to the role.

Laws in several Western countries forbid professional interviews from addressing topics that would, in most other situations, be considered normal getting-to-know-you questions like age, religion, or where you graduated high school. Where I live, some of these topics are actually forbidden.

When it comes to intimate or romantic relationships, there's a sense of right and wrong or confidence and shame when it comes to conversation topics. With your partner, what conversation topics do you share and what topics do you refuse to share? What topics are easy to bring up in a conversation or argument, and which topics are you sweeping under the rug entirely to avoid conflict?

A professor of clinical psychology named Dr. Eric Sprankle posted on Twitter: "It's a lot easier for couples to argue about porn use than it is to have a vulnerable conversation about a sexual desire discrepancy, relational boundaries, insecurities, coping mechanisms, the role of masturbation in the relationship, and why one partner is aroused by pirates."[25]

So, welcome to the next dial on the Boundaries Dashboard – Topics! The Topics boundary consists of the topics you discuss in this relationship, and it also includes consideration of the topics you don't discuss.

Topics also matter in your relationship with yourself. Your thoughts are the topics that you either choose to think about, distract yourself from, or push out of mind.

THE SCIENCE OF YOUR THOUGHTS

I comment on the science of "feelings" in a few places in this book, and now since this chapter is about the boundary of topics, it's time to comment on the equally significant science of your "thoughts."

I look at every thought as a "topic" that is born within you, and you can share those topics of thought in a live conversation or you can keep them private within the conversation of your own mind and heart for consideration and processing or just for safekeeping.

As a matter of fact, and as a mind-blowing development in science, whenever you bring up a topic, whether it's only in the privacy of your own mind or in a live conversation, your brain is producing something that is now becoming measurable by scientific equipment.

I'm not talking about science fiction, but it sounds like it. Scientists are on their way to reading your mind with technologies that convert brain activity to images, interpreting and decoding thoughts straight from the brain. For example, if you go search for "brain-computer interfaces (BCIs)," you'll learn about technologies that allow a direct communication pathway between the brain and an external device or computer.

Scientists intend to use these kinds of power for good, like helping paralysis patients communicate or bringing back memories to those with Alzheimer's. However, Dr. Rafael Yuste, Director of the NeuroTechnology

Center at Columbia University, says we have advanced so far in the capability to read minds that it also now needs to be addressed as a legal matter of human rights[26] to make sure that the contents of our brains are not decoded without our consent.

I also learned from Dr. Yuste that the Republic of Chile made a constitutional amendment protecting cerebral activity and its data. This new law makes the protection of information that comes from the brain a basic human right. "Neuro-rights" is now a thing.

I mention all of that so you can begin to understand the importance of topics and that they now matter more than ever because of profound advancements in science to measure them in the brain and new legislation needed to protect them.

Thoughts physically exist; that is, if "physically exist" means that thoughts are associated with measurable physical processes, then in that sense, they are physical phenomena.

I hope this helps you understand that the topics you entertain in your mind matter. Maybe one day you will able to see your own thoughts born on a screen before you can name them, like a sonogram of a child in utero.

THE DYNAMIC RELATIONSHIP BETWEEN SELF-VIEW AND WORLDVIEW

If I were to break up every possible topic into categories and place them in order of importance, I would place the topics of emotional states and thoughts as the most important subjects.

Second in importance would be self-view and worldview.

I see everything else in the universe as subcategories of the above topics.

Self-view and worldview are two different but interdependent topics, and I believe that they determine our every decision and action.

Your self-view is how you view yourself – spiritually, religiously, intellectually (including academic or scientific viewpoints), morally, and/or philosophically.

Your worldview is how you view the world around you – spiritually, religiously, intellectually (including all academic or scientific viewpoints), morally, and/or philosophically.

A helpful metaphor to illustrate the difference between self-view and worldview is that of a microscope versus a telescope.

Self-view is like a microscope that looks inside and up close. Whenever someone speaks about a self-view topic, they're sharing something that expresses their own sense of self-worth or understanding of themselves in any area of life. If someone says, "Nah, I don't want to go for that job. I'm not good enough," that falls into the self-view bucket.

Worldview, on the other hand, is like a telescope that looks far away and outside. It's a topic in which one talks about either their beliefs or someone else's belief's about the external context they live in, including the people around them, society, culture, the world, and humanity. If someone says, "Nah, I don't want to work for that company. They don't have a sense of social responsibility," that falls into the worldview bucket.

Worldview includes moral subjects of right and wrong, as well as the more lighthearted sense of what's cool and not cool. Worldview also includes topics about what others feel and believe. Talking about the worldviews of others often helps us determine ours. As a matter of fact, much of our worldview comes from others sharing theirs.

Chapter 13: Topics Dial

The relationship between self-view and worldview is dynamic, constantly adjusting or changing. If your beliefs change in one, then it likely impacts the other. So, if you change your mind about your self-worth (self-view), then the consequence might be that your ideas about the world will also change, and vice versa when you change your mind about the world around you.

Everything you believe and observe about yourself and your inner world can possibly change when your beliefs and observations about your outer world change, and vice versa.

So, because of that interdependency and dynamic, self-view and worldview are equally powerful and equally deserving of your attention. If you need to start somewhere to change your life, there are no greater topics to explore than what you believe about yourself and the world around you.

THE POWER OF DIVISION

Let's return to the topic of the human relationship that you're working on in this book.

At some point in time there has been or will be one or more topics you want to discuss with that person while the need festers somewhere deep inside of you to bring it up in conversation – but you don't know where to start.

Well, one of the powers of the Topics boundary is to divide a difficult topic into smaller more manageable ones. Sometimes the act of dividing a topic into more digestible pieces has the power to bring peace to enemies and get warring lovers cuddling in bed again.

Dividing a topic means finding a subtopic or a related topic that is smaller and easier to reach an agreement on.

You might want to talk about something, but your feelings are too strong. So, what if you pick apart that heavy topic into bite-sized subtopics with less emotional charge, and reach peace focusing on one at a time? Aim first for a small win that's healthier and easier for you to process.

It's like cutting a piece off the steak that you can chew rather than shoving the whole 300 grams into your mouth at once. Break it down.

Each person has their own emotional pain and pleasure thresholds, and you know your own thresholds better than anyone else. If it hurts to try and chew the entire porterhouse steak in one bite, then take out a fork and knife.

Third-degree emotions happen when you bring up too many topics at once without dividing and focusing. Jeff Guenther, a Licensed Professional Counselor, made this point beautifully when he gave this advice to romantic partners: "Stay focused on the specific thing that made you feel bad because it allows your partner to more easily be accountable."[27]

For example, it can cause an emotional explosion if you bring up the entire history of someone's behavior by saying, "You're always ignoring me." However, if you divide up the complex topic of someone's history and focus the present incident – "For the past hour, I have felt ignored" – it can have a very different and more positive outcome.

The words "always," "never," and "all the time" can come across as overwhelming because, without specifying a precise time or date range, they cover an incalculable amount of time. Time itself has not yet ended, so a thing cannot be "always" or "never" or "all the time." Even though they are not intended to be understood literally, those words can easily trigger third-degree emotions because they communicate something exaggerated or untrue to some degree.

Dividing up emotionally charged topics can help bring people closer or, at least, offer more chances of a deeper and higher quality emotional exchange.

CHAPTER 13 EXERCISE

TOPICS DIAL INSPECTION

TITLES AND DATE

So now it's time to take out your Dashboard Diary.

Put today's date on top and write the title "Topics Dial."

Underneath the title, write: "My Top Motivator: _____" and in the blank space, write your motivator that you discovered in Chapter 6: Fuel Check. Underneath that, write "My Second Motivator: _____" and in the blank space, write your second motivator from that same chapter.

After that, split the page into three columns. Title the first column "Green," the second column "Yellow," and the third column "Red."

Part Three: Get Roadworthy

FIRST COLUMN: GREEN LIGHT TOPICS

This is the column to identify topics that trigger green dashboard lights for you in this relationship.

What does it mean for your Topics boundary to trigger green lights?

A green fuel light means the topic aligns with your motivators in some way.

A green oil light means the topic agrees with (doesn't conflict with) your self-care.

A green battery light means the topic involves consent (expressed and sought).

A green temperature light means the topic shifts your own emotional state into the first-degree range of emotion.

In this column, think about topics that currently trigger green lights for you in this relationship that you would like to maintain and continue at this time. Also in this column, think about new topics that you believe have a good chance of triggering green lights and that you'd like to experiment with.

I suggest you aim to write down a minimum of five topics if you can, but write as many as you'd like. If you feel stuck, use the Brainstorming section toward the end of this exercise to generate ideas.

Here are some examples of what someone might write in the first column:

1. My current wins in life since we last spoke

2. Her current wins in life since we last spoke

3. My nephews

4. Physical health – mine, hers, and those we love, including nutrition and exercise

5. Funny pop culture stories

6. Inspirational events that have happened in the world

7. Positive experiences from her childhood

SECOND COLUMN: YELLOW LIGHT TOPICS

This is the column to identify topics that trigger yellow dashboard lights for you in this relationship.

What does it mean for your Topics boundary to trigger yellow lights?

A yellow fuel light means you feel unsure whether the topic aligns with your motivators.

A yellow oil light means you feel unsure whether the topic agrees with (doesn't conflict with) your self-care.

A yellow battery light means you feel unsure whether the topic involves consent (expressed and sought).

A yellow temperature light means that the topic triggers an emotional state that you're unsure is healthy or unhealthy for you.

Part Three: Get Roadworthy

I suggest you aim to write at least a couple of topics in this column, but write as few or as many as you'd like. If you feel stuck, use the Brainstorming section toward the end of this exercise to generate ideas.

Here are some examples of what someone might write in this second column:

1. The guy I went on a date with last week

2. My thoughts on human sexuality

3. Her current living situation

4. Her romantic life

THIRD COLUMN: RED LIGHT TOPICS

This is the column to identify topics that trigger red dashboard lights for you in this relationship.

What does it mean for your Topics boundary to trigger red lights?

A red fuel light means the topic does not align with your motivators in any way.

A red oil light means the topic clearly conflicts with your self-care.

A red battery light means the topic does not respect consent (expressed or sought).

A red temperature light means the topic shifts you into an unhealthy emotional state.

Chapter 13: Exercise

In this column, think about topics that currently trigger red lights for you in this relationship and that you would like to adjust, discontinue, or replace with something healthier or better.

I suggest you aim to write at least a couple of topics in this column, but write as few or as many as you'd like. If you feel stuck, use the Brainstorming section toward the end of this exercise to generate ideas.

Here are general examples of what someone might write in this third column:

1. Gossipy subjects about other people that have no clear and healthy purpose

2. Anything concerning her business venture that I genuinely do not support

3. My feelings about her poor decisions (not without a mediator, anyway)

4. Her ex-husband

5. My thoughts and feelings about certain theological topics

6. Her thoughts and feelings about certain theological topics

BRAINSTORMING FOR ALL THREE COLUMNS (FOR REFLECTION ONLY)

To help stir up more ideas for your three columns, here are some brainstorming questions you may want to think about, depending on the type of relationship this is. Read the questions, see if they generate any ideas, and then return to your three columns of the above exercise if you feel inspired to add to or update what you wrote in your three columns.

- ○ When it comes to conversation topics about physical health and biological needs (including medical health, physical fitness, maintaining hygiene, proper nutrition, fresh air, etc.), what needs to change or stay the same?

- ○ When it comes to conversation topics about financial health (income, savings, investments, expenses, cashflow, planning, spending habits) as well as paying for things or sharing finances, what needs to change or stay the same?

- ○ When it comes to conversation topics about restful activities, low energy downtime, and relaxation, what needs to change or stay the same?

- ○ When it comes to conversation topics about play, uplifting excitement, celebrating, having fun, and sharing fun activities, what needs to change or stay the same?

- ○ When it comes to conversation topics about career, trade, or business, hiring or managing people, contracted services, change of career activities, and anything business-related, job-related, or career-related, what needs to change or stay the same?

- ○ When it comes to conversation topics about emotions and thought life in general (feelings or ideas), what needs to change or stay the same?

- ○ When it comes to conversation topics about your self-view (how you view yourself and self-worth), what needs to change or stay the same?

- When it comes to conversation topics about worldviews (spiritual, religious, intellectual, moral, or philosophical life), what needs to change or stay the same?

- When it comes to conversation topics about learning something, doing something new, and discovery or exploration of anything and everything in general, what needs to change or stay the same?

- When it comes to conversation topics about time management, scheduling, calendar, and planning or prioritizing time, what needs to change or stay the same?

- When it comes to conversation topics about environments (home, work, or other environments), what needs to change or stay the same?

- When it comes to conversation topics about your relationship with this person or other human relationships, what needs to change or stay the same? Remember this includes any human relationship – strangers, friendships, acquaintanceships, biological and adopted family relationships, romantic, dating, or sexual relationships, professional and business relationships, local community groups, neighbors, organizations, and political/national relationships.

HIGH FIVE TIME

As with previous exercises, let's end this chapter with the much-needed reminder of how celebrating even the smallest of successes builds and sustains momentum.

So, how will you celebrate your win of completing this exercise?

Part Three: Get Roadworthy

Go find a mirror and give yourself a high five or think of something quick and new to do, however small.

If you'd like to step up your game or simply do this as your little celebration ceremony for this chapter, I challenge you to take a selfie of whatever way you decide to celebrate and then share it to my Facebook, @boundariescheck, or share it on your own social media and tag me @boundariescheck with the hashtag #chapter13.

You've finished the Safety Inspection for the Topics boundary! When it comes to this boundary, you have metaphorically taken apart the electronics connected to this dial and inspected it. Now you've identified which wires are working well for you and which need your attention or replacing.

If you close this book and suddenly come up with more ideas, remember to come back and write them into your Diary.

CHAPTER 14

THIRD PARTIES DIAL

(14 minute read)

ILLUSTRATION

A couple plan to get married. They hire a wedding planner who makes their lives better throughout the eight months of planning. The wedding planner is a third party in the engaged couple's relationship.

A business owner and her office staff have an adversarial relationship. She hires a consultant to come up with ways to fix that. The consultant is a third party in the relationship between the owner and the staff.

Two neighbors share a quiet and peaceful small neighborhood together, happy with the prestigious reputation of their street. Then a plot of land between them is sold to a new neighbor who brings down the value of the other two homes through neglect of their property and noise disruptions day and night. The disruptive third neighbor is now the third party to the relationship between the two peaceful neighbors.

While you read this book, if you notice that my ideas impact your ideas, feelings, thoughts, beliefs, or behaviors in your relationship with the other person, then as author of this book, I become a third party to your relationship.

Any third person (or group) who noticeably impacts one or both people in a relationship, either positively or negatively, becomes a third party to the relationship. A third party influences your personal feelings, ideas, thoughts, beliefs, or behaviors in this relationship.

In one sense, you can argue that all of humanity is a third party to your relationship, but when it comes to managing boundaries, the only third parties you directly name and which get your attention are the ones that you believe are noticeably impacting your relationship at this time.

Either you or the other person in the relationship can identify a third party.

THIRD PARTY IMPACT

For privacy's sake I haven't named the author of this social media post or even named the platform, but here's a copied-and-pasted story that offers you an example of the negative impact that a third party can have on a human relationship – in this case, a romantic one.

> So, I have come to visit *my fiancé and stay with him for a few months, since I have been studying abroad for school. I've tried to be friends with* one of *his newer friends that I've met and have made efforts in speaking to her and getting to know her, as I like to know that my partner has good friendships around him that support the relationship. I have just found out that she has been telling him that she thinks I'm getting in the way of their friendship and that their friendship hasn't been the same since I've been*

here. I have literally been nothing but nice to this girl, and I haven't done anything but be here to spend time with my partner. I feel as though she is jealous that his time is being spent with me, which is making me think she might be interested in him. Am I right? When she is around she never tries to speak to me when he's with me, and she's always asking him for favors and for him to drop her places. All of this makes me feel like she is attached to him. What do you all think?

Reading that, for me, was like watching pea and ham soup spill all over someone's brand-new diamond-studded white dress from Dolce & Gabbana. I thought, "What a mess!" Third parties can really make or break any relationship. The lesson there, for me, was simply how impactful a third party can be.

Third parties can also be very positive experiences for a human relationship.

Third parties can inspire two people to have a stronger relationship. Common examples are a great counselor, a great friend, or a great community of supportive people.

In a professional relationship, an inspiring executive can directly and positively impact relationships between managers and staff. They say that CEOs "set the tone" for the company. They are often a significant third party in staff and manager relationships in an organization.

A great example of this from my own experience was the CIO at a multinational company – a multibillion-dollar organization – who was both very intelligent and very humble; he also was free and courageous enough to be both innovative and quirky and let his direct reports be themselves. That set the tone, trickled down to the guy who reported to him, and from that guy to the woman who reported to *him* (my manager), and then down to me.

Our CIO may not have realized this, but in my relationship with my manager he gave me a license to be "me" to a degree that I hadn't experienced before.

He wasn't afraid of being over the top, so I wasn't afraid either. Or rather, I was much less afraid than I ever was before. That same fearless humility was the strength that also made him an incredible leader who could boldly push the company forward with new technology and innovation.

There are executives and people at the office who are like that CIO. But there are also political leaders, parents, siblings, acquaintances, friends, and lovers like that, too. They inspire you to be better in other relationships, too. That's one of the positive impacts of third-party relationships.

Some personalities empty our physical and mental batteries of energy, leaving us with little or no energy for others, while other personalities charge us up to the point where we can charge others up from the energy we received.

That empowering third party can be someone transitory in our lives, too, like a stranger at the grocery store who was extra kind to you and made you believe in the goodness of humanity again.

Simply put, third-party relationships impact this one that you have with the other person, and they need your attention.

THE MOST IMPACTFUL THIRD-PARTY RELATIONSHIP

Here's a trivia question. Out of all the third-party relationships in your life, which one impacts your relationship with the other person the most?

Give yourself a few seconds to look away from this page so that you can take a guess. The answer is in the next paragraph.

When it comes to the Boundaries Dashboard, the most important third-party relationship to your relationship with the other person is the one you have with yourself.

Yes, when it comes to your relationship with the other person, your relationship with yourself is the most impactful third-party relationship. Your relationship with "you" is the most unavoidable, continual, and influential of them all.

You can physically distance yourself from every other relationship, but you can't physically distance yourself from you.

Sleep provides a sense of mental distance from oneself for a little while. Thank God for sleep so I can at least take a break from me!

If you don't have a good relationship with yourself, you'll feel trapped and exhausted even on vacation.

When it comes to the other person, your relationship with yourself is the most important of all third-party human relationships to get right, and the amount of work and attention needed to get this right is massively underestimated.

At any point in the day, there can be many warring needs in you – to find meaning, to eat, to sleep, to experience sexual intimacy, to earn money, get rest, learn or experience something new, to manage biological health and medical needs, to respond to the people demanding your attention, and so much more. Put simply, you have the job of negotiating inner-world peace, and that is how you will bring peace to others and in the world around you – by creating it inside of you first.

You have a very complex mix of opinions and demands from within your nervous system to listen to and negotiate a peace agreement with.

THIRD PARTIES TO YOUR RELATIONSHIP WITH YOU

We can take this another level deeper.

Your "relationship with you" also has third-party relationships that impact it. Other people impact your relationship with you; they can increase your sense of life and health or they can take away from it.

Sometimes you need a third party to jump in to help you negotiate your internal conflicting needs.

Third parties can help you sort out your inaudible cries from within and recognize your "voices" of conflicting needs and desires. A third party can help you be creative with a solution, to help you understand things you don't know yet, and to help you come up with the right direction for your relationship with you.

A third party in your relationship with yourself might be a good friend, an inspiring author or speaker, a therapist, a teacher, or a professional personal coach.

Your relationship with yourself dictates sanity and your ability to make happy and healthy boundaries with everyone else; that's why your relationship with you is the most important third-party relationship in your relationship with the other person.

And that is why the oil light exists on the Boundaries Dashboard – to keep track of the health of your relationship with yourself and its impact on the health of the relationship you have with the other person.

The oil light from Chapter 5 signals your condition of self-care, and self-care is just another way of referring to your relationship with yourself.

What's different about your boundaries in your relationship with yourself compared to everyone else is that you control the decisions in this relationship with yourself. When it comes to the other person, you don't control them or their boundaries.

The first step in managing your relationship with you is to take the Boundaries Health Check for your relationship with yourself and identify the light color. Call it out. Name it. That dashboard light color represents the status or condition of your relationship with you.

If your precious oil light goes yellow or red, you simply check the six boundaries to see which of the six dials might improve your relationship with you.

Maybe it's time to change environments (the Territories boundary).

Maybe it's time to bring in another person or group to share expertise and/or information with you (the Third Parties boundary).

Maybe it's time to do good things for yourself like give yourself more sleep and buy more nutrition-packed food for yourself (the Treasures boundary).

Maybe it's time to shut down current levels of access to you on social media or maybe it's time to open up new ones (the Tools boundary).

Maybe it's time to start intentionally thinking about new and different things by reading a book, or keeping a journal or gratitude list, or learning new ways of thinking (the Topics boundary).

Part Three: Get Roadworthy

Maybe it's time to adjust the length of time and frequency of any or all of the boundaries I just listed (the Time boundary).

It's a simple turn of any of the six "dials" on your dashboard. Experiment one by one to figure out what actions and decisions may need a dial turned up, turned down, or maintained at the same level.

Part Three: Get Roadworthy

CHAPTER 14 EXERCISE

THIRD PARTIES DIAL INSPECTION

TITLES AND DATE

So now it's time to take out your Dashboard Diary.

Put today's date on top and write the title "Third Parties Dial."

Underneath the title, write: "My Top Motivator: _____" and in the blank space, write your motivator that you discovered in Chapter 6: Fuel Check. Underneath that, write "My Second Motivator: _____" and in the blank space, write your second motivator from that same chapter.

After that, split the page into three columns. Title the first column "Green," the second column "Yellow," and the third column "Red."

Part Three: Get Roadworthy

FIRST COLUMN: GREEN LIGHT THIRD PARTIES

This is the column to identify third parties that trigger green dashboard lights for you in this relationship.

What does it mean for a third party to trigger green lights?

A green fuel light means the third-party relationship aligns with your motivators in some way.

A green oil light means the third-party relationship agrees with (doesn't conflict with) your self-care.

A green battery light means the third-party relationship involves consent (expressed and sought).

A green temperature light means the third-party relationship shifts your own emotional state into the first-degree range of emotion.

This column is for third-party relationships that you would like to maintain and continue at this time.

List as few or as many as you'd like. If you feel stuck, use the Brainstorming section toward the end of this exercise to generate ideas.

Below are some examples of what someone might write in the first column. I have added some explanations in brackets just so you can understand third parties better, but do not feel obligated to write this bracketed information in your list.

1. My friendship with Lisa. (She gives me inspiration and wisdom for this relationship.)

Chapter 14: Exercise

2. The New Recipe Club I belong to. (This group gives me something productive to do while he is working on Wednesday evenings.)

3. My love and fanship of my favorite author. (He keeps my worldview healthy for this relationship.)

4. My citizenship relationship with Australia. (This political relationship keeps my tension levels lower in this relationship with the other person, giving me a sense of freedom where we live.)

SECOND COLUMN: YELLOW LIGHT THIRD PARTIES

This is the column to identify third parties that trigger yellow dashboard lights for you in this relationship.

What does it mean for a third-party relationship to trigger yellow lights?

A yellow fuel light means you feel unsure whether the third-party relationship aligns with your motivators.

A yellow oil light means you feel unsure whether the third-party relationship agrees with (doesn't conflict with) your self-care.

A yellow battery light means you feel unsure whether the third-party relationship involves consent (expressed and sought).

A yellow temperature light means that the third-party relationship triggers an emotional state that you're unsure is healthy or unhealthy for you.

List as few or as many as you'd like. If you feel stuck, use the Brainstorming section toward the end of this exercise to generate ideas.

Below are some examples of what someone might write in this second column. I have added some explanation in brackets to help you understand third parties better, but do not feel obligated to write this bracketed information in your list.

1. His coworker (She sends him personal text messages, looking for his attention that's not work-related, and I'm unsure of her intentions.)

2. Our landlord (Their poor management impacts our ability to upgrade our living space.)

3. Our bank (Not sure they give us the banking options we need to hit our mutual financial goals.)

4. His best friend's brother (He keeps coming over unannounced, interrupting us).

THIRD COLUMN: RED LIGHT THIRD PARTIES

This is the column to identify third parties that trigger red dashboard lights for you in this relationship.

What does it mean for a third party to trigger red lights?

A red fuel light means the third-party relationship does not align with your motivators in any way.

A red oil light means the third-party relationship clearly conflicts with your self-care.

A red battery light means the third-party relationship does not respect consent (expressed or sought).

A red temperature light means the third-party relationship shifts you

Chapter 14: Exercise

into an unhealthy emotional state.

List as few or as many as you'd like. If you feel stuck, use the Brainstorming section toward the end of this exercise to generate ideas.

Below are some examples of what someone might write in this third column. I added explanations in brackets only to help you better understand "third parties," but don't feel obligated to write any bracketed explanations in your list.

1. My relationship with myself (Neglecting to make my follow-up doctor visit and treatment impacts my health and my energy level to do things with him that we both want to do. Making the doctor's appointment will flip the dashboard lights from red to green again.)

2. My relationship with my ex (His stories showing up in my social media feed cause unhealthy feelings in this relationship.)

3. My relationship with "that" family member (Their attitude brings me down consistently and puts me in an unhealthy and strange mood, impacting my ability to feel fully present with him.)

BRAINSTORMING FOR ALL THREE COLUMNS (FOR REFLECTION ONLY)

To help stir up more ideas for your three columns, here are some brainstorming questions you may want to think about. Read the questions, see if they generate any ideas, and then return to your three columns of the above exercise if you feel inspired to add to or update what you wrote in your three columns.

- What, if any, third-party relationships help or hinder your physical health in this relationship? As an example, a mutual friend who encourages illegal drug use might hinder your physical health and a mutual friend who encourages health and fitness might improve your physical health.

- What, if any, third-party relationships help or hinder your financial health in regard to this relationship?

- What, if any, third-party relationships help or hinder your downtime and relaxation that's needed for you to feel present in this relationship?

- What, if any, third-party relationships help or hinder your sense of playfulness, excitement, celebrations, and/or general fun activities that you need in this relationship?

- What, if any, third-party relationships help or hinder the business, trading, professional services, or anything business/job/career-related in this relationship?

- What, if any, third-party relationships help or hinder your emotions and thought life (feelings or ideas) when it comes to this relationship?

- What, if any, third-party relationships help or hinder your self-view (how you view yourself and self-worth) in this relationship?

- When it comes to this relationship, what, if any, third-party relationships help or hinder your worldview (spiritual, religious, intellectual, moral, or philosophical life)?

- What, if any, third-party relationships help or hinder your desire or ability to learn new things, do something new, grow, discover, or explore in this relationship?

- What, if any, third-party relationships help or hinder your time management, prioritizing, scheduling, and calendar management in this relationship?

○ What, if any, third-party relationships help or hinder the environments that you share in this relationship? As an example, perhaps a third-party relationship is bringing one or both of you into unhealthy environments or adding unhealthy elements to existing environments. On the other hand, maybe a third-party relationship is bringing one or both of you into healthier environments, or adding healthy elements into existing environments.

HIGH FIVE TIME

Repeating is what your heart and organs do all day long to keep you alive and growing, so it's totally cool to repeat things that sustain and grow your heart and mind. Celebrating your smallest of wins is one of those things.

So, how will you celebrate your win of completing this exercise? Go give yourself a high five in the mirror or pick another little way of acknowledging your effort.

If you like this idea, I challenge you to take a selfie of your high five or whatever celebration you choose, and then share it to my Facebook, @boundariescheck, or share it on your own social media and tag me @boundariescheck with the hashtag #chapter14.

You've finished the Safety Inspection for the Third Parties boundary! When it comes to this boundary, you have metaphorically taken apart the electronics connected to this dial, and you've inspected it. Now you've identified which wires are working well for you and which need your attention or replacing.

If you come up with more ideas later, come back and write them into your Diary anytime.

CHAPTER 15

TIME DIAL

(10 minute read)

THE MAGIC DIAL ON THE DASHBOARD

Time. It's the most unique dial on the Boundaries Dashboard. That's because it is the boundary that determines the amount of time and frequency of all five of the other boundaries.

The Territories dial controls what choices you make about the physical environment and physical space that you share with the other person, but you turn the Time dial up or down to change the amount of time and the frequency that you agree to share that territory.

The Treasures dial controls what you invest or don't invest in this relationship, but you turn the Time dial up or down to adjust the length of time and the frequency that you invest or don't invest it.

The Tools dial controls what communication technologies you agree to use or not use, but you turn the Time dial up or down to adjust the length of time and the frequency that you use it or don't use it.

The Topics dial controls the number of topics that you choose to talk about (or not talk about) with the other person, but you turn the Time dial up or down to change the amount of time and the frequency that you choose to discuss those topics or not discuss them.

The Third Parties dial controls the boundaries of all other relationships that impact this one, but you turn the Time dial up or down to change the amount of time and frequency that you choose to spend with or for those other relationships.

As with all boundaries, your Time dial settings will change as the road of this relationship changes; there are different seasons of life as you grow, as you experience more of the world, and as your physical, mental, biological, financial, and emotional needs change.

However, we're in this season of your life right now, so in the exercise in this chapter, we'll be looking at your time boundaries for this season of the relationship.

THE DOSE MAKES THE POISON

During one of my most difficult seasons with a particular family member, I was able to have a decent conversation on the phone if it lasted 30 minutes or less. It was like clockwork; as soon as 30 minutes hit, it felt like my foot had suddenly slipped off a tightrope over top of the Grand Canyon. Thirty minutes proved to be the maximum time for keeping it healthy.

Everything seems to have its healthy maximum. Water is healthy, and we need it to live, but too much of it can flood your organs and you will literally drown. Life-giving water can turn excessive and dangerous.

Washing your hands is great, but studies show that washing them too much can damage your skin and give germs a place to grow and thrive. And vitamins are essential for life, but apparently too much of them can lead to heart problems, muscular issues, bleeding issues, and more.[28]

Modern medicine has given humanity the opportunity to live longer, but in the wrong quantity and frequency, medicine can end our lives suddenly.

Soft little droplets of water falling on your skin doesn't sound so dangerous, right? Ah, but turn up the Time dial (amount of time and frequency), and it becomes a method of torture. One soft little droplet of water falling repeatedly on the same spot on your skin for a long period of time becomes a cruel interrogation method otherwise known as Chinese Water Torture.

In small doses, something as life-giving as water can be such an awesome experience but increase the length of time and frequency of those water droplets, and it can become a legitimate torture device.

The dose of anything can give life or destroy it.

Hydrogen cyanide is a highly toxic chemical but, in small doses, cyanide can be found in certain foods like almonds and cherry pits and is harmless to humans. Formaldehyde is a carcinogen and toxic at high concentrations, but it is naturally produced in the human body and found naturally in small amounts in some fruits and vegetables.

It's been the same for me when it comes to each of the six boundaries, but most powerfully with the Time boundary: with the right turn of the dial on the Boundaries Dashboard, even poison can be brought down to harmless levels.

For me, time has been the easiest of the six boundaries to measure, quantify, and adjust, and that may be what makes it so powerful.

CHAPTER 15 EXERCISE

TIME DIAL INSPECTION

TIME DIAL SETTINGS

This exercise is different from the other boundaries exercises. That's because each answer you give will be paired with one or more of the other five boundaries.

Unlike the other boundary dials on the Boundaries Dashboard, the Time dial never turns up or down alone. For example, a certain territory might be healthy for you both to share, but what amount of time and frequency keeps it healthy?

A certain communication tool might have become unhealthy for you both to use, but what time and frequency adjustments could potentially make it healthy again?

Talking about a certain topic may be healthy, but what length of discussion makes it turn in the wrong direction?

Part Three: Get Roadworthy

A third party to this relationship, like a good friend or counselor, may be doing good for you and this relationship, but what amount of time and frequency of time with that person changes that story for better or worse?

In other exercises throughout this book, you focused on one boundary at a time, but in each of the three columns of this exercise, you'll look at the Time boundary together with any one of the other five.

TITLES AND DATE

So now it's time to take out your Dashboard Diary.

Put today's date on top and write the title "Time Dial."

Underneath the title, write: "My Top Motivator: _____ and in the blank space, write your motivator that you discovered in Chapter 6: Fuel Check. Underneath that, write "My Second Motivator: _____" and in the blank space, write your second motivator from that same chapter.

After that, split the page into three columns. Title the first column "Green," the second column "Yellow," and the third column "Red."

FIRST COLUMN: GREEN LIGHT TIMES

In this column, list each of the other five boundaries and write down amounts of time and the frequency of that time that already work well for you. In other words, these time frames and frequencies trigger green dashboard lights for you in this relationship.

Chapter 15: Exercise

What does it mean for your Time boundary to trigger green lights?

A green fuel light means the Time boundary aligns with your motivators in some way.

A green oil light means the Time boundary agrees with (doesn't conflict with) your self-care.

A green "battery light" means the Time boundary involves consent (expressed and sought).

A green "temperature light" means the Time boundary shifts your own emotional state into the first-degree range of emotion.

I suggest you aim to write down a minimum of five Time boundaries if you can, but write as many as you'd like. If you feel stuck, use the Brainstorming section toward the end of this exercise to generate ideas.

Here are some examples of what someone might write in this first column:

1. Territories boundary (including body boundaries): Her house – 30 minutes once a week is currently working for me; also big hugs hello and goodbye each visit.

2. Treasures boundary: Sending her gifts twice a year – once for her birthday and then for Christmas.

3. Tools boundary: Video or audio calls maximum 45 minutes once a week.

4. Topics boundary: When it comes to frequency, it's healthy to bring up these topics in every conversation: her latest business and marketing wins and challenges, her health and fitness progress and challenges, and funny stories and videos.

Part Three: Get Roadworthy

5. Third Parties boundary: Our mutual friend Chris who hangs out with us about once every month or two.

SECOND COLUMN: YELLOW LIGHT TIMES

In this column, think about each one of the other five boundaries and write down amounts of time and the frequency of that time that trigger yellow dashboard lights for you for that boundary.

What does it mean for your Time boundary to trigger yellow lights?

A yellow fuel light means you feel unsure whether the time boundary aligns with your motivators.

A yellow oil light means you feel unsure whether the time boundary agrees with (doesn't conflict with) your self-care.

A yellow battery light means you feel unsure whether the time boundary involves consent (expressed and sought).

A yellow temperature light means that the time boundary triggers an emotional state that you're unsure is healthy or unhealthy for you.

I suggest you aim to write at least a couple of Time boundaries in this column, but write as few or as many as you'd like. If you feel stuck, use the Brainstorming section toward the end of this exercise to generate ideas.

Here are general examples of what someone might write in this second column:

1. Territories boundary: More than 5 minutes sitting close together makes me feel a little nervous.

2. Treasures boundary: It feels awkward if he takes me to dinner any more frequently than once a month; I'd rather split the bill.

3. Tools boundary: I don't want to text any more than two minutes in my day. (Happy to use voice call or voice memos after that.)

4. Topics boundary: I won't discuss the possibility of us dating for more than one minute, because I already told him how I feel about that.

5. Third Parties boundary: Spending any more than one hour with him and our other friend Jen gets weird. (I can't pinpoint why just yet.)

THIRD COLUMN: RED LIGHT TIMES

In this column, list each of the other five boundaries and write down amounts of time and the frequency of that time that trigger red dashboard lights for you in this relationship.

What does it mean for your Time boundary to trigger red lights?

A red fuel light means the time boundary does not align with your motivators in any way.

A red oil light means the time boundary clearly conflicts with your self-care.

A red battery light means the time boundary does not respect consent (expressed or sought).

A red temperature light means the time boundary shifts you into an unhealthy emotional state.

Part Three: Get Roadworthy

In this column, think about times that currently trigger red lights for you in this relationship and that you would like to adjust, discontinue, or replace with something healthier or better.

I suggest you aim to write at least a couple of Time boundaries in this column, but write as few or as many as you'd like. If you feel stuck, use the Brainstorming section toward the end of this exercise to generate ideas.

Here are some examples of what someone might write in this third column. I've included explanations in brackets, but you don't have to:

1. Territories dial: Staying in her home for more than three days in a row. (Drives my stress levels through the roof.)

2. Treasures dial: Sitting with her at home doing nothing more than five hours a week promotes an unhealthy sedentary lifestyle. (I'd rather set a maximum "do nothing" time.)

3. Tools dial: Phone calls more than five minutes go downhill quick. (Phone conversations without video means I can't see her facial expressions which makes her complex personality extremely difficult to interpret.)

4. Topics dial: If I spend any amount of time at all discussing any topic with the intention of seeking her approval. (It has regularly come back to bite me.)

5. Third Parties dial: Sharing my close friends with her for any amount of time. (She consumes them with gossip.)

BRAINSTORMING FOR ALL THREE COLUMNS (FOR REFLECTION ONLY)

To help stir up more ideas for your three columns, here are some brainstorming questions you may want to think about, depending on the type of relationship this is. Read the questions, see if they generate any ideas, and then return to your three columns of the above exercise if you feel inspired to add to or update what you wrote in your three columns.

- When it comes to environments and/or body boundaries that you share or don't share with the other person (your Territories boundary), what amounts of time and/or frequency help or hinder you in this relationship?

- When it comes to the investment of your energy or effort – physical, material, financial, emotional, and mental (your Treasures boundary), what amounts of time and/or frequency help or hinder you in this relationship?

- When it comes to anything that can be used to communicate (your Tools boundary – whether it's a sending tool, receiving tool, or access tool), what amounts of time and/or frequency help or hinder you in this relationship?

- When it comes to the time spent on conversation topics you talk about (your Topics boundary), what amounts of time and/or frequency help or hinder you in this relationship?

- When it comes to any relationship outside of this one that influences your ideas, feelings, thoughts, beliefs, or behaviors in this relationship to any noticeable degree (your Third Parties boundary), what amounts of time and/or frequency help or hinder you in this relationship?

Part Three: Get Roadworthy

HIGH FIVE TIME

Say it with me for the last time: Celebrating even the smallest of successes builds and sustains momentum.

So, how will you celebrate your win of completing this exercise?

It's time for a small win celebration – a high five to yourself in the mirror (because it's fun and it works) or any other small thing you decide to do, whatever it is.

To step up your game or simply do this as your little celebration ceremony for this chapter, I challenge you to take a selfie of your celebration and share it to my Facebook, @boundariescheck, or share it on your own social media and tag me @boundariescheck with the hashtag #chapter15.

You've finished the Safety Inspection for this boundary! When it comes to your Time boundary, you have metaphorically taken apart the electronics connected to this dial and inspected it. Now you've identified which wires are working well for you and which need your attention or replacing.

If you close this book but then come up with more ideas, come back and write them into your Diary anytime.

PART FOUR

MAP YOUR TRIP

CHAPTER 16

RELATIONSHIP ROADMAPS

(11 minute read)

WHERE YOUR ROADMAP BEGINS

Whether it's Google Maps on our smart phone or a good-old fashioned printed map that takes two hands to open, throughout history, we humans have depended on maps to orient ourselves and find the best roads to travel.

We encounter unexpected roadblocks or dangers quite regularly in life, and a map helps navigate around those; it gives us landmarks and guideposts to look for to get us back on track.

It's the same in human relationships; if you can hold a map of the relationship in your hands – whether on a digital device or on paper – it greatly increases your chances of feeling purposeful, meaningful, and more empowered, especially in hard times. A documented relationship roadmap will orient you and help you find a strong sense of direction,

Part Four: Map Your Trip

especially when you feel stuck.

And that's what you're going to create in Part Four "Map Your Trip."

Your relationship roadmap will help orient your decisions and actions with the other person in this relationship. Because of the strong direction it gives, it will also help you find the right boundaries for yourself in other human relationships. It will even help you attract the right human relationships into your life that will agree with and amplify your sense of purpose in this relationship and in your relationship with yourself.

Having a relationship roadmap helps you know what roads are best for you to take with the other person.

And if a relationship road disintegrates, and one or both of you stop traveling this life together, you still have your map that is yours alone to remind you where you're headed.

In this book, I guide you through creating yours. Your relationship roadmap will one day become the story of your life – the places you travelled and goals you accomplished on your own and those you shared with the other person. If or when you go through this book for a different relationship in your life, you will create a unique roadmap for that relationship, too.

Depending on changes to the landscape and new developments, the roadmaps you see on Google Maps or the printed map booklets at the convenient store all get updated. Your relationship roadmap is no different. Yes, you'll stick to it and it will guide you, but if a major life change happens, or a critically important project comes along, then it's time to calculate if any of your intended destinations need a quick adjustment or update.

So where do you begin to create your map for this relationship?

Your roadmap starts with identifying what I call your "destinations." Destinations are what your relationship roadmap is made of.

The upcoming exercises will take you through the process of creating one.

WHAT ARE DESTINATIONS?

When it comes to your relationship roadmap, your "destinations" are your long-term goals. By "goals" I mean the collection of your most important expectations, hopes, visions, and experiences that you see yourself moving toward or "driving toward" in life.

If destinations are "long-term goals," then why don't I ditch the word "destination" and just stick to the term "long-term goals"? Here's why. A "goal" is a sports metaphor, and it typically brings to mind a visual of one field and someone kicking or throwing a ball directly into a basket or past a certain and specific marker of some sort, whereas the metaphor of a "destination" brings to mind the idea of driving to a new place and your arrival can happen in a large number of ways.

Your "destination" is more of an indirect and complex journey that involves many metaphorical fields of land, not just one, and it involves many small goals to hit along the way. Reaching a destination isn't quick and straight-forward as kicking a ball into a net. The "rules of the game" may change with each small goal along the way, too.

I will still use the phrase "long-term goal" here and there in this book, but only strategically.

Ok, I define destinations as "long-term" goals, but how much time does that mean? "Long-term" depends on your personal capacity to see ahead in your life. A "long" amount of time is defined uniquely for each individual, depending on their situation and stage in life, but as a coach, I typically define long term as six months to a year for most coaching clients.

However, in some cases where a client faces a major transition in life, "long term" can mean as little as several weeks or a few months. For example, someone may have recently experienced an unexpected event that throws their entire future into question, and in that case, they cannot see months ahead and so are taking life day-by-day and moment-by-moment. In that case, "long term" might mean as little as two weeks.

And how many destinations does a person have? As a personal coach, my client may have several destinations to work toward over a long period of time, but in each coaching conversation, the client chooses their top or most important destination to discuss and work toward.

Throughout this book, I have been taking you through the same process that I would go through in a live one-on-one coaching conversation: first we get clarity, and then we create action. In this book, we first took a full inventory of your boundaries in Part Three, and now we will identify specific directions you'd like to go in this relationship here in Part Four. In Part Five, you will have all of the previous chapter exercises to help you create your very next step of action along with a repeatable process for you to continue until you reach your intended destinations.

In coaching, while I refer to a client's long-term goal as their "destination," I also refer to all of their short-term goals on the way to their destination as their "next stops." Next stops are the many small plans of action that you take in order to reach your destination. I will go into more detail later in the book.

Another important thing to note about your destinations is that they can be either yours alone or shared. Examples of destinations that are yours alone might be to lose a certain amount of body fat or to learn a new skill. An example of a shared destination would be opening a business together with the other person or competing together in a local contest.

If or when the other person has identified their destinations, the overlap of both of your journeys creates the rich stories of your relationship.

Destinations are not just a nice thing to identify and work toward. Rather, to be in a human relationship without recognizing the direction you're going is confusing. A human relationship without clear intentions can feel like driving in heavy fog.

On *The Dan Kennedy Fitness and Lifestyle* podcast, a show I have listened to religiously, I remember one of his fascinating guests said something that stuck with me: "Wishy-washy intentions make wishy-washy outcomes."

I remember the topic of that episode was about getting what you want in life, including in relationships. That quote is another way of saying that a blurry vision of what you really want in this relationship will produce blurry outcomes. No wonder human relationships can be so confusing!

I call the process of identifying your destinations "mapping your trip," which gives this part of the book its title. Mapping is a process, and we'll do it together in these next chapters.

WHAT DESTINATIONS DO

Destinations do tons of work for you. They help with prioritizing and decision-making in all areas of life, but perhaps most fundamentally, identifying your destinations keeps you true to yourself and to the other person in every human relationship.

Destinations give you something genuine to share with the other person in each relationship, and during those seasons of life when there is no one else, you have destinations of your own that give you something rich and meaningful to aim for in your relationship with your own soul.

Your destinations on the relationship roadmap keep you knowing who you are and what you want from this life, which in turn will help you find your place in your community and in the world. Because of that, I'd go so far to say that the best indicator that someone is ready for dating, or a career, might be when they have sketched out a relationship roadmap for their own life. Whether it's a professional or personal relationship, a roadmap gives each party in the relationship a way to determine compatibility and a way to identify what bonds them together.

DESTINATIONS ARE NOT FEELINGS – THEY CREATE THEM

Destinations are not feelings, but they do cause them.

In a human relationship, if your goal is to feel certain emotions or maintain an emotional state in the relationship, then that is not a destination; rather, having a destination is what allows you to achieve that emotional state.

When it comes to the relationship roadmap, a destination requires you to make a number of boundary adjustments, which either help create or protect an emotional state.

Each of the six boundaries individually creates feelings, and the six boundaries also create feelings when mixed together in certain quantities like a recipe. Different combinations of those six ingredients come together and emotionally "taste" differently.

You reach your destinations as the result of making a combination of many boundary decisions – places and spaces to share, things you aim to do or accomplish or maintain together, communication technologies you wish to use, topics of conversation you wish to integrate into your lives, adding other human relationships that help or assist this one, and finally, destinations are also the frequency and quantity of time that you aim to spend together or doing any of those things.

In other words, the idea here is that the roads toward your destinations on your relationship roadmap consist of – and only of – your decisions about the six boundaries, and those decisions create your feelings and thoughts.

FEELING LOST VS. FEELING ACCOUNTABLE

Ever feel lost in a relationship?

If you feel lost in a relationship, perhaps you have not defined what you really want or need for your own life, and so everything – including other human relationships – seems a bit blurry.

Or perhaps you know what you want or need in life, but you feel lost because you and the other person have not identified long-term goals to share together.

Or perhaps you already arrived at an intended long-term destination with the other person but never mapped out a new one, so now you feel a sense of aimlessness.

Or perhaps the long-term destination that you're both headed toward doesn't align with what you genuinely want out of life, or it conflict in some way with your sense of purpose.

Part Four: Map Your Trip

As a child, you followed the relationship roadmaps that your parents and other authorities set out for you, and then as you grew your language abilities, you became increasingly more capable of naming goals of your own; in other words, you learned to identify and communicate the things you need, expect, hope for, wish for, and want.

You didn't think in terms of a "roadmap" or "destinations" back then, but as you grew, you slowly learned to identify what you were aiming for, and those aims did not always agree with the ones that your childhood authorities laid out for you.

For some reading this book, maybe your childhood authorities didn't lay out many or any long-term goals for you, and that left you feeling lost.

Whatever the relationship, a feeling of being lost often makes us disoriented. Identifying and documenting your personal expectations, experiences you'd like to have, hopes, and goals for your future – or what I call your "destinations" – has all the potential to give you a sense of moving forward. Additionally, when you write down your destinations, that document becomes a witness to something true and deep within you, an artifact in the history of you, and it becomes an external source of accountability.

Over the years, I've come across mentions of several studies showing that the act of writing down your goals is strongly associated with goal success in both personal and professional contexts, and those who write those goals in detail are significantly more likely to hit their goals than people who don't write them down.

SHARED DESTINATIONS

After you identify your own personal destinations for your relationship roadmap, you can then discover which of them you'd like to share or currently share with the other person. You can also discover which ones might bring you closer together, and which ones might drive you apart.

Back in high school, my best friend at the time and I shared the same science class, shared a certain sense of humor, and we both had a great love for dancing. We both shared the "destinations" of going to raves and clubs together, goofing off, and hanging out with other people who love the same things.

My destinations with my high school best friend were tremendously fun and a bit wild, so once I became very religious, stopped partying, stopped having fun, and left for university to become a somewhat rigid academic, we had nothing to share anymore so our relationship road ended. (Good news! Years later I have, for the most part, recovered from being boring!)

I tell you that story as an example of how shared destinations are what bring two people together and keep them traveling on one relationship road.

It's the same for all kinds of human relationships.

A shared destination may appear differently on two people's roadmaps, and they are still shared. For example, in a professional relationship, one person's destination might be to get paid for house cleaning services and the other person's destination might be to receive the regular weekly service of a house cleaner. Shared destinations can work very well and make economies thrive.

Two people often have very different things they're looking to get out of a human relationship. The big question is this: is each person's destination something that can be shared with the other? That will determine the length of their relationship road.

Part Four: Map Your Trip

Imagine a married couple where the husband sees himself sharing his life with only his wife until old age, but his wife sees herself enjoying life both with him and their future children. The road of their relationship could possibly diverge into separate lives if they don't revise the destinations on their relationship roadmaps.

Or imagine two people meet on a dating app, where one person only sees a one-night stand, and the other person excitedly sees a potential future together. One person sees only sharing bodies for one evening, and the other sees sharing daily conversations, dinners, and many dates ahead.

That's the importance of shared destinations; they keep you on the road of a human relationship. They give you purpose and direction. When you feel no real sense of purpose for the relationship, or you are each headed in opposite directions, a "dead end" relationship road sign comes into view very quickly.

When it comes to the relationship you're focusing on in this book, the first step to knowing which of your destinations to share is to first identify your own destinations for your life – big or small. Later in Part Four where we map your trip, I will walk you through the exercise to identify yours.

CHAPTER 17

MY ROAD LENGTH

(8 minute read)

In your Boundaries Health Check, you looked backward in time to evaluate yourself in this relationship, and we called that period of time your "time frame." It was historical.

In contrast, from this page forward in this book, we're going to look forward in time. We'll look at the roads ahead and the farthest distance you can see yourself going in this life and relationship right now, and this is what I call your "relationship road length" or "road length" for short. It is within this period of time that we will map all of your destinations.

On a digital map, if you zoom out too far, you can't see the roads anymore. If you zoom too closely, you can't see what's ahead for your journey. So, your relationship road length will zoom out just enough for practical decision-making and considering all your foreseeable options.

A map, whether physical or digital, also doesn't include entire roads for various reasons. Maybe the cut-off part is still being built, maybe it's shut down, or maybe the road is not governed by the map's country or region. Likewise, while you might have many years or even decades

Part Four: Map Your Trip

ahead in a human relationship, there will be parts of the journey that you just can't yet see.

Later in this part of the book, you will measure the current "road length" of your relationship. Your "road length" refers to how far ahead you can comfortably see your own life right now and how far ahead you can comfortably see yourself in your relationship with the other person. Those two road lengths can be very different amounts of time.

However, in this current chapter, we're going to focus on your road length in your relationship with you. This will be one measurable amount of time. Then, separately in an upcoming chapter, we'll focus on your road length in your relationship with the other person.

Just as some roads are excluded on a real roadmap, some of your roads may stretch farther than you can see or plan for right now. When mapping your trip, we are only concerned with how much (or how little) you can clearly see right now.

In your relationship with you, your road length is the farthest length of time you can see yourself doing something in this world that we live in. It is the farthest most "zoomed out" view of your life, the longest you can comfortably see ahead. It's the farthest measure into the future that you can easily see yourself either maintaining something (keeping it the same because it is working well, such as a diet or exercise or lifestyle), turning down something (removing or reducing it), or turning up something (increasing, growing, achieving, or changing).

In your relationship with yourself, for example, your road length can be something as simple as "I comfortably see myself just living into my 90s," or it can be as complex as, "I can comfortably see myself building empires until I'm 110."

If you can't see yourself on Earth doing something past a certain measure of time such as one month from now or a decade, then that measure of time is your road length. Anything past what you can see comfortably is like an unstable or unconstructed road. When it comes to the Boundaries Dashboard, a road is not a "road" unless it's constructed – planned, paved, and safe to drive on with a clear start and end, or else it's not properly a road.

Where I'm from, in order for a pathway to be recognized as a "road" by a city, town, county, or state, it has to have certain width requirements, safety standards, surface types, engineering and signage, and other legal considerations. It's the same with your relationship roadmap and road length.

On your relationship roadmap, if there is an uncomfortable degree of uncertainty of the road's stability, then it fails the standard of being considered a "road." Send in the road construction crew or close it off, unless you want to drive into a ditch or drive off a cliff!

So, it might be that you can comfortably see yourself existing on planet Earth for the next 50 years, or it might be you can comfortably see only five months – or even five weeks – ahead. The farthest amount of time that you can comfortably see yourself maintaining or achieving anything for yourself– whether it's days, weeks, years, or decades – that is your "road length."

DIFFERENT EYESIGHTS

At different stages of my life, my road length was very short. When I was a child, the next day was the farthest I could see. As a teen, I remember there was a time I could only see as far ahead as the next date that my friends and I planned for another night out at a New York City club or rave.

Part Four: Map Your Trip

Different people have different lengths of eyesight, too. Some people have 20/20 vision, while others are born with visual impairment of 20/70 vision or worse and can only see clearly at 20 feet what people with normal vision can see clearly from 70 feet away.

Regardless of whether it's lifestyle or something we're born with, we each see different lengths ahead, literally with our eyes and metaphorically with our visions for our lives.

At some points in my life, I didn't know yet what town, state, or country I would live in beyond a month's time.

In 2013, I decided to travel for one month. On Facebook, I made a post to all my friends and asked who had a room available for me to stay, and several of them responded. I had very little idea what I would do with my life after this trip. One month was my road length.

So, I emptied the apartment where I lived, ended the lease, and journeyed from Staten Island, New York City to the other side of the world, with my first stop in Brisbane, Australia.

After a few weeks in Brisbane, the oven-like heat and the size of the spiders had me so repulsed that I didn't know how I could ever stay. But the Australian I met and dated in that time, as well as his precious family and friends, all proved themselves to be some of the most beautiful, smart, and kind humans I know.

Being around such an inspiring Australian family fed a deep sense of wonder inside of me about humanity. Because of them, I tolerated the heat and decided to use a high-powered vacuum for the occasional monster-sized spider.

The longer I observed Australians, the more optimistic I felt about my life, and so the longer ahead I could see some of the things I'd like to do with my life.

During my first week in Australia, the farthest I could see in my life was only the next 30 days. A 30-day road length! After the first three or four years in Australia, I could start to see at least another five to ten years in Australia. My road lengthened as I found things I loved in life and in Australia.

Thanks to the influence of Australia's vibrant health and fitness culture, I can now see myself lifting weights into a very old age, even into my 90s (don't laugh!). When I lived in New York City, I did not and could not see that many years ahead.

Now, I have a longer road length that spans decades and stronger internal vision. I can comfortably see myself into a very old age making far more whole-hearted decisions, not half-hearted ones, eating in a way that gives me energy (not in a way that gives me refined-sugar lethargy), and getting a minimum number of hours of sleep every night.

So, right now as you read this book, think about the farthest amount of time ahead you can comfortably see for yourself and your own life. Maybe you can easily imagine yourself in your 90s. Maybe the farthest you can comfortably see your life right now is the next two weeks.

In this chapter's exercise, you'll write the longest time frame that you can most comfortably see ahead.

COMFORTABLE IS THE MAGIC WORD

As you now know, your personal road length on your relationship roadmap is the farthest ahead you can comfortably see yourself doing something – anything! – here on this amazing planet Earth.

I'm using the word "comfortable" a lot and emphasizing it on purpose. The period of time you choose for your road length must feel comfortable in order for this process to work. Picking a period of time that feels uneasy or *un*comfortable is like driving on a road with potholes and ditches. The Boundaries Dashboard malfunctions on unfinished roads, so we don't pick periods of time that seem unstable.

Check in with your nervous system to find what period of time feels good to you. If an amount of time doesn't come to mind quickly, then set an alarm for one minute. In that one minute, ask yourself: what can I picture myself doing many decades from now?

If "many decades" of time feels at all uncomfortable or scary, then change the length of time until it does feel comfortable. For example, if decades doesn't feel right, then imagine years. If years doesn't feel right, imagine months. If months doesn't feel right, then imagine weeks.

Likewise, if a time frame feels too short, then lengthen it. If a year feels too short, lengthen it to five years. If five years feels too short, lengthen it to a decade. And so on, until the unit of time feels comfortable for you.

In this next exercise, you'll be writing it down.

CHAPTER 17 EXERCISE

MY ROAD LENGTH

Open your Dashboard Diary and write down today's date and the title, "My Road Length."

Underneath that title, pick one of the six units of time listed below, and then write a number to go with it – for example, "2 weeks" or "1 year" or "2 decades."

When selecting a unit of time and a number, ask yourself, "What's the farthest ahead I can comfortably see for myself and my own life?" In that amount of time, you can see yourself maintaining something that's working well for you, accomplishing something, improving something, or generally experiencing something that generates a good feeling.

Here are the six units of time to choose from:

- Days
- Weeks
- Months
- Years

- Decades
- Lifetime

As a reminder, if the length of time you selected makes you feel at all nervous or scared because of how long it is, then shorten the time until it feels right. The key is that you write down an amount of time that is the farthest ahead you can see, while still feeling comfortable.

Another way to look at it is this: aim for an answer that triggers a first-degree emotion, as described in Chapter 8 in the section "Three Degrees."

Ready? Write down the farthest ahead you can comfortably see.

As with every other chapter, your outcome for this book depends on completing this exercise.

CHAPTER 18

MY DESTINATIONS

(12 minute read)

YOUR LONG-TERM GOALS

Now that you have defined your road length, it's time to think about your collection of expectations, hopes, visions, experiences, and goals that you see for your own life during that time, and then in the next chapter, we'll look at those you share with the other person. Right now, we're focusing on you alone because knowing what's inside of you will help you know what you have to share with others.

Just as each person in a human relationship has their own dashboard to control, each person also has individual destinations to drive toward. For example, both people in a professional relationship might be driving toward a shared destination of starting a business together, but each person also has their individual destination in some other area of life such as perhaps staying fit, eating healthy, building a home, investing in stocks, or learning something new.

By first identifying destinations (long-term goals) in your relationship with yourself, you can afterward align your decisions and actions in life with other people. Feeling driven toward something in life also helps you overlook small problems that can otherwise seem out of proportion.

A destination also helps you know what dials to adjust on your dashboard to keep you headed in the direction that's healthy for you, and ultimately, healthy for the relationship.

In this chapter's exercise, I'll help you identify your personal destinations. Since destinations are what you want to drive toward in life, a good way to get clarity on those is to first identify what you *don't* want to drive toward in life. In other words, identifying what you *don't* want often helps you get clear on what you *do* want.

Through the following pages, you'll be gathering raw material for building your roadmap, and it is intended to help you better identify potential destinations.

UNSTUCKING

When you stop and look ahead at what you desire for your life and your destinations, your mind will most likely wander and think about all the things you don't want in life – don't want to be broke, don't want to be overweight, don't want a career you hate, or one of a million other "don't wants."

I find that when we neglect taking the necessary next step of converting our "don't wants" to "wants," we often find ourselves feeling stuck in repeated negative patterns in life. For example, I had a friend who said that every girlfriend he ever had ended up cheating on him. So I said, "Ok, unfaithful is what you don't want. Have you ever thought about what character traits to intentionally aim for in a girlfriend? Next time you consider making someone your girlfriend, only date someone who is faithful. Consciously look for the faithful type."

Not long after that, boom. He found her, a faithful girl who was exactly what he desired.

Converting "don't wants" to "wants" helps you identify a target and move toward powerful destinations in your life.

The key, when thinking about your destinations, is to "unstuck" yourself in two steps: first, by consciously recognizing the moment you have a "don't want" thought, and then second, using what you don't want in order to identify what it is that you do want.

"Unstucking" yourself is a two-step process. Recognize that you don't want choices A, B, or C, and then convert A, B, and C into something you do want, such as D, E, or F.

Don't want to date an impatient person? Convert that into consciously looking for a patient person to date.

Don't want the job you have? Convert that to a goal of figuring out what job you do want.

Don't want to live in a certain way? Then convert that "don't want" to a goal of how you do want to live.

Don't want to look a certain way? Then convert that "don't want" to a goal of figuring out how you do want to look.

Our "don't wants" are important because they reveal our tastes and tell us who we aren't. However, if we don't take the next step to convert them to "do wants," then our lives take no clear direction, and we end up in miserable cycles of "stuckness."

For example, when it comes to dating, I know that I don't want an unsupportive and unreciprocated intimate partnership in which I feel unsafe. If I stay stuck in a vision of what I don't want, I end up avoiding situations where I can meet someone wonderful all because I'm in a state of resistance.

So, I follow the two steps to get unstuck. First, I recognize my "don't want" and, second, I simply convert that thought to a "do want." I *do want* an intimate partnership of mutual support, reciprocation, and protection emotionally, physically, sexually, mentally, and financially.

Aha! I finally have something to look for, to aim for, to drive toward. On the road of my life, I'm no longer resisting what I don't want; rather, I'm attracting what I do want. I feel unstuck, free to move forward in life.

The conversion helps you get clarity on your destinations.

TOLERATIONS

Speaking of identifying your "don't wants"....

What have you been tolerating in your relationship with yourself? In other words, what have you been putting up with that is making you feel stuck? Those questions are "step one" of unstucking yourself.

For each of the six boundaries, I'm about to give you a series of questions about what you're tolerating in your relationship with you. These questions are purely for your reflection, not to write down answers. Read each question, then stop and think. The purpose here is to prepare you for an upcoming exercise where you will identify what you "do want." Here we go!

Treasures Boundary

What might you be tolerating about your own decisions and actions when it comes to your physical health, fitness, hygiene, nutrition, or biological needs?

When it comes to your mind and body's need for downtime, doing physically relaxing things, and chilling-out, what, if any, of your personal behaviors or habits are you tolerating?

What are you currently putting up with in regard to your management of your financial health? It might have to do with your income, savings, investments, expenses, cashflow, planning, spending habits.

Uplifting activities, celebrations, and having fun are vital for a healthy relationship with yourself. What are you allowing to block you from those experiences?

In your career, trade, or business, where do you believe you're compromising your values or accepting less than what you truly desire?

Topics Boundary

What emotion or thought habits are you allowing instead of confronting?

What worldview are you allowing yourself to adopt, even though deep down you know it goes against your better judgment? This includes your philosophical, spiritual, religious, moral, or intellectual life.

What about your view of yourself needs to change? This includes your self-worth and your ideas about who you are and who you want to be.

When it comes to your own personal learning, novelty, discovery, and exploration, what are you overlooking?

Time boundary

What about your personal time management needs to change? This can include making time for yourself and all the ways you manage your time in general.

Territories boundary

Environments include everything from sounds to visuals to culture, and they include home spaces, workplaces, personal space, or any place you visit. What environments or characteristics of environments are you putting up with that drain your energy?

Tools boundary (communication tools)

Think about all of the communication tools that you can use to encourage yourself, keep yourself accountable, and improve or prioritize your life. What tools are you using or not using that are preventing you from reaching your full potential?

Third parties boundary

Consider the human relationships that influence your relationship with yourself the most right now. They may be friendships, acquaintanceships, family relationships, romantic or sexual relationships, professional relationships, community groups, or political/national groups.

At this point in your life, which human relationships hinder the health of your relationship with yourself the most?

THE POWER OF BRAINSTORMING

"Brainstorming" is one of the most powerful activities you can do to find new and exciting options for just about anything.

This method is used by leaders, coaches, and successful people everywhere, and it's used in every context from solving personal problems to high level corporate executive meetings.

Here is the number one rule for brainstorming: a brainstorm is a 100% judgment-free zone. For a designated period of time, all ideas are treated as valid, no matter how weird or boring or wild or shocking. No answer is right or wrong; otherwise, it's just not "brainstorming" anymore.

If you set aside 10 minutes for the brainstorm, then those 10 minutes are for letting any and all ideas flow; that's the central rule of the game.

An idea might sound weird or wrong, but it often strangely or magically ends up making a valuable contribution that leads to the final answer. Its weirdness or "wrongness" can trigger new and different ideas that somehow lead to a powerful conclusion.

The exercises here in Part Four will guide you through several brainstorms. My hope is that they will get your creativity flowing and generate ideas you may not have thought about before.

So, when you see a brainstorm exercise in this chapter and upcoming chapters, remember it's your own personal 100% judgment free zone.

CHAPTER 18 EXERCISE

MY DESTINATIONS BRAINSTORM

It's time to convert the "don't wants" you thought of earlier into "do wants." It's time to get unstuck.

This is a brainstorming exercise where you create lists of ideas of what you'd like to see for yourself and your own life, and this will serve as raw material later when you name your destinations and build your roadmap.

Remember the rule of brainstorms: this is a 100% judgment-free zone, so use this exercise to freely write whatever you think of, even if it seems too good to be true or even impossible. There's something magical about including "the impossible" as it often seems to open expand our creative problem-solving abilities.

There are no wrong answers! And this exercise is not a commitment to make any changes to your life, either; it's only a brainstorm! So, be very playful and experimental with yourself when answering all of the following questions.

Part Four: Map Your Trip

And now's the time to open your Dashboard Diary, write today's date on top and the title "My Destinations Brainstorm."

Underneath the title, write: "My Top Motivator: _____" and in the blank space, write your motivator that you discovered in Chapter 6: Fuel Check. Underneath that, write "My Second Motivator: _____" and in the blank space, write down your second motivator from that same chapter.

And underneath all of that, write down the title "Road Length" and the amount of time you wrote down for "My Road Length" in Chapter 17's exercise. This way, you know what time frame to keep in mind for every question below.

Below are your six questions to answer in your Dashboard Diary, and they are each concerned only with your own life; the next chapters will cover anything that you share with the other person.

Also, every question is only concerned with the amount of time that your road length covers.

If you feel stuck on what to write down, return to the earlier section in this chapter titled "Tolerations" to generate ideas.

QUESTION #1 – TREASURES BOUNDARY

Think about how you invest your physical, financial, mental, and material energy into your own life and self-care. In other words, think about the effort you put into these six areas of your life:

- Physical health and fitness, hygiene, nutrition, and general biological needs
- Financial health – income, savings, investments, expenses, cashflow,

Chapter 18: Exercise

- planning, and spending habits
- Uplifting activities, playfulness, celebration, and having fun
- Physically relaxing things and chilling-out type of activities
- Career, trade, or business
- Learning, novelty, discovery, and exploration

Here's question #1: If you were most true to yourself and your motivators, what would you maintain (keep the same), turn down (remove or reduce), or turn up (increase, grow, achieve, or change) by the end of your road length?

Remember that each of the six boundaries are like a volume dial, and there are three kinds of decisions:

- Turn down, which means you want to reduce or remove something.
- Keep at its current volume, which means you want to maintain and support something that's working well for now.
- Turn up, which means you want to achieve, grow, complete, obtain, or revise something, and it may also include replacing a part of what you're doing already with something experimental or different.

In your Dashboard Diary, write a numbered list of answers that come to mind when you think of that question.

In your list, write as few or as many as you wish.

QUESTION #2 – TOPICS BOUNDARY

This question is about your self-care in the three areas below. If you were most true to yourself and your motivators, what would you maintain, turn down, or turn up by the end of your road length?

- Your emotion or thought habits
- Your worldview, including your philosophical, spiritual, religious, moral, or intellectual life
- Your view of yourself, including your self-worth and your ideas about who you are and who you want to be

In your Dashboard Diary, write a numbered list of all answers that come to mind when you read that question.

In your list, write as few or as many as you wish.

QUESTION #3 – TIME BOUNDARY

This question is about your personal time management, including making time for yourself and the ways you manage your time in general.

If you were most true to yourself and your motivators, what would you maintain, turn down, or turn up by the end of your road length?

In your Dashboard Diary, write a numbered list of all answers that come to mind when you read that question.

In your list, write as few or as many as you wish.

QUESTION #4 – TERRITORIES BOUNDARY

This question is about your environments and spaces, including everything from sounds to textures to visuals to culture in general. Think of your home spaces, workplaces, or any place you visit, as well as your personal physical space or what I call your "body boundaries."

If you were most true to yourself and your motivators, what would you maintain, turn down, or turn up by the end of your road length?

In your Dashboard Diary, write a numbered list of all answers that come to mind when you read that question.

In your list, write as few or as many as you wish.

QUESTION #5 – TOOLS BOUNDARY (COMMUNICATION TOOLS)

This question is about any communication tools that you use to encourage yourself, keep yourself accountable, remind yourself of your wins, remember promises to yourself, or simply organize your thoughts. This can include any tool at all – physical things like paper or something you hang on the wall, all the way to digital tools like smart phone apps or other devices.

If you were most true to yourself and your motivators, what would you maintain, turn down, or turn up by the end of your road length?

In your Dashboard Diary, write a numbered list of all answers that come to mind when you read that question.

In your list, write as few or as many as you wish.

QUESTION #6 – THIRD PARTIES BOUNDARY

This question is about the human relationships that noticeably influence your relationship with yourself right now. These may be friendships, acquaintanceships, family relationships, romantic or sexual relationships, professional relationships, local community groups, or political/national groups.

If you were most true to yourself and your motivators, what would you maintain, turn down, or turn up by the end of your road length?

In your Dashboard Diary, write a numbered list of all answers that come to mind when you read that question.

ALL SET FOR NOW

Wow! Well, if you finished the above exercise, then that is a big deal. You have now written a list of potential destinations for your life right now; that's what your numbered lists represent from this exercise.

How will you celebrate the work you just completed? At the very least, please take a moment to proudly pat yourself on the shoulder for me.

Did you do it?

Okay, good. Thank you.

You're all set for now. In an upcoming chapter, we'll come back to the answers that you listed in the brainstorm above.

Part Four: Map Your Trip

CHAPTER 19

SHARED ROAD LENGTH

(5 minute read)

HOW FAR CAN YOU SEE?

While your "road length" is the farthest ahead you can comfortably see your own life right now, your "shared road length" is the farthest you can comfortably see ahead in your relationship with the other person.

You will see different shared road lengths for different relationships at different times in your life. While I can only comfortably see six months ahead in my relationship with my client because that's the length of our contract, I can easily see decades into the future in my relationship with my dad. I can only see two minutes with the grocery clerk, and I can see at least one year ahead with my hairdresser.

A road length might be minutes, hours, days, weeks, months, years, or decades. Your road length is however far ahead you can comfortably see on the road of this relationship, and your destinations will be what you choose to drive toward within that time.

Part Four: Map Your Trip

SHORT ROADS

Imagine driving on a rural road where you can see only as far ahead as your headlights show you. The road might be much longer than you can see, and you may intend to drive on it for a very long time, but all you can see is the small bit of road that your headlights spill onto.

That's what a human relationship can be like. Sometimes several factors out of your control prevent you from seeing how far the road stretches, like nighttime driving. Other times, you can clearly see far ahead as you do on a sunny day.

A short road length does not mean that the road cannot continue past the headlights; it only means that this is the only length ahead that the headlights can illuminate. In other words, a short road length means that you are missing information or experience that would enable you to see farther.

You may have a great job, but the contract is only for one year, so you can comfortably see only 12 months ahead. You may have just found a potentially great romantic relationship, but you have known them for a few weeks, so you can only see a few weeks or months ahead. You may have a friendship with someone who lives nearby, but you know that you're moving to another city in two months and you're not sure if or when you're returning; so, you might only comfortably see the friendship for the two months ahead while you're still living in the same town.

The full length of the road will reveal itself as you drive, as the headlights hit the pavement ahead, and as the sun comes up and illuminates the journey of the relationship.

No matter how long or short, if it's a length of time that feels comfortable and you're honest about it, then it is the right road length for this moment.

SOME EXAMPLES

Remember that the key phrase for a road length is what you can "comfortably see." Requiring a sense of "comfort" when I come up with a road length means that I will come up with a period of time that is honest to myself and practical.

For example, when it comes to dating apps, I typically keep a first "date" to one hour, because if I'm honest with myself, this is what makes me feel safe. It's also practical, since it keeps expectations and pressure low. So, before I meet a dating app "match" in person for the first time, I only see a road length of 60 minutes.

Those 60 minutes are all I can honestly and comfortably see sharing with him until I sit down and get to know him better. Sometimes I sit down and know right away that 60 minutes is going to be the end of our shared road length.

On rare occasions, I sit down for a first date and can comfortably see a road length of weeks or months of getting to know the guy better. Whether the guy thinks the same is a topic of discussion to have with him, but each of us must first develop our own vision in order to discover if we both see the same road ahead or not.

Job interviews can be much like meeting someone from a dating app because you never know the personalities you're going to meet once you're face to face. I remember one woman interviewing with me via video chat, and her manner of speaking and body gestures were as if someone had injected horse tranquilizer into her bloodstream moments before our call. She acted as if she couldn't care less that we were having a professional conversation about a potential business relationship.

As soon as I experienced her sloth-like mannerism, I saw a maximum road length of ten minutes. I raced to end the conversation as professionally as I could and respectfully turned off that shared road as quickly as possible.

Whatever time frame feels peaceful for you – that's the shared road length for you right now, and it's honest.

ROAD LENGTHS MAKE DECISIONS EASIER

Road lengths existed in your mind before you had a name for them. They have helped you make decisions. For example, when you could only comfortably see yourself maintaining a relationship with another person for another few days, you didn't and likely wouldn't commit to anything that locked you into a five-year contract with them.

In any human relationship, a road length makes your decision-making and action-taking much easier.

When you can identify a comfortable time frame that you easily see yourself maintaining your part of the relationship, then it becomes clear whether or not to commit to anything like buying tickets for the both of you to an event that's many months away, signing any kind of contract that impacts or involves the other person, signing up for memberships together, financial commitments or major purchases for them or with them, or making any kind of long-term promises.

Of course, it's good to know the road length that the other person has in mind as well, but you must first know yours in order to discover if the two agree. Road lengths would be a conversation topic to consider sharing, once you have completed your work on your Boundaries Dashboard.

So, what's your road length in your relationship with the other person? You'll find out in the next exercise.

CHAPTER 19 EXERCISE

SHARED ROAD LENGTH

Open your Dashboard Diary, write down today's date and the title, "My Shared Road Length."

Underneath that title, pick one of the six units of time listed below, and write a number to go with it – for example, "2 weeks", "6 months," or "3 decades."

What's the farthest ahead you can comfortably see yourself maintaining your part of this relationship with the other person? In that period of time, you might see yourself continuing to share something that's working well for you, accomplishing something, improving something, or generally experiencing something with the other person.

Units of Time:

- Days
- Weeks
- Months
- Years
- Decades
- Lifetime

Part Four: Map Your Trip

As a reminder, if the length of time you selected makes you feel at all nervous because of how long it is, then shorten the time until it feels right. They key is that you write down a length of time that feels comfortable.

Another way to look at it is to aim for an answer that triggers a first-degree emotion (as described in Chapter 8 in the section "Three Degrees").

Ready? Write down how far ahead you can comfortably see.

As with every other chapter, your outcome for this book depends on completing this exercise.

CHAPTER 20

SHARED DESTINATIONS

(16 minute read)

WHERE'S THIS HEADED?

If you get into the car and start driving without any idea of where you're going, then I think it's fair is it to say you're "headed nowhere in particular."

It's the same with any human relationship.

If you have nothing to aim for in a human relationship, then it would also be fair to say that "the relationship is headed nowhere."

Right now, your relationship with the other person is either: (a) headed somewhere in your mind, which means you have something or some things you'd like to share with them; or (b) not headed anywhere in your mind, but you'd like to figure it out because you're not sure what you'd like to share with them; or (c) fading out of existence.

If you feel a clear direction with the other person, well done! The exercises in these chapters will help you map the best routes.

If you feel like you're more aligned with option "b" above, then here's the good news: right now, you're in a discovery phase. In a discovery phase, you don't know where the relationship is headed, but your aim is to explore what you need or want in that relationship.

Discovery itself is a purpose and direction. When you don't know where you're headed, it's OK to be in this stage of research and development.

Sometimes we jump in the car with no particular destination, but rather we aim to explore potential destinations. So, you hop in the car and go for a drive. You become a combination of a researcher and a tourist, investigating what grabs your attention and what might become a destination for the future.

That's discovery.

Even when you're on the search for something to aim for, that's still an aim.

If you're not moving towards a destination or intentionally on the hunt for one, then you may soon find a "dead end" sign on the road of this relationship or end up crashed in the gutter, stuck in an emotional ditch.

Maybe you have heard the ancient saying, "Where there is no vision, the people perish." It's the same in this relationship. Without an aim, it will die. The opposite, then, is also true: a relationship with a destination will live.

"So, where's this headed?"

It's a question on the minds of CEOs every day. The destination of the company hangs on decisions made daily. Is the company on a path to meet its profit goals for the year?

It's a question in the back of minds of anyone who wonders if their friends will continually be "too busy" for them. Where is this friendship headed?

It's in the back of minds of family members who lose touch with another family member and wonder if everyone's happier this way. Where is this headed?

It's in the forefront of the mind of the employee who hears about budget cuts about to happen at the company they work for. Where is this headed?

Now think about your relationship. Where is it headed for you?

It's perfectly OK to have only one or even just a few very simple and "normal" sounding destinations. Maybe the destination is sharing meals in the evening. Maybe it's going with the other person to the doctor's office for an annual checkup. Maybe it's sharing a joke more often.

Maybe the destination is more complex.

A wife may see raising children, buying a home, and retiring at old age with her husband as major destinations in her mind.

A businessman may see making a $250K net profit in a year and then selling the business to their business partner as a destination.

A person who just had a great time on a first date may see themself going on a second date. Someone else might sit down on a first date and see years ahead – a house and kids with the other person.

Looking at the road ahead in this relationship means looking into the future toward your collection of expectations, experiences you'd like to have, hopes, and goals for this relationship. Your collection of all those things that you intentionally aim to share with the other person are your "shared destinations."

Part Four: Map Your Trip

When your own personal collection of expectations, experiences you'd like to have, hopes, and goals do not directly involve the other person, they are simply your own destinations.

I once heard someone say that "clarity is kindness." In other words, not being clear about what you really want in a human relationship is unkind. Refusing to identify your needs and wishes in a relationship leaves the other person confused and unable to support you or know how to make the relationship work.

So, you might say that identifying your destinations and your shared destinations is kindness.

SHARED DESTINATIONS

Is there anyone *not* guilty of this?

In the privacy of our own minds, we assume the other person shares the same collection of expectations, experiences we'd like to have, hopes, and goals for the relationship when, in fact, they have not expressly said that they share them; and even if they have stated that they shared them, we don't check to see if they have the same pictures in mind that we do.

A client might assume that you're available on weekends, but you're not. You might assume a client shares an understanding with you of all the terms and conditions of the agreement you both signed, when they actually don't.

A manager might assume you want to spend your lunch break eating with the team, when, in reality, a team lunch only feels like more work and your brain desperately needs a mental break to recharge. You might assume your manager knows all the work you've been slaving away at, when in fact they've been too busy to notice.

A family member might assume they can call you at all hours of the night or day to just shoot the breeze, when in fact it upsets your work, much-needed sleep, and other commitments. You might assume a family member knows how you feel, when they don't.

In a marriage, a spouse might expect intimacy to happen every other day continuously, while their partner expects it to be frequent the first six months and then taper off after childbearing.

We also assume that someone consents to something because they have consented in the past. However, that's an assumption that people's wants or needs never change.

The way we make assumptions reminds me of something I saw in my first year of university that stuck with me ever since. I can still see it vividly in my mind. It was simply a sign that hung on one of the doors of the math department that said, "One false assumption, and logic does the rest."

In other words, an entire history of a relationship can be based on just one false assumption.

And eventually that unstable foundation breaks the relationship.

And that's why we start human relationships off on a firmer foundation by identifying our destinations from the beginning.

Are you ready to identify yours?

In this chapter's exercise, you'll identify your destinations that you wish to share in this relationship, aka your "shared destinations."

Each person in a relationship has their own destinations that they wish to share with the other person. Assuming that you already know the other person's destinations is like an unintentional hijacking of the other person's car; you're grabbing their wheel and steering in a direction they never consented to.

So, when you think of your shared destinations – your collection of expectations, experiences you'd like to have, hopes, and goals for the relationship – keep in mind that these do not also appear on the other person's roadmap unless they consent to and understand what they are consenting to.

And consent requires a conversation. But before you can bring up the topic of what you see yourself sharing with the other person, you must first identify and name those shared things. And that's what you'll be able to do in this chapter's exercise.

SAME STOPS, DIFFERENT EXPERIENCES

A "relationship road" is a metaphor that represents the experiences you share with the other person. On this road, you are the driver of your car, and the other person is the driver of theirs.

You are both sharing experiences, whether it's doing business together or getting life organized or just having fun. One or both of you propose ideas for goals to reach together – long-term or short-term – and/or things to maintain together, and these are your shared destinations.

Sometimes destinations change, but having them keeps us moving on the road and learning what we need and want from our lives. Detours and rerouting happen on any kind of journey, but that doesn't stop you from traveling.

Chapter 20: Shared Destinations

In this relationship, a shared destination is a personally significant place in life or business that you travel to with the other person. It gives you something to accomplish or experience with and/or for the other person.

The other person has destinations of their own to share with you. Sometimes your destinations have the same name, but you each experience them through your own nervous systems, and you each contribute something a little different to get there.

You might both have a destination to buy a house together, for example, but each of you contributes differently to the process and offers unique personality strengths that make the purchase happen. One person may use their natural flair for numbers to calculate investment potential, while the other person uses their strong social skills to find a winning real estate agent.

Once the home is bought, one of you shouts with the excitement that you've been visualizing you'd feel, and the other person falls onto the couch with a deep sense of relief and relaxation that the purchasing process is over.

A shared destination on your relationship roadmap is shared, but you own yours and the other person owns their shared destination. For example, you own your body, but you share it with an intimate partner. You are responsible for your destinations in the same way that you are responsible for your own body, whether you share it or not. You take your own body to the doctor when it's sick; you don't take anyone else's body on behalf of yours. Likewise, your shared destinations in this relationship are ultimately yours to identify, care for, and nurture.

Your heart physically beats inside of your body, not inside of theirs. So, you must look after it first and foremost. Now it's time to look deeper inside of you to brainstorm your destinations in this relationship.

EXAMPLES OF SHARED DESTINATIONS

To get ready for this chapter's exercise, here are several general examples of shared destinations that cover several types of human relationships – from a relationship to a group of people to a relationship to another individual, and from relationships with strangers, to intimate partners, to business partners, to family.

Many of these might seem like small goals, but the size or complexity of a destination will vary based on each person's unique emotional, physical, financial, and psychological resources. The time frame to reach these destinations would also vary based on each person's unique "road length."

Note how none of these destinations force the other person or group, but rather they propose or invite the other to respond, share, or participate.

Relationship: my partner and I

Destination #1 – Initiate physical intimacy at least two times a week.

Destination #2 – Research and investigate to help us determine our next joint-investment project.

Destination #3 – Propose that we cut down on watching the news because of the negative mood it brings into the house and find something uplifting and agreeable to replace it with.

Destination #4 – Propose and agree on a regular schedule of discussing the topic of shared destinations to ensure we're on the same path.

Chapter 20: Shared Destinations

Relationship: my sibling

Destination #1 – Maintain a clean guest room free of clutter for their quarterly visits.

Destination #2 – Respectfully back out of any conversation that feels like gossip and find healthier alternatives.

Destination #3 – Propose an annual holiday away during winter at the ski lodge where the family can all stay together.

Destination #4 – Bring up the conversation topic of boundaries and what we each think is healthy for us.

Relationship: my best friend

Destination #1 – Do whatever it takes to keep our weekly meetup on my calendar, the one where we share our latest dating stories.

Destination #2 – Buy tickets for our favorite comedian's show.

Destination #3 – For her birthday, surprise her with a gourmet cooking class together.

Destination #4 – Cut down the number of times I agree to go out to eat with her, so I can save money.

Relationship: me and a local community organization

Destination #1 – Maintain my level of membership by attending all of the decision-making meetings this quarter.

Destination #2 – Remove myself from the weeknight volunteer schedule.

Part Four: Map Your Trip

Destination #3 – Round up a group to start a new chapter of the organization that is only for singles.

R̲e̲l̲a̲t̲i̲o̲n̲s̲h̲i̲p̲: ̲ m̲e̲ ̲a̲n̲d̲ ̲t̲h̲e̲ ̲c̲o̲u̲n̲t̲r̲y̲ ̲w̲h̲e̲r̲e̲ ̲I ̲a̲m̲ ̲a̲ ̲c̲i̲t̲i̲z̲e̲n̲

Destination #1 – Start and complete the passport renewal process.

Destination #2 – Figure out a better way to understand each candidate so I can make better voting decisions in the November election.

Destination #3 – Don't say not-so-nice things about my country unless they clearly come from a compassionate and constructive intention.

Destination #4 – Pursue a role in government in order to speak up for those without a voice.

R̲e̲l̲a̲t̲i̲o̲n̲s̲h̲i̲p̲: ̲ M̲e̲ ̲a̲n̲d̲ ̲a̲l̲l̲ ̲o̲f̲ ̲t̲h̲e̲ ̲p̲e̲o̲p̲l̲e̲
w̲h̲o̲ ̲v̲i̲e̲w̲ ̲m̲y̲ ̲p̲r̲o̲f̲i̲l̲e̲ ̲o̲n̲ ̲d̲a̲t̲i̲n̲g̲ ̲a̲p̲p̲s̲

Destination #1 – Continue to restrict my dating app usage to the two-hour window after work.

Destination #2 – Create and refine a safer process of how to select who I meet up with in person.

Destination #3 – Create a list of lessons I've learned from emotionally impactful interactions on the app.

Destination #4 – Stop responding to messages when poor effort is put into their messages, profile photos, and/or profile description.

342 | The Boundaries Health Check™

CHAPTER 20 EXERCISE

SHARED DESTINATIONS BRAINSTORM

Similar to Chapter 18's "My Destinations Brainstorm" exercise, your ideas in this exercise will serve as raw material later when you build your roadmap.

This is a brainstorm exercise where you think about the period of time that you named as your "shared road length" in the last chapter and imagine everything that you'd like to see yourself doing (or not doing) in this relationship, or what you'd like to share (or not share), within that time.

Remember, the rule of brainstorming is that it is a 100% judgment-free zone; so, feel free and creative with whatever you write. Include the impossible, if it's something you truly need or desire. There are no wrong answers!

This brainstorming exercise is not a commitment to make any changes to your life, either; it's only a brainstorm in order to assist you later when creating your relationship roadmap. So, be honest, playful, and experimental with yourself when answering all the following questions.

Part Four: Map Your Trip

And now's the time to open your Dashboard Diary and write today's date on top along with the title "Shared Destinations Brainstorm."

Underneath the title, write: "My Top Motivator: _____ " and in the blank space, write your motivator that you discovered in Chapter 6: Fuel Check. Underneath that, write "My Second Motivator: _____ " and in the blank space, write down your second motivator from that same chapter.

And underneath all of that, write down the title "Shared Road Length" and the amount of time you wrote down for your "Shared Road Length" in Chapter 19's exercise. This way, you know what time frame to keep in mind for every question below.

Here are the six questions to brainstorm in your Dashboard Diary.

QUESTION #1 – TREASURES BOUNDARY

Here's the first question to answer in your Dashboard Diary: If you were most true to yourself and your motivators, what would you maintain, turn down, or turn up by the end of your shared road length?

Consider all kinds of treasures:

- Things you do for or with the other person in the area of physical or medical health, physical fitness, hygiene, nutrition, and safety
- Things you do for or with the other person in the area of financial health – income, savings, investments, expenses, cashflow, planning, and spending habits
- Things you do for or with the other person for the sake of uplifting activities, playfulness, celebrations (big or small), and having fun / creating a space where fun might happen
- Things you do for or with the other person for the sake of physically

Chapter 20: Exercise

relaxing and chilling-out type of activities
- Things you do for or with the other person for the sake of career, trade, or business
- Things you do for or with the other person for the sake of learning, novelty, discovery, and exploration

Remember that each of the six boundaries is like a volume dial, and there are only three kinds of decisions:

- Turn down, which means you want to reduce or remove something.
- Keep at its current volume, which means you want to maintain and support something that's working well for now.
- Turn up, which means you want to achieve, grow, complete, or revise something, and it may also include replacing a part of what you're doing already with something experimental or different.

Read the above question again, and in your Dashboard Diary, write a numbered list of all answers that come to mind when you read it. In your list, write as few or as many as you wish.

If it helps, set a timer on your phone or other alarm device to give yourself space to think about this, i.e. maybe set it for anywhere from 2 to 5 minutes.

QUESTION #2 – TOPICS BOUNDARY

When it comes to this relationship, think about how you share (or don't share) conversation topics. Three general categories of conversation topics are below, and there are potentially many more subtopics.

Question #2 is this: If you were most true to yourself and your motivators, what topics would you maintain, turn down, or turn up by the end

Part Four: Map Your Trip

of your shared road length?

- Emotions, thoughts, or thought habits (yours, theirs, and/or someone else's)
- Worldview, including your religious, intellectual, moral, or philosophical life (yours, theirs, and/or someone else's)
- Your view of yourself, including your self-worth and your ideas about who you are and who you want to be

In your Dashboard Diary, write a numbered list of all answers that come to mind when you read that question.

In your list, write as few or as many as you wish.

If it helps, set a timer on your phone or other alarm to give yourself space to think about this, i.e., maybe set it for anywhere from 2 to 5 minutes.

QUESTION #3 – TIME BOUNDARY

Think about how you choose to spend your time in this relationship, how much quality time you devote, the frequency that you spend that time, and how you schedule or manage your time in this relationship.

If you were most true to yourself and your motivators, what Time boundaries would you maintain, turn down, or turn up by the end of your shared road length?

In your Dashboard Diary, write a numbered list of all answers that come to mind when you read that question.

In your list, write as few or as many as you wish.

If it helps, set a timer on your phone or other alarm device to give yourself space to think about this, i.e., maybe set it for anywhere from 2 to 5 minutes.

QUESTION #4 – TERRITORIES BOUNDARY

Think about the environments and spaces you share in this relationship, including all five senses – sounds, sites, textures, smells, and tastes. Consider home spaces and workplaces, the overall culture, and environment of any place you visit together.

This boundary also includes your personal physical space or what I called earlier in this book your "body boundaries."

If you were most true to yourself and your motivators, what Territory boundaries would you maintain, turn down, or turn up by the end of your shared road length?

In your Dashboard Diary, write a numbered list of all answers that come to mind when you read that question.

In your list, write as few or as many as you wish.

If it helps, set a timer on your phone or other alarm device to give yourself space to think about this, i.e., maybe set it for anywhere from 2 to 5 minutes.

Part Four: Map Your Trip

QUESTION #5 – TOOLS BOUNDARY (COMMUNICATION TOOLS)

Think about all the communication tools that you can use with or for the other person – physical or digital. Also remember that this includes sending, receiving, and access tools as described in Chapter 12.

If you were most true to yourself and your motivators, what tools would you maintain, turn down, or turn up by the end of your shared road length?

In your Dashboard Diary, write a numbered list of answers that come to mind when you read that question.

In your list, write as few or as many as you wish.

If it helps, set a timer on your phone or other alarm device to give yourself space to think about this, i.e., maybe set it for anywhere from 2 to 5 minutes.

QUESTION #6 – THIRD PARTIES BOUNDARY

Think of any human relationships that are noticeably impacting your relationship with the other person at this time. They may be friendships, acquaintanceships, biological or adopted family relationships, intimate relationships, professional or business relationships, local community groups, neighbors, organizations, or political/national groups.

If you were most true to yourself and your motivators, what third party boundaries would you maintain, turn down, or turn up by the end of your shared road length?

Chapter 20: Exercise

In your Dashboard Diary, write a numbered list of answers that come to mind when you read that question.

If it helps, set a timer on your phone or other alarm device to give yourself space to think about this, i.e., maybe set it for anywhere from 2 to 5 minutes.

ALL SET FOR NOW

Wow. That "wow" isn't just a nice filler word; it's a genuine emotion of mine as I think about you getting this far into the work of *The Boundaries Health Check*. You have now written a list of potential shared destinations for yourself in this relationship; that's what your numbered lists represent from this exercise, and coming up very soon in this book, these will help you to start building your relationship roadmap.

As I write these words, I feel a deep satisfaction from the fact that you have travelled this far with me as the author.

So, how will you celebrate the work you just completed? At the very least, please take a moment to proudly pat yourself on the shoulder for me.

Did you do it?

Oh, good. Thank you.

CHAPTER 21

MY RELATIONSHIP ROADMAP (EXERCISE)

(14 minute read)

ARE YOU A PAWN ON A CHESSBOARD?

In a song titled "Erase This" by Evanescence, there's a powerful verse that says:

> I can't wash these sins away
> This sinking feeling everyday
> I'm waking up in someone else's life.

Whenever I hear that line, "I'm waking up in someone else's life," I relive the hollow memories deep in my chest about a time when I lacked strength to voice my own genuine desires for my life. And I realize how far I've come since those dark days.

Before I found the courage to feel and identify my own pure desires for all areas of my life – such as my career, my money, and my relationships

– I felt like a chess piece being moved around in the game of everyone else's life. I remember waking up in the middle of the night next to the man who was my partner at that time, looking around the bedroom in the dark, and asking myself, "Who is this? Where am I?"

I felt light years away from my own soul and my sense of self. My situation in life at that time was far more a product of what I thought others wanted for me rather than what I genuinely desired for me. I felt that my feelings didn't matter as much as everyone else's.

I woke up each morning with far more of a sense of "what's going to happen to me today?" rather than "what will I make happen today?"

There were a few reasons I was able to break through that mindset, but personal coaching was one of the key reasons I was able to get back in touch with "me." Regular conversations with a skilled and qualified personal coach helped me identify and then vocalize my needs and desires in a safe space and kept me accountable to take action.

To this day, I continue to work with a personal coach to keep myself aware of my needs and desires and take action.

The exercises throughout this book and this chapter use personal coaching techniques, and my hope is that they help you in any part of your life where you feel like you're in the dark and you're asking yourself, "Who is this? Where am I?"

Identifying your genuine needs and desires, and then mapping the direction for your life, gives your life back to you, puts "you" back into your own skin. It gives you control of your own chess board rather than being the pawn pushed along by someone else's finger.

In this exercise, you're becoming a mapmaker of your life by plotting your destinations where you'd like your life to head over a certain period of time. You're now becoming a player in the challenging and rewarding game of life, no longer the pawn in someone else's.

YOUR BUILDING BLOCKS

Welcome to the last Chapter of Part Four, "Map Your Trip." This is where you plot out destinations on your relationship roadmap. If you completed all the previous exercises, then you have the four solid building blocks to create your map.

Your four building blocks are in your Dashboard Diary; they are your personal road length, your shared road length, plus your two brainstorm lists – your destinations and your shared destinations.

Creating this map signifies you being true to yourself and sincere about the direction you'd like to go in this relationship.

This chapter walks you step by step through the mapmaking process, and it fully relies on what you have written down in your Dashboard Diary for previous exercises, so have your Diary on hand.

Before we start mapmaking, I'll give you a general vision of what a relationship roadmap might look like.

WHAT YOUR MAP MIGHT LOOK LIKE

You can have a strong desire to do something in life, but that thing is not very healthy for you. You can also have something you know you "should do" in your life that's wonderfully healthy for you, but you don't have tons of desire to do it.

Part Four: Map Your Trip

The relationship roadmap plots your destinations according to the two independent factors of "desire" and "health."

Just as a map has four directions (North, South, East, and West), your relationship roadmap is also broken into quadrants. The four quadrants are separated by two intersecting arrows. The greater the "desire" and "health" of a destination, the farther to the "North" and "East" it will appear on your roadmap.

On a compass (aka the intersecting arrows) that you would see on a typical roadmap, the East-West arrow is called the "horizon," and the north-south arrow is called the "meridian." However, on the relationship roadmap, the east-west arrow represents amount of "desire," and the north-south arrow is amount of "health."

Your compass on the relationship roadmap has the same four letters that a normal compass would have – N, S, E, and W, but those four letters mean something different on the relationship roadmap.

The "N" means "Nutrient-rich" or "Nourishing," as in, "This is nourishing for my life." And the "S" means "Satisfactory" or "Sufficient," as in, "This is sufficiently healthy for me."

All of your destinations are healthy to some degree because they follow from the exercises in previous chapters, but some of your destinations are going to be (metaphorically) more nutrient-dense than others. In other words, some destinations might have more life-giving qualities than the others.

The "E" on the compass means "Eager," as in, "I am eager to do this," and the "W" means "Willing," as in, "I am willing to do this." Eagerness refers to a strong enthusiasm, anticipation, or keenness to do or experience something. Eagerness is proactive and full of energy towards a particular task, event, or opportunity.

Willingness, on the other hand, indicates a readiness or openness to do something, but it's not the same high level of enthusiasm as feeling "eager." Willingness is a calm and intentional kind of desire.

While both "willing" and "eager" express a level of desire to do something, "eager" carries a stronger sense of excitement, energy, motivation, and anticipation.

To help you understand how "willing" and "eager" changes in each quadrant, I've sketched the compass below and added marks along each arrow – 1 through 10 represents a growing intensity.

The relationship roadmap that you draw in an upcoming exercise will not need to contain these numbers (unless it helps you to add them).

When you plot a destination on your roadmap, you can imagine the increasing intensity that you see below – the higher the number, the greater your sense of desire and health for that destination.

Part Four: Map Your Trip

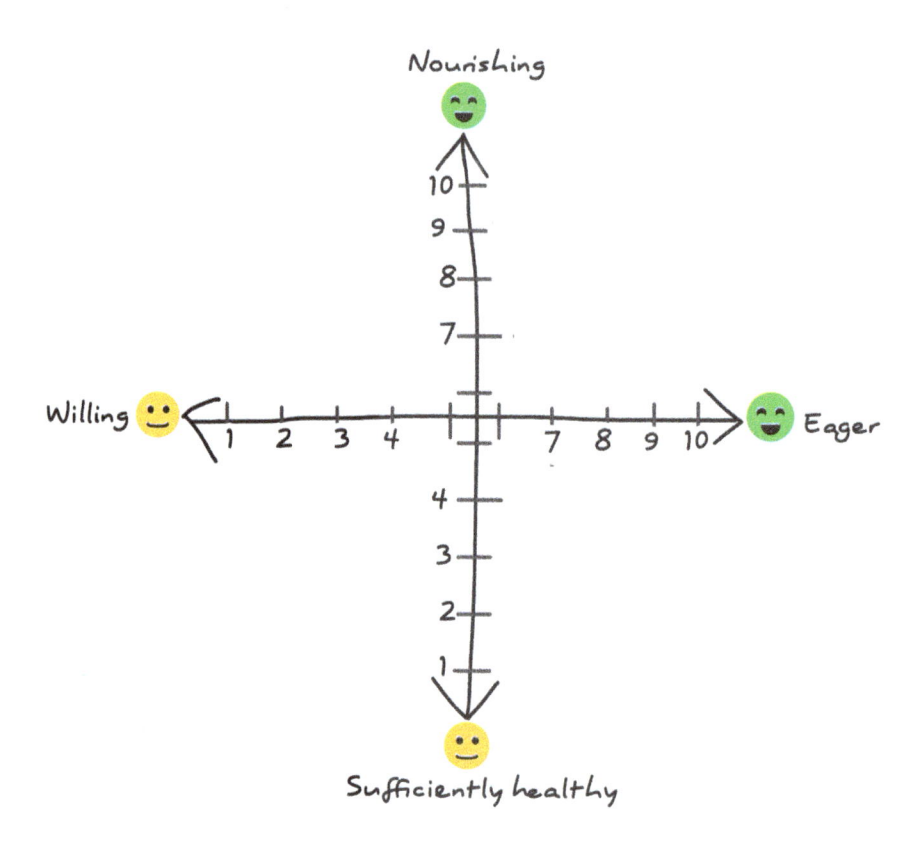

Nourishing 🙂

10, 9, 8, 7

Willing 🙂 ← 1 2 3 4 | 7 8 9 10 → 🙂 *Eager*

4, 3, 2, 1

Sufficiently healthy 🙂

Every destination on your map is something you have some degree of desire to do, and which provides some degree of health to you. However, some destinations will provide a sense of greater health than others, and some you will desire more than others.

You can see in the drawing how the levels of desire and health increase from left to right and from bottom to top, with the highest intensity of desire and health being at the top right ("Northeast") corner and a general sense of desire and health being at the bottom left ("Southwest") corner.

So, now you know what the North-South (health) and East-West (desire) compass arrows represent.

Chapter 21: My Relationship Roadmap (Exercise)

Below is an example of how it can look when you map your destinations on a relationship roadmap.

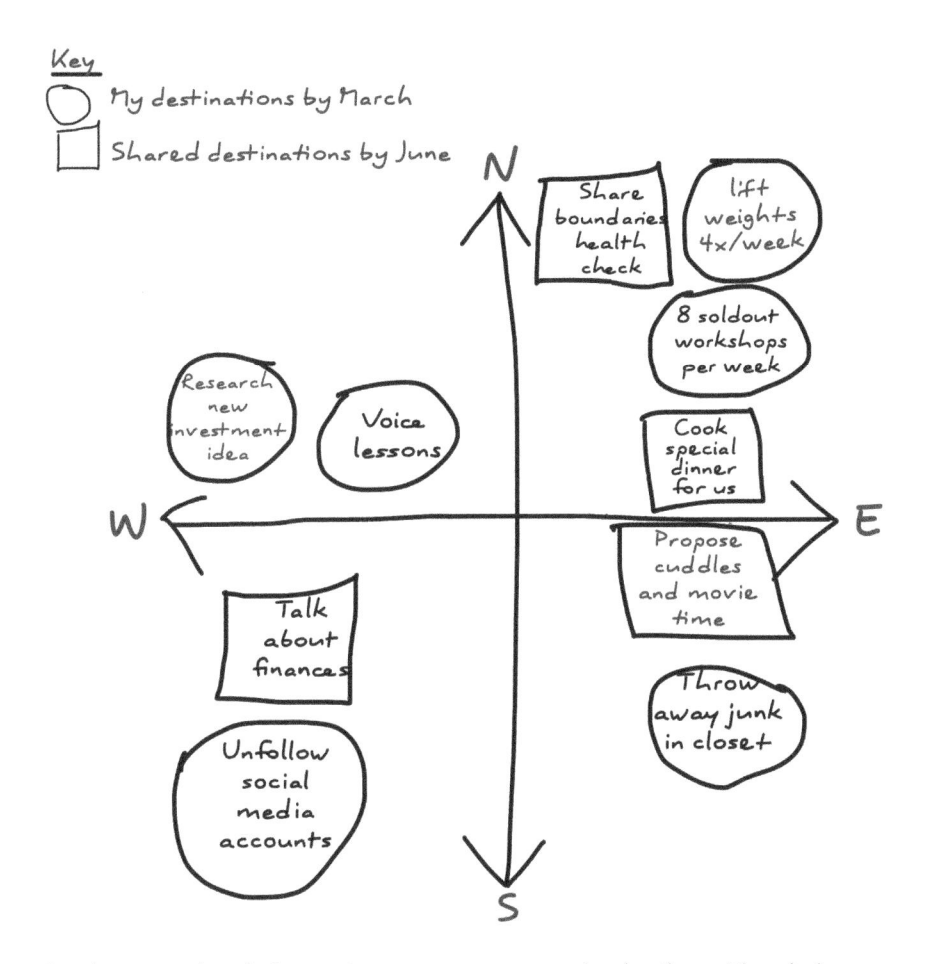

Key
○ My destinations by March
☐ Shared destinations by June

```
                              N
                    ┌──────────┐  ┌──────┐
                    │ Share    │  │ lift │
                    │boundaries│  │weights│
                    │ health   │  │4x/week│
                    │ check    │  └──────┘
                    └──────────┘
                              ╱‾‾‾‾‾‾╲
                             │8 soldout│
                             │workshops│
                             │per week │
    ╱‾‾‾‾‾‾╲                  ╲_____╱
   │Research│   ╱‾‾‾‾╲       ┌──────┐
   │  new   │  │Voice │      │ Cook │
   │investmt│  │lessons│     │special│
   │  idea  │   ╲____╱       │dinner│
    ╲_____╱                  │for us│
                              └──────┘
W ←─────────────────────────────────────→ E
                              ┌──────┐
                              │Propose│
                              │cuddles│
                              │and movie│
                  ┌──────┐    │ time │
                  │ Talk │    └──────┘
                  │about │
                  │finances│   ╱‾‾‾‾╲
                  └──────┘    │Throw │
                              │away junk│
       ╱‾‾‾‾‾‾╲               │in closet│
      │Unfollow│               ╲_____╱
      │ social │
      │ media  │
      │accounts│
       ╲_____╱
                              ↓
                              S
```

On the map, the circles and squares represent destinations. The circles are your destinations, and the squares are your shared destinations. Where you plot your destinations along the two arrows represents your degree of desire to achieve the goal, and the relative healthiness of the goal.

All circles happen within the amount of time you wrote down for your road length, and all squares happen within the amount of time you wrote down for your shared road length.

Part Four: Map Your Trip

Your relationship roadmap may have far more or far fewer destinations than this example. Your destinations may be more complex or simpler. You may have one circle and many squares, or you may have one square and many circles. So, understand that this example is only to illustrate how it might look.

As an alternative design, instead of putting each destination into a square or circle, you might instead choose to write a list of destinations in each of the four quadrants with your circles and squares next to each destination. The symbols indicate which are shared and which are your own, like the following example.

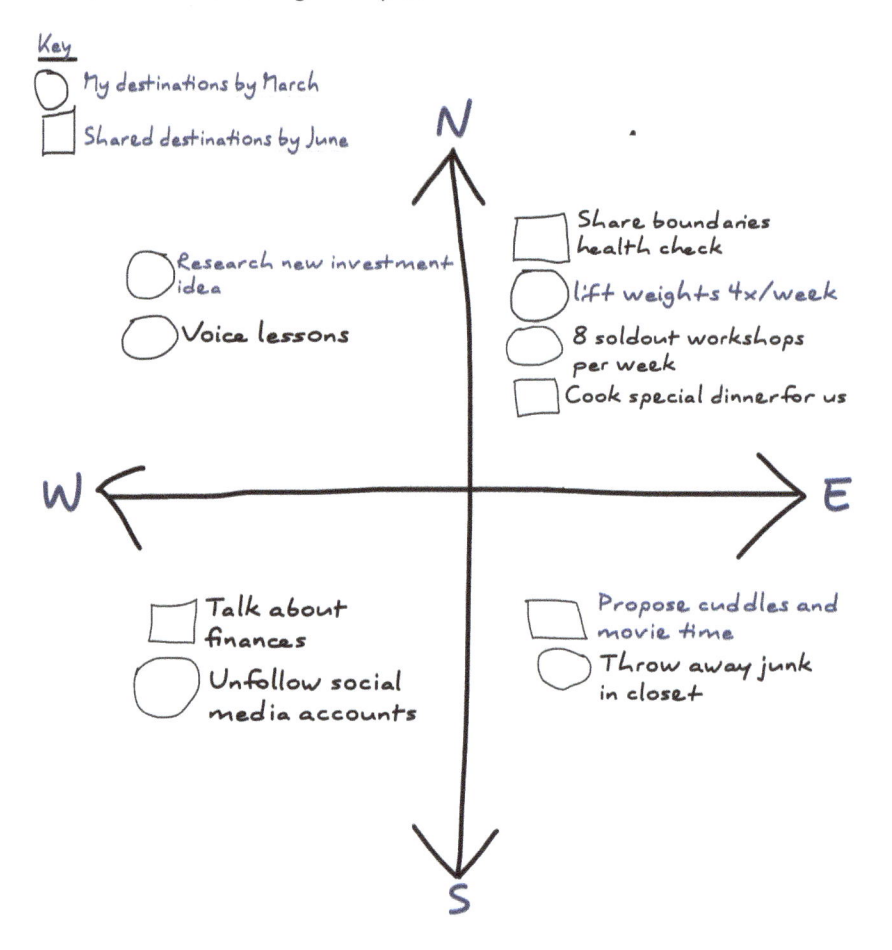

Key
○ My destinations by March
▢ Shared destinations by June

NW quadrant:
○ Research new investment idea
○ Voice lessons

NE quadrant:
▢ Share boundaries health check
○ Lift weights 4x/week
○ 8 soldout workshops per week
▢ Cook special dinner for us

SW quadrant:
▢ Talk about finances
○ Unfollow social media accounts

SE quadrant:
▢ Propose cuddles and movie time
○ Throw away junk in closet

So, those were examples and illustrations to help you get an idea of what we're about to do together. Are you ready? Got your Dashboard Diary in hand?

I will now walk you through each of the three steps.

MAPPING, STEP 1: CREATE YOUR KEY

A "key" on a map is a small section on the page, off to the corner or the side, that explains the meanings of the symbols used on the map. The key on your relationship roadmap will have two symbols.

The two symbols on your map are a square and a circle, and each symbol has two meanings: the circle represents both your personal destinations and your road length, and the square represents both your shared destinations and shared road length.

As you can see in the two relationship roadmap examples in this chapter, the key is on the top left. You can see a circle with a date next to it, and a square with a date next to it. On your relationship roadmap, the dates will be based on the road length exercises you did in the "My Road Length" and "Shared Road Length" exercises in Chapters 17 and 19.

Here are instructions on how to do that. Step 1, here we go!

Open to a blank page in your Dashboard Diary.

Side note: You're about to draw a circle and a square. However, if you're using a digital notebook as a diary and don't know how to insert a square or a circle, one solution is to use a capital letter "O" for the circle and use two brackets with two spaces in between "[ ]" to represent a square.

Part Four: Map Your Trip

Now, let's get started for real. Your first step is to write the word "Key" in small letters on the top left of the page, just like you saw in the earlier examples.

Under the title "Key," draw a small circle. Next to the circle, write down a date... but what date? Look at the amount of time you wrote down for "My Road Length" in Chapter 17's exercise and then add that amount of time to today's date.

For example, let's pretend your road length from Chapter 17 is "one month." If today's date is January 1st, then you would add 30 days (one month) to today's date. Then, in the Key next to the circle, you would write "by January 31st." Easy!

Underneath the circle, draw a little square. Next to the square, write down a date... but what date? Look at the amount of time you wrote down for your "Shared Road Length" in Chapter 19's exercise and then add that amount of time to today's date.

For example, let's pretend your shared road length from Chapter 19 is "six months." If today's date is January 1st, then you would add six months to today's date. Then, in the Key next to the circle, you would write "by June 30th."

So, did you do it? If not, then now's your moment. Continue reading after you have finished your Key.

The dates next to your circle and square are like expiration dates, so you know when your vision may need refreshing. I don't know about you, but I just felt things get real! Putting down a date somehow makes a vision burn more clearly and brightly.

Just as geographical maps change over the course of human history to reflect changing boundaries and place names, your map is made to be useful during a particular period of time. Now you have a time period for your map.

MAPPING, STEP 2: DRAW YOUR COMPASS

Sidenote: We're about to draw a compass. However, if you're using a digital Dashboard Diary and find it hard to draw a compass, then you can simply insert a table with four sections or four quadrants. If you do that, then name the top left quadrant "Desire, Very Healthy," the top right "Great Desire, Very Healthy," the bottom left "Desire, Healthy," and the bottom right "Great Desire, Healthy."

If you're using a good old physical diary, draw a double-headed arrow left to right across the middle of the page, dividing the page into two sections. Just like in the example I gave you earlier, write a "W" on the end of the left side of the arrow, and write the letter "E" on the end of the right side. These stand for Willingness vs. Eagerness.

Draw a double-headed arrow top to bottom, down the center of the page. This creates four sections. Write the letter "N" on the top of the arrow and an "S" on the bottom. These stand for Nutrient-rich vs. Sufficient (or Satisfactory) for your health.

Now you have four equal-sized sections or quadrants, and your destinations and your shared destinations will go into them in Step 3.

MAPPING, STEP 3: PLOT YOUR PLACEMARKS

When mapmakers create roadmaps, the cities, towns, and other important places that they plot onto the map are called "placemarks." On your relationship roadmap, your placemarks are your destinations.

You're the mapmaker, and so you'll decide what destinations belong on your relationship roadmap. Your placemarks will include a mix of both

Part Four: Map Your Trip

your destinations and your shared destinations that you listed in your previous brainstorming exercises from Chapters 18 and 20.

When I look at a map of my local city, not everything in the city appears on it. The beautiful statue at the top of the main street is not there. The gorgeous artwork on the side of the building isn't on there. The new store that just popped up on the corner hasn't made on there yet. Sometimes cool parts of a city don't even make it onto the map, but they exist. They just don't get a placemark.

Only placemarks that fit the purpose of the map and fall within its relevant time frame will get a place on the map, and it's the same for your relationship roadmap. Only destinations that make your dashboard lights glow green and only destinations that fit your road lengths get a place on this map.

In the exercises "My Destination Brainstorm" from Chapter 18 and "Shared Destination Brainstorm" from Chapter 20, you listed destinations under each of the six boundaries. For Step 3, it's time to pick and plot your top destinations onto your relationship roadmap.

First, let's look at how to start plotting your own destinations (not the shared ones).

In Chapter 18's exercise "My Destination brainstorm," you answered six questions in your Dashboard Diary. Each of your answers to those six questions is a potential destination to plot onto your roadmap. Look at all the destinations you wrote down.

Out of all your answers to those six questions, which one or two destinations come closest to being both highly desirable to you and very healthy for you? Identify those top destinations.

Do you find it hard to pick only one or two? If so, then first give each destination a rating. On a scale from 0 to 10, write down next to each destination how much you desire it (10 being the most desire) and give it a rating from 0 to 10 on how healthy it is likely to be for you (10 being the healthiest). Then pick the destinations that have the highest total scores (desire + health).

After you select the top one or two destinations, write them in the top right quadrant of your relationship roadmap. Leave room in the quadrant for several more destinations which might be added later in this exercise. Remember that the healthier a goal seems to you, the higher it will be placed on the "N" arrow, and the more you desire it, the farther right it will be placed on the "E" arrow. So the top right quadrant means both high health and high desire.

After writing your destinations into the top right quadrant of your roadmap, either circle each destination inside of the quadrant or, to save space, simply draw a small circle next to it. The circle indicates that this is a destination of yours (as opposed to a shared destination).

Let's now look at how to start plotting your shared destinations.

In Chapter 20's exercise "Shared destination brainstorm," you answered six questions. Each of your answers to those six questions is a shared destination. Look at all the shared destinations you wrote down.

Out of all your answers to those six questions, which one or two destinations come closest to being both highly desirable to you and very healthy for you? Identify those top destinations.

If you find it hard to pick only one or two, then give each destination a rating. On a scale from 0 to 10, write down next to each destination how much you desire it (10 being the most desire) and give it a rating from 0 to 10 on how healthy it is likely to be for you (10 being the healthiest). Then pick the destinations that have the highest total scores (desire + health).

After you select the top one or two shared destinations, write them in the top right quadrant of your relationship roadmap. Leave room in the quadrant for several more destinations which you might add later in this exercise. Remember that the top right quadrant means high health and high desire.

After writing your shared destinations into the top right quadrant of your roadmap, either draw a square around each destination inside of the quadrant or draw a small square next to it (use the same method you used for your personal destinations). The square indicates that this is a shared destination.

What goes inside the other three quadrants?

Plot at least another six destinations on your roadmap, and use either a circle to indicate it is your destination or a square to indicate that it's your shared destination. Pick and plot as many as you feel comfortable into any of the four quadrants.

In the top left quadrant, write destinations that feel very healthy and somewhat desirable to you. Write as few or as many as you would like, and include any mix of your own destinations and your shared destinations.

In the bottom right quadrant, write destinations and/or shared destinations that feel healthy and are highly desirable to you. Write as few or as many as you would like.

In the bottom left quadrant, write destinations and/or shared destinations that are generally desirable and healthy. Write as few or as many as you would like. This quadrant means it's still desirable and healthy, just not as high as the other quadrants.

After you fill in the quadrants, you have completed your relationship roadmap. I wonder how it feels for you right now to have mapped out the most important goals for you and this relationship.

However, there is an even more important next step in the coming pages.

You have now completed Part Four of this book, but in Part Five, you will learn how to use your relationship roadmap to prioritize and manage your personal decisions and actions in your relationship with yourself and the other person.

Every time you update the relationship roadmap that you created today, or whenever you create a relationship roadmap for a new relationship, that is your chance to re-evaluate your destinations. You can carry over your destinations to the new map or revise them. Most important, however, is to celebrate each destination you have reached or maintained over the period of time in your map's key.

We're about to get driving. Are you ready to get on the road and start traveling to your map's first stop?

PART FIVE

PLAN YOUR NEXT STOP

CHAPTER 22

AN INTRODUCTION TO YOUR NEXT STOP

(4 minute read)

TWO PARTS TO EVERY DRIVER'S TEST

At age 16, when I applied for a New York driver's permit, I had to pass two parts of a driver's test – first, a written test where I sat at a desk, and second, a live road test, where I sat behind the wheel of the car and drove. I had to pass both parts to get my license.

Learning the theory is an essential part of learning how to drive a car, but taking it on the physical road in real traffic where human lives are potentially at risk is a whole other level of skill and knowledge.

I passed the written test, but I nearly failed my live driver's test. I wasn't ready for a license, which was proven by the fact that I crashed my first two cars in the first few months of having my license – a Toyota Corolla and a Nissan Sentra. Thank God for insurance that helped me get a nice big, safe Volvo as my third and final car of my teenage years.

It's just like that in human relationships. We can understand and even ace the theory of how human relationships work on paper, but then once we get out on the road for the live "road test," we can easily crash the car. In other words, we know what to do theoretically but haven't done it in practice.

Part Five of this book marks the start of your driver's test. Now that you know the theory, let's take your metaphorical car for a drive to one of your destinations on your relationship roadmap.

The driver's test is a simple eight-step process that you can repeat for each destination on your relationship roadmap. Then after you follow this process to reach a destination, start at the beginning of the same eight-step process again to arrive at your next destination.

WHAT IS A NEXT STOP?

As a personal coach, my coaching client is the driver of their own life; and in each conversation, my job is to ask them carefully selected, timely, and powerful questions that help them decide which way to turn their steering wheel on their way to their long-term goal, aka their destination.

First, through a series of questions, I identify which destination they want to work toward right now in life. Then, for a client to reach their destination, we schedule consistent one-on-one conversations, and in each of those conversations, I use coaching skills and techniques to help them get clarity on their next short-term goal that will help them progress to their long-term goal.

For example, if their destination is to switch careers, then in each conversation, I review with them what happened since our previous conversation, and then I help them design their next step of action or "next

Chapter 22: An Introduction to Your Next Stop

stop" on their road to their career shift. The next stops that come out of each conversation might be signing up for an event that helps them get more clarity, doing a skills and passions audit, designing a vision board or vision statement, contacting key people to setup meetings for advice or networking, or any number of actions.

As another metaphor to understand next stops, think of how in baseball, there are four bases. When a player runs and touches all four bases in sequence – first, second, third, and fourth, they are awarded a "run." Touching each base is like completing a "next stop" toward your long-term goal. Once you've touched all bases, you've reached your long-term goal.

In each conversation, my client and I identify whether they have hit their short-term goal – kind of like checking to see if they "touched base," and if they did, then we design their next stop on their way to their destination.

In Part Five, you'll see that each next stop involves you identifying what I call a "baby step" forward toward your destination. Completion of a baby step is yet another metaphor that represents you progressing one step closer to your long-term goal.

That's how it works in a live conversation, but this is a book. So, I've converted the process for you to do it without me. Now that you have created your relationship roadmap, each "next stop" refers to the time that you intentionally set aside to follow the simple process over the following pages. The process follows the same content as live personal coaching conversations.

I will walk you through the process of picking one destination on your relationship roadmap that motivates you the most right now and then designing your next stop toward that destination.

Part Five: Plan Your Next Stop

Once you complete your next stop, you simply set aside the time in your calendar to return to this same exercise and repeat the same eight steps for every "next stop," until you reach your destination. Then once you reach your destination, you can start the same process over again with a brand-new destination on your roadmap.

Part Five: Plan Your Next Stop

CHAPTER 23

GET HOOKED INTO YOUR GOAL (EXERCISE)

(15 minute read)

Just as a fisherman catches a fish by using bait on a hook, I'm about to introduce you to the process of getting your heart and mind hooked into your destination.

It's a simple series of steps to follow, and I call it "baiting." I call it baiting, not because I know much about fishing (because I don't), but rather because there are eight steps and they all start with the letter "b." If you put the letter "b" and the number "8" together, like "b-8," and say it out loud, it sounds like "bait."

I published the baiting process in my first book, *The Science of Personal Coaching*.[29] I copied the basic steps over to this book and made a few updates.

So, now it's time to get into your metaphorical car, put your hands on the wheel for the road test, and allow the baiting process to convert your knowledge of the Boundaries Dashboard into action.

Part Five: Plan Your Next Stop

When we walk through the eight steps of baiting, I will challenge you to pick a destination that you most genuinely desire and a next stop that you believe you can easily achieve. After you complete your first next stop, simply return to this page, start again at Step 1, and repeat the baiting process to plan your second "next stop." Do the same thing for each next stop until you reach your destination.

It's time to take out your Dashboard Diary.

Put today's date on top and write the title "My Next Stop."

OK, ready? We're going to start this trip with a bang!

STEP 1: THE BANG

Did you know that the exclamation point ("!") was called a "bang" in the 1950s? It's a fun symbol that represents strong emotion, excitement, or emphasis. When it comes to the baiting process, the "bang" represents the amount of desire or drive that you feel when you envision arriving at your destination.

In this step, you will pick one destination from your relationship roadmap. The Destination that you choose to work toward will require a significant amount of "bang," and that is because you likely will give up or get lost partway through the journey if the vision does not compel you.

So, in this first step, it's time to look at all of the destinations on your relationship roadmap to see which one compels you the most. Remember that both your own destinations and your shared ones can powerfully impact your relationship with the other person. So, pick either type!

If you feel certainty right now about which destination you're going to drive toward first, then this step will be easy. If you don't feel certainty, then here's what to do.

Let the word "bang" represent how much excitement the destination generates or how life-giving it is when you picture yourself reaching the destination.

On a scale of 0 to 10, with zero meaning that you do not feel excited, and 10 meaning you feel the most excited, which destination triggers a score of 8 or above for you?

If you score an 8 or above for more than one destination, then pick the one with the highest score from among those.

Once you find a top scoring destination, open your Dashboard Diary, write today's date, and "Destination" as the page title.

Underneath the page title, write "Step 1," then write your top scoring destination and the score you gave it.

If your score is a 7 or below for all destinations on your roadmap, then how can you adjust or change any of those destinations so that it gives you a score of 8 or above? One of the ways to figure that out might be to ask yourself: "How can I integrate my motivator (see Chapter 6) into any of these destinations to increase the 'bang'?" Another question to ask yourself is: "What could I change about this destination to make it more meaningful, fun, or exciting?"

STEP 2: THE BABY STEP

I call Step 2 "The Baby Step" because it's the way the universe works – one step at a time. No human baby comes out of the womb as an adult, and neither will your destination be all grown up as soon as you conceive it. Rather, it will take smaller steps of growth to achieve it.

So, now's the time to identify the next and smallest step to take toward your destination. Your very next action toward your destination should be small enough that you feel fully confident you can make it happen within the next one to seven days. In coaching, it's more important to set goals you can accomplish rather than goals that will have a huge impact. That's because the "win" of the achieving the goal will create momentum and inspiration to continue, whereas the self-doubt created by failing to achieve it can slow you down.

That's right, it's worth repeating: Keep your next step small enough that you can make it happen within a time frame of no more than one week.

Your next step is your "next stop" toward your destination.

In your Dashboard Diary, write down the title "Next Stop," and then write only a few words to describe your next step toward your destination. Think of a way to say it that can be as short as a title of a movie or slightly longer if needed. I recommend aiming for five or seven words maximum, but the shorter the better.

Apparently, the longest movie title ever was from a 2005 horror movie spoof called *Night of the Day of the Dawn of the Son of the Bride of the Return of the Revenge of the Terror of the Attack of the Evil, Mutant, Hellbound, Flesh-Eating Subhumanoid Zombified Living Dead, Part 3.*

Hah! I have faith that you can title your baby step more concisely than that 37-word movie title!

Ok, so what's the name of your next baby step toward your destination?

The title you write down now becomes the name of your next stop on the journey toward your destination.

STEP 3: THE BACKLOG

In Step 2, you birthed your next stop into the world and gave it a name.

However, if you take a few moments to think about the next stop toward your destination, you may realize there is a list of other things that you also need to do. You might also think of a list of alternative next steps. This is where the "backlog" comes in.

If you think of a list of other things to do, you can park them here in your Dashboard Diary, where they will wait for the right time for your attention.

This list may be very short or it may be very long, but make sure it's a list and not a paragraph! Creating it as a list is important so that you can easily check the steps off in the future.

In your Dashboard Diary, write the title "The Backlog" and write a list, however long or short, of other or alternative steps that come to mind when you think of your next stop.

Each time you come back to the baiting process, flip back to your previous backlogs to see if anything needs to replace your next stop. Flipping back to your backlogs from previous next stops can be enlightening.

If needed, go back to Step 2 to rename your baby step (aka your next stop). Cross out the old one and write your new next stop title in its place.

Then, when you're ready, let's move on to Step 4.

Part Five: Plan Your Next Stop

STEP 4: THE BOOKING

When you book a hotel room or a flight or a dinner, you select times and dates and put everything into some kind of calendar. That's what this step is for – figuring out the length of time that your next stop will take on your calendar.

The "booking" for your next stop could involve you putting one hour into your calendar on Sunday to complete a step or it may mean scheduling 20 minutes on three separate days.

Not sure how long your next stop will take to complete? Simply estimate the least amount of time this next stop could take and the most amount of time, and then pick the middle of the two estimates. For example, if the least it could take is 20 minutes and the most 60 minutes, then I pick the average of those two numbers and schedule 40 minutes.

Once you calculate that estimate of how long it will take, look at your calendar and see how to fit it in, either by splitting it up or fitting it all into one spot.

Maybe you decide to sit down for 10 minutes three times over the next five days. Maybe you will spend 60 seconds every day over the next week. Pick whatever works for you, however small or large the window(s) of time.

In your Dashboard Diary, write down "The Booking" and answer these five questions:

1. What is your estimate of the time it will take to complete your next stop?

2. What do you see as the earliest date you could complete this next stop by?

3. What do you see as the absolute latest date you could complete the next stop by?

4. What days and times will you put into your calendar to complete this? If you are splitting your actions into several times slots over one day or several days, list them all here.

5. What reminder method will you use to organize this booking? Some examples include reminder lists, alarm clocks, Google calendar, a paper taped to the wall, a physical calendar using pen and paper, or something else.

STEP 5: THE BANKING

So, you've covered the "bang," the "baby step," the "backlog," and he "booking." Now it's time for the "banking"!

A bank is a store of value. In a bank, a valuable thing might be cash, money, jewelry, a valuable document, or gold kept in a bank's vault. Similarly, in this step, you'll identify a valuable thing that will signal that you have completed the next stop. That "thing" can be an accomplishment or something tangible.

Whether it's quite small or very large, what is an observable event or item that will mark your completion of this next stop toward your destination? Here are some examples:

- A notification pings you to confirm that your next stop is completed (i.e., the cha-ching sound of sending a payment, or the "message sent" pop-up after sending a message).
- A person says something to confirm it's completed.
- You deliver a message to someone.

- You have changed the state of something.
- You have gained new knowledge.
- A clock or timer confirms you spent the time on this that you planned.
- You received a receipt or a certificate.
- You can point to a tangible change in your body or nervous system.
- You receive an email that contains information you looked for.
- You will have a new page or document that you didn't have prior to the task.
- You receive money or something else of value.

In your Dashboard Diary, write down "The Banking" and list one thing that will signal that you have completed your next step toward your destination.

STEP 6: THE BATTLE

Step 6 is to prepare for battle. Whether it's a sports team or an army, winners prepare for attack ahead of time.

I am non-military and not a sportsman either, but I know vaguely that an army might prepare itself by building strong bases and practicing defensive tactics, and a sports team may prepare by practicing how to stop the other team from scoring, learning different tactics and formations, and studying how their opponents play. Whether it's as serious as war or as exciting as a competition, the quality of your preparation will often determine whether you reach your goal or not.

The "battle" in your journey toward your destination refers to the physical, mental, or emotional preparation you need on the field as you meet obstacles along the way.

Depending on your next stop, your battle preparation can be as minor as bringing an umbrella, asking a friend to babysit while you work, or stocking up on extra coffee. It can be as large as hiring a top professional advisor to give you expert advice, buying a fancy and expensive new outfit that makes you feel confident, taking a one-day trip alone, or maybe even hiring a personal coach to prepare you with a healthy mental mindset for the day of your task.

Regardless, the first step is identifying your opponents, whether human or machine or nature itself, and then planning your strategy to overcome them.

Sometimes something beyond your control will stop you, even when you have prepared. The key is to make a conscious effort to note what you learned about the opponent or obstacle so that you can use that knowledge to better prepare for it in the future.

In your Dashboard Diary, write down "The Battle" and make two columns. Title the left column "The Opponent" and title the right column "Strategy."

In the "Opponent" column, write a numbered list of anything at all that you believe can get in the way of completing your next stop. In the "Strategy" column, for each numbered item you listed as an Opponent, think about what you can do ahead of time to help reduce its likelihood or its impact, or to avoid it altogether.

The strategies column could contain any kind of tool, action, person, or other preparation activity that will likely help you prepare for each battle. Think about "failed" attempts in the past, identify potential ways around them, and list ways to do things differently this time.

Here are examples of things I might write in the "Opponent" column:

1. Feeling too tired.

2. No one is available to help.

3. Not believing in myself.

4. I don't have enough information.

5. Jane might say no.

Here are corresponding examples that would go in the "Strategy" column:

1. Get 9 hours sleep the night before and/or have an extra energy drink.

2. Ask a friend ahead of time if they are willing to be on call if I need help.

3. Use personal coaching techniques to boost my belief in myself.

4. Accept the fact that I only need to know one thing and find that out first.

5. Prepare to thank Jane even if she says no and ask her directly what it will take to for her to be comfortable saying yes.

STEP 7: THE BELIEF

In your Dashboard Diary, write down "The Belief" and your score to the following question: On a scale of 0 to 10, with zero meaning you don't believe at all and 10 meaning you fully believe, how believable is it that you will complete your next stop?

Chapter 23: Get Hooked into Your Goal (Exercise)

If you score an 8 or above, then continue directly to Step 8.

If your score is a 7 or below, then it's time to go back to Step 1 and go through each step of the "baiting" process to identify what you need to change in order to get a score of 8 for this question.

As you walk through your Step(s) again, make sure you update all answers to Steps 1 through 7.

STEP 8: THE BACKBONE

A backbone provides crucial support; it holds you up and keeps you alive. When it comes to your next stop, support can mean accountability of any kind, whether it's an alarm you set for yourself or a handwritten reminder that you stick on your mirror. Support can also mean a person – a friend, coach, or family member – who agrees to help you in some big or small way with your next stop.

Sometimes the only support I need is a big piece of paper taped to my door to remind me. Other times I need an entire list of supports to reach my next stop, like a personal coach, a piece of paper, an alarm clock, and at least nine hours sleep.

When it comes to your next stop, think about both non-human and human forms of support that might help you complete it.

You might also want to think about successful support strategies you've used in the past that worked well for you and how they may or may not help again.

In your Dashboard Diary, write "The Backbone" and answer the question: What kind of additional support or accountability, if any, will you put in

Part Five: Plan Your Next Stop

place to ensure you complete this next stop?

GRADUATION: HOW WILL YOU CELEBRATE?

Graduation ceremonies happen when you progress from one level to another, and these events can be very big or very small. No matter how big or small, people tend to have a sense of "missing out" or of incompletion when they aren't able to participate in their graduation ceremonies.

A graduation creates momentum. Each graduation acts as a final acknowledgement of what you have done and gets you ready for the next stage. The momentum created by the acknowledgment is the most important reason to do it.

As you know from previous exercises in this book, I believe that the secret potion for success is celebrating the small wins, and so in this chapter, it's time to plan out ways that you will acknowledge your effort and show up for yourself after you complete your next stop.

This final part of the baiting process is for you to write down a menu of ideas, and then after you complete your next stop, you do one of the things you wrote down.

Every time you reach this part of the "baiting" process, you keep acknowledging and celebrating in one of the ways that you planned.

But what if you don't complete your next stop? If you don't complete it, then the win to celebrate will be identifying any new information you gained about yourself in the process. Observations and information that you learn about yourself become ammunition for a future win.

All learning matters. In team sports, individual contributions are valuable, even if they don't directly result in a score. In ice hockey, players can earn "assists" by helping set up a goal, which reflects their valuable contribution to the team's success. In basketball, while the main objective is to score baskets, players can also earn points for their team through free throws when they are fouled by an opponent. So, even a foul can turn into an opportunity to score.

Whether you hit your target or not, a ceremonious ending to the baiting process scores emotional points that will create momentum.

Yes, celebrate the small wins when you complete the next stop – and also when you didn't complete it but learned something in the process.

So, what big or little thing can you plan to do to congratulate yourself? Maybe it's a high five to yourself in the mirror or to someone else nearby. Maybe it's a simple smile to and for yourself. Maybe it's a quiet but pronounced inner thought telling yourself, "Good job." Maybe it's turning on your favorite song and giving your hips a little bump to the rhythm. Maybe there's a special coffee you think is a bit pricey, but for the special occasion of completing this next stop, you'll get it.

In your Dashboard Diary, write the title "Momentum Celebration" and list a couple of options for how to celebrate your completion of your next stop. I've started a brainstorm below to stir ideas.

- Turn on one particular song that makes you feel great and upbeat.

- Do something to memorialize the win, like taking a photograph or creating something artsy.

- Set aside an intentional amount of time to reflect and meditate on the positive feelings associate with the win.

- Sit somewhere that you don't normally sit, perhaps somewhere with a beautiful view where you can reflect on your win.

- ○ Take a little time off work or extend a lunch break to either relax or do something fun.

- ○ Watch a funny or inspiring video or show.

- ○ Read part of a magazine or book that makes you happy or listen to an uplifting podcast or audiobook.

- ○ Bake, cook, or buy something you'd love to eat or drink.

- ○ Do one of those personal development challenges like an affirmation or a high five in the mirror.

- ○ Share the news with someone you know who will certainly celebrate your win with you.

Here's another way to celebrate your win and/or be grateful for what you've learned. Come and find me on social media as @boundariescheck, and leave a comment with the hashtag #IWON so I can see it! Any and every time you complete your next stop, I invite you to do that, whether you've fully completed it or simply learned what to do differently next time.

Think of this celebration as the period at the end of a sentence (or the "full stop," as we say in Australia). There are eight steps in the baiting process that brings you to each stop toward your destination, and this celebration is your graduation ceremony.

PART SIX

USE THE GLOVE COMPARTMENT

CHAPTER 24

COMMUNICATING BOUNDARIES

(15 minute read)

A glove compartment is where you might store important and helpful essentials like emergency napkins, vehicle registration, or an extra pair of sunglasses.

Part Six of this book is like a glove compartment full of essentials, which is why I titled this part, "Use the Glove Compartment."

So, here we are.

The next stop in your journey of this relationship might involve communicating new boundaries, and if you feel any hesitation about doing that, then you can grab some quick tips in this chapter.

While boundaries can include things that you joyfully propose or agree to, boundaries can seem much harder to communicate when you believe the other person might act negatively in response. So, this "glove compartment" focuses on the more tricky boundary conversations and topics.

SAY IT NONVERBALLY

Your actions and decisions speak louder than words.

Words are only a fraction of what you communicate to the other person in this relationship. You also "say" things through your actions and decisions – how long you stay, what time you decide to leave, where you agree to go and what environments you choose, where you don't agree to go and what environments you move away from, who you spend time with and who you don't, and what you do or what you don't do.

While many times it's best to directly and verbally state your new boundaries ahead of time, other times it might be more impactful to introduce your new boundaries with a new action. In other words, sometimes it's best to let your behavior be the introduction to the new, healthier you and clarify it formally with words later if needed.

And when it comes to nonverbal messages, there's also your facial expression.

And your body gestures.

Maybe even the scents you wear are sending a message about your degree of self-care and how you want others to feel good around you.

Nonverbal communication is powerful.

When coworkers keep interrupting your focus, you can wear visible noise-canceling headphones, signaling your need for concentration, without saying a word.

Leave the office on time every day, showing colleagues you value work-life balance.

Suggest alternative times for social gatherings, without directly saying "no, I need that time to do other things."

Rearrange your living room so that the television is no longer the main feature, communicating a desire for more conversation.

After work, turn on an auto-reply for work emails, indicating that you're not available 24/7.

Surprise your partner with small acts of kindness, expressing affection and support without words.

In a busy household, signal your need for self-care, downtime, and investment in your personal interests by creating a reading nook or an exercise corner. Then, use it.

Host home-based and no-alcohol social events to communicate your need for more genuine social connections, rather than going to the loud and crowded clubs where you feel disconnected.

Leave your phone in another room during quality time with loved ones, a behavior that says how important it is for you to be present and fully engaged.

So, what does all of this mean for you right now as you read this book? It means that you have many choices about how you communicate a new boundary, and many times the words themselves have little to do with what you say.

WHAT DOES YOUR VOICE SAY?

When you choose to directly communicate your boundaries with words, what are you actually communicating beyond your words with the sound of your voice? The audible patterns of your voice might say something very different than the words you speak.

Behind your words, your intentions speak through at least eight qualities: speed or tempo, breathing pattern, volume, articulation or pronunciation, emphasis, tone (emotional quality), rhythm, and vocal pitch (the rise and fall of voice or the musicality). These non-verbal characteristics have the power to turn your words into their opposite meaning.

"Sure" said with a wavering voice means the opposite of certain.

"I'm fine" with a trembling voice suggest the speaker is far from fine.

"Oh great!" points to the opposite meaning when spoken with a sarcastic tone.

"I really appreciate it," said with a flat and apathetic vocal pitch indicates the opposite of genuine appreciation.

Because of the power of voice to completely change the meaning of words, I've found it's often better to think about the quality of my voice before thinking about the words I want to say.

Rather than thinking "What do I want to say?", it is more powerful to think "How do I want my voice to make the other person feel when I say it?" This kind of preparation takes work, and for me to do it well, I have to set aside the time and effort for each and every message. It's like writing and rehearsing a song.

Every sentence you say is like a song; your words are the lyrics and the music is the mood you deliver through the eight qualities of your voice. When your music matches your lyrics, clear communication happens. That's why it's hilarious when someone comically takes a popular gangster rap song and sings it opera-style; the music and lyrics clash and confuse. In a classical opera voice, try singing the rap lyrics "Yo, I'm livin' da thug life, hustlin'" and you'll feel the dissonance. It's a sense of inauthenticity; something doesn't match up.

So, remember the power of the music in your voice when it's time to deliver your message.

THE 7% RULE

A body language researcher found that a face-to-face conversation is 55% nonverbal, 38% vocal, and only 7% verbal.[30] This means that in a face-to-face conversation, your body, face, and voice change how your words are interpreted.

If the words you choose only account for 7%, then how much time, effort, and attention do you invest into the other 93% of your message?

In other words, how much do you think about your body language, your facial gestures, and the characteristics of your voice?

Imagine someone for the first time tells you the words, "I love you," but the corner of their nose is curled in disgust and their voice sounds annoyed. A little confusing, right?

Have you ever noticed yourself saying words that your voice and facial expression seem to disagree with, even a little bit? If you said yes, then that is most likely because your temperature light is flashing yellow or red. In other words, your emotional state is sitting in an unsure or unsettled temperature range (as described in Chapter 8), and the truth about your uncertainty is beginning to erupt like a volcano.

Part Six: Use the Glove Compartment

True emotion is like hot lava seeping through the cracks of a mountain. The lava is 93% of what you communicate, and it runs over top of your words. Your words are only 7% of what's going on; that's why I call it the 7% rule.

MASTERING THE MOUNTAIN

When the sound of your voice contradicts your words, the contradictory message flows over your words and melts away their meaning. So, how do you conquer a volcanic mountain?

Just like any dangerous natural phenomenon, you prepare ahead of time.

First, in each situation, the courageous decision to commit to vulnerable honesty will save you from needing to practice the "right" words. Mark Twain, the famous American writer, said, "If you tell the truth, you don't have to remember anything."

Second, for each situation, instead of focusing on practicing the 7%, practice the 93% ten times more. A great way to think of preparation is to rehearse the "music" of your message like a song.

Think of your emotional state as the melody, quality of your voice, and all instruments, and then think of your words as the lyrics that sit lightly over top. Pick the right music for your message and rehearse it ahead of time. Do this every time you have an important message to share.

I have used this mental rehearsal technique for interviews throughout my career. Twice I was promoted in the job interviews – given a higher-level role than what I applied for, and another time I was one of the top three chosen for a second interview out of an original pool of over 800 applicants. I've also had to sit in front of senior executives a number of times throughout my career, and I use the same technique to prepare.

Leading up to interviews and key meetings, I take time to stop and visualize myself sitting in front of the suited and intimidating people or person facing me. In that visualization, I practice feeling and maintaining a calm and attentive tone. I don't even need to think about the actual words I want to say, because I knew that when you carry the right "music" in your heart, your words don't matter as much.

When you decide that you're going to be a calm listener and stick to "honesty is the best policy," the right words tend to show up, even if you stumble into them.

When I wrote my book *The Science of Personal Coaching*, I named this visualization technique "fast forwarding." It's a personal coaching tool, and it's a staple in my way of life, business, and communication. To "fast forward" is a mental rehearsal; it's skipping ahead in your imagination to a specific point in time to play out how you want to feel from the beginning to the end of the situation.

Now, if you were to write out a speech, you would sit down and, in your imagination, you would walk through what to say. You'd imagine the points you want to make. Similarly, with fast forwarding, you sit down and, in your imagination, you walk through what you want to feel. You'd imagine the tone and emotions you want to maintain, the person you want to be.

When fast forwarding, I sit down and picture all sorts of emotions that may come at me in the specific situation, whether that's sitting in a chair in front of a group of suited executives or getting on a call to share bad news with someone I love. I picture myself running through the entire event, emotionally responding the way that I'd like to. It's like a professional athlete's warm-up routine before a big competition.

I picture the other person making me feel uncomfortable, scared, or nervous about something, and then I envision how it would feel within my chest to respond honestly, vulnerably, and bravely. The key to effective fast forwarding is that I feel it throughout my body and particularly in my chest, from beginning to end. I don't only picture it in my mind.

It's like playing a child's game of "make believe" when you practice it all in your imagination, and then it ends up becoming a true story. It's as if the mental rehearsal makes the brain believe that you have done it already, so that when you're sitting down "for real" in front of the person and you recall what you rehearsed, the brain confidently thinks, "I've done this before. I got this!"

QUICK SCRIPTS

We have looked at how important it is to visualize the "music" or attitude of your message, and now it's time to look at preparing your "lyrics" or words.

Words will naturally flow from a genuine heart, but it can certainly boost your confidence to know that you have a few key words, lines, or phrases to help you say what you mean. In this section, I'll share an assortment of statements that might help you communicate about your boundaries.

These are in no particular order and are only for inspiration. I suggest you read the ones that seem useful to you out loud so that you can hear yourself say them, as a type of warm up. Everyone speaks with a slightly different style, so take some of these and make them your own by swapping words or altering the structure so that it feels natural and matches the way you talk.

Most of these examples are about expressing a potentially conflicting

Chapter 24: Communicating Boundaries

opinion, a different plan of action, or a decision to change something for yourself. These are usually the more difficult kinds of messages to communicate.

I love the phrase "back yourself," which means to believe in your capabilities. I am convinced that saying these kinds of statements out loud helps build that mental muscle of confidence in your capability to communicate your needs.

Note that the blank spaces in some examples are for you, when the time comes, to fill in the specific information that you're sharing with the other person.

Here we go!

- I have _____ minutes right now, then I'll be heading off.

- No, but thank you for offering.

- I'm not sure; so, instead, how possible is it to do it this way?

- This subject brings me down. What other subjects would you like to chat about?

- I don't know if this is right for me, at least for right now.

- I'd love to try _____ instead. What do you think?

- I would rather cut out _____.

- I need to _____ in order to be honest and true to myself.

- I need some space to think about that before I make a decision.

Part Six: Use the Glove Compartment

- ○ I need some time to process my thoughts before I respond to that.

- ○ I'm going to take some time to process so I can better communicate what I think.

- ○ That action / those words hurt, so I need to make choices that are healthier for me.

- ○ I feel angry, and I want to sort that out before I respond.

- ○ I feel confused, and I want to sort that out before I respond.

- ○ I don't feel ready yet to talk about that.

- ○ I don't know yet.

- ○ I'm not sure, so it's a no for now.

- ○ Until I find something healthier for me, I'm going to reduce the amount of _____ because it doesn't feel right for me right now.

- ○ Your decisions and actions impact me, and mine impact you. Because of that, I'm going to _____.

- ○ We're each responsible for our own decisions and actions. Because I'm respsonsible for mine, I'm going to _____.

- ○ Both of our feelings matter and are always valid, and something about this just doesn't feel right to me.

- ○ Something about _____ doesn't seem right to me.

- ○ I need some time for this one.

Chapter 24: Communicating Boundaries

- How can we negotiate this so it's healthy for both of us?
- This doesn't feel healthy for me.
- Something never felt right about the way I was doing it before, so I'm going to start trying new ideas.
- Something about that doesn't line up with where I'm headed.
- When it comes to _____, that's not the direction I'm headed in.
- Something about _____ doesn't feel right, so I think I'll give a try.
- I need to change something to make this healthier for me.
- To be loyal to myself, I need to _____.
- To maintain to my sense of peace, I need to _____.
- To be loyal to myself, I need to do something different, so here's what I'm going to change about what I do / what I say / what topics I share.
- I don't like to respond until I feel more certain/confident about how I feel / what I think.
- I like to give myself time to think about my options.
- I'll take a little time and get back to you on that.
- There's another option that feels more right for me.
- I don't know the words yet for it, but something just doesn't feel right to me about that.

Part Six: Use the Glove Compartment

○ I respond during these hours or days: _____.

○ I'm going to wait a bit to think about what's healthiest for me.

○ I am going to back out of this (conversation topic / plan / activity / commitment) for now because I want to have the right state of mind and heart for it.

○ I don't think it's healthy to continue a conversation if, for whatever reason, I'm not feeling heard.

○ My feelings matter, and I don't think it's right or healthy for me to belittle them or discount them in any way.

REMOVE "YOU"

In a tricky conversation, the difference between controlling vs. respecting the other person can be as simple as removing the word "you" and restating the sentence starting with "I". Instead of using the words "you" and "your," make "I," "me," and "my" the subjects and objects of your sentences.

In other words, any time you notice your emotional state slipping into a second- or third-degree range, or if you notice a possibility that the other person is misunderstanding your message, then stop and convert the sentence to one that's empowering. Remove "you" and "your." Use only "I," "me," or "my" statements.

For example, instead of the command "You should not say that," you can say, "I need to back out of this because it doesn't feel right for me." And then take the action you need to take.

Instead of the implicit "you" in a command such as "Don't do that," instead say, "That's not healthy for me."

Instead of "Don't you shout at me," you can say, "I'm happy to have this conversation when we can both speak calmly. I'll propose a couple of dates and times for a chat soon."

Instead of "You're being mean," say, "I feel terrible hearing that, so I'm going to leave and give myself time to process what's healthy for me right now."

Instead of "That's your problem," say, "I feel that's out of my control."

Instead of "You invited me here for no reason," say, "I don't see any value for me to add here, so I'm going to go shortly."

The next time a tricky conversation comes up, remove "you" and watch how it acts as a kind of train track to move the conversation in a better emotional direction.

THE INVITATION

When you adjust boundaries, you don't always need a formal declaration like, "From now on, I am going to change the way I _____." Of course, that is appropriate or needed in some situations, but in other situations it may be awkward for everyone. I know it's awkward, because I've done it too many times.

Until I saw others model an alternative, I didn't know any other way. It's a technique where you simply give the other person a heartfelt notice of an upcoming change. Giving notice is a graceful alternative, and I call it "the invitation" approach.

When you throw a party, you send invitations and ask for an "RSVP,"

Part Six: Use the Glove Compartment

which is simply a request to find out if the person will attend or not. People can RSVP yes or no, but regardless of whether they attend or not, the party still goes on.

When it comes to communicating a new boundary, let the other person know clearly ahead of time and treat it as an invitation. In the shortest and sweetest way possible, present your new and healthier direction that you will be heading in the near future and offer the other person to travel that road with you.

For example, instead of saying to a client, "I am charging too little and undervaluing my work, so I have raised my package prices," instead I can say, "In one month's time, my new package price will be _____ to better fit my changing availability and the demand for my services. When our current contract expires, I hope we can work together through one of these new packages."

Another way to think of the invitation approach is to think of it as inviting the other person to a graduation ceremony to celebrate the upgrade of your healthy boundaries. It's like saying, "I'm going to celebrate this new journey for my life, and I will understand if you can't make it or you have other plans, but I'd love for you to join me."

In other situations, you can present the invitation as simply as, "I realize _____ is not working for me anymore, and so over the next few weeks, I decided that I will start _____. I understand if you can't, but I'm really hoping that I continue to share _____ with you."

And yet another way to think of this is as an invitation to a conversation about healthier decisions. For example, "I'm going to start taking some needed time for myself and head home a bit earlier from now on. How much do you relate to the need to take some time for yourself?"

Knowing your intentions are pure, the calmness in your tone will give off a sense of peace like incense.

If, by chance, you express that peace and health are your priority and the other person argues against that need of yours, then you have discovered how little that person regards the health of the relationship. That information will help you make better decisions when it comes to who you choose to invest yourself into.

CHAPTER 25

GOVERNING STYLE

(4 minute read)

DISCOVER YOUR RELATIONSHIP GOVERNING STYLE

Just as you find many different forms of government across the world, you will also find different forms of governing styles across your personal and professional relationships.

What's a governing style in a personal or professional relationship? It's the degree of consent that is sought and expressed in the relationship. In the political or national relationship between you and your government, your degree of consent determines the form of government. In your personal or professional relationships, your degree of consent also determines the form of government, or simply the way decisions are made.

For example, if consent is not sought by the people for its decisions, a government can be called a dictatorship. The more consent that is sought from its people, the more freedom and opportunities a country is considered to have. New forms of government may emerge, but in this age, a democracy is a government that seeks consent from its people (i.e. voting) and also expresses its consent through the law-making process.

In each of your human relationships, you have a different way of seeking and expressing consent, which is a form of government or more casually what I like to call "your governing style." And the degree of consent you seek and express in each relationship differs from parent-child, to CEO-employee, to doctor-patient, to husband-wife.

In this short chapter, we look at the way you make decisions in your relationship with the other person, which determines your relationship's governing style. Your decision-making varies to some degree in every relationship, so we are looking at your dominant governing style.

Your relationship government style also applies to your relationship with yourself as much as it does with everyone else. For example, some of the happiest moments in my life were when all parts of me made peace on a decision; when all of me said "yes" with a sense of reason, pure-heartedness, and calm. There was a healthy internal consensus between heart, soul, mind, and body.

In your relationship with the other person, your degree of expressing and seeking consent distinguishes one governing style from another. How often do you check whether the other person agrees with your decisions that impact them or the relationship? How often do you express agreement or disagreement with the other person's decisions that impact you or the relationship?

Oppressive governing styles don't only exist on a large scale at the level of nations and countries. Oppressive governing styles happen small scale, too, in individual relationships.

When it comes to decisions that impact the other person, if the majority of your decisions do not seek the other person's consent and they are unhappy about that fact, then that's a "relationship dictatorship." If a majority of the time you do not check whether the other person agrees with a decision but you do it anyway... yep, you're the big "D."

(Dictator, that is.)

However, it's not a dictatorship if the other person consents to you making decisions on their behalf. A relationship government style in which the other person "elects" you to make decisions for them in the relationship can be called a "relationship republic." The other person consents to you making the decisions for them, unlike a dictatorship where the other person's consent is irrelevant.

A relationship governing style in which you both healthily debate and vote for each decision on what's good for the "country" of your relationship is a "relationship democracy."

If you do not have any particular way that you make your decisions in this relationship, then perhaps your style is "relationship anarchy." Anarchy, in simple terms, means "no government." In anarchy, there is no agreement around how decisions are made, and while that can sound liberating to some people, chaos and conflict can erupt often and make it hard to work together.

So how do you narrow down your governing style in this relationship? Think about the majority of decisions you make in this relationship and identify whether or not you expressed consent to the other person or sought consent from them. Your decision-making style is your governing style.

The other person can evaluate their governing style on their own, since they are the only ones who can hear their own internal voice of consent.

To do this more precisely, create a blank page in your Dashboard Diary, and draw five columns. Title the first column "Date," the second one "Decision" (what decision was made?), the third "Subject area" (this is the area of life or business that the decision relates to), the fourth "My consent was sought" (answer yes or no), and the fifth "The other person's consent was sought" (answer yes or no). Complete a minimum of 10 entries about your decisions in this relationship, filling in all columns, and then see which relationship governing style emerges.

Over time, you'll see a pattern emerge of how often your and their consent matters to you.

A certain governing style might show up only in certain key areas of decision-making like finances or health.

After a minimum of ten recorded decisions, look at what patterns start to show up for your decision-making in the relationship.

If you did not seek consent from the other person for the majority of decisions in this relationship, then your governing style for this relationship resembles a dictatorship.

If the other person consented to you making decisions on their behalf for the majority of decisions, then your governing style for this relationship resembles a republic.

If both you and the other person openly and respectfully debate to negotiate on decisions in the relationship, then your style resembles a democracy.

If consent is unpredictable for the majority of your decisions, then your style is like a form of anarchy.

Is it time for government reform? If so, maybe it's time to add it to your relationship roadmap.

CHAPTER 26

MY TAKE ON TOXICITY

(3 minute read)

In my personal life, I define a "toxic relationship" in two ways. First, it's a relationship in which a qualified mental health professional has identified it as toxic; or second, it's a relationship that scores red lights in the Boundaries Health Check assessment contained in this book (see scoring described at the end of Chapter 3).

With the Boundaries Health Check, I can actually measure toxicity.

The concept of "toxicity" is helpful because it identifies patterns of behavior that cause harm, but I use this term only to refer to a relationship, a pattern of behavior in a relationship, or an interaction.

I won't call a *person* "toxic."

Yes, a person can act dangerously and require correction, or in extreme cases, deserve prison when their toxic behaviors break the law. But for me, it's their behavior and interactions in a human relationship that I would label as "toxic," not their entire being.

Using the phrase "toxic person" or telling someone "you are toxic" hints

Part Six: Use the Glove Compartment

that the person is irredeemable and allows no room for the possibility of growth, learning, or change. So, naming the *behavior* toxic, as opposed to naming the *person* toxic, creates a subtle shift of perception from hopelessness to potential, however small that potential is.

In nature, after all, we sometimes see things that appear toxic in one situation become healing in another situation, all depending on the interaction. Here's a fun illustration of that, based on science.

Memes are often lighthearted metaphors that actually point to deeper and more complex realities.

I saw a meme that used three cartoon characters to show the surprising reality of how a "toxic" chemical can switch to healthy, depending on the interaction.

The meme shows an image of a frightening monster, and next to the monster are the words:

"Sodium (Na) is highly reactive, explodes in contact with water."

Below that, there's a second scary monster, and next to this second monster are the words:

"Chlorine (Cl) is a poisonous/deadly gas."

Further down below the two scary monsters, it shows the popular, friendly, and fun-loving cartoon monster Shrek, and next to him it reads:

"Sodium Chloride (NaCl) is a food preservative and flavoring agent that you consume from the local supermarket."

The meme shows that the two chemicals, sodium (with the chemical symbol "Na") and chlorine (with the chemical symbol "Cl"), are each destructive like monsters on their own. But when they come together and form sodium chloride (NaCl), they are no longer destructive. NaCl is table salt, the stuff you put into your food.

In other words, in a fun way, the meme highlights the fact that two otherwise dangerous chemicals can interact in a way that preserves life instead of destroying it.

I checked this fact with my friend Ben, a professional chemical engineer, who said, "Yes that is correct. Chlorine was the first chemical weapon used in WW1. Sodium metal reacts violently when exposed to water (they store it in oil to prevent it reacting). Yes, sodium chloride (NaCl) is table salt and the main salt in sea water."

In contrast to NaCl, there are also chemicals that are hazardous when they interact but safe when kept separate. In other words, there are chemicals that act like two friendly Shreks when separate but turn into devils when they interact. So, you can say that the interaction either makes or breaks the monster.

Humans can be like that, too. In human relationships, people can become like dangerous monsters or friendly fun-loving creatures, depending on who or what they mix with. The mix makes or breaks the poison.

Yes, the person who is called "toxic" may indeed have damaging behaviors and so require safe distance, learning, and correction; however, if we label an entire person as "toxic" as opposed to labeling only their particular behaviors, then I have a lot of questions. Here are a few of them.

How does labeling someone "toxic" help the person correct their behavior?

How much does this reinforcing label end up being counterproductive?

How does this label help the person understand their power to change?

When a student is struggling with a subject, does a good teacher call them names and give up on them or does a good teacher identify the areas where the student needs help and offer avenues for improvement so that the student can find their strengths?

We humans are among the most complicated, dangerous, beautiful, and wonderful chemical reactions in the universe.

Some human interactions bring out the behaviors of a terrible monster, bursting from the chest like in the film *Alien*, while others bring out the behavior of a friendly monster like Shrek.

Call out the interaction.

Identify the behavior.

Measure the toxicity of the relationship.

Not the person.

CHAPTER 27

DATING BOUNDARIES

(14 minute read)

As in Rule #5 of the six rules of every human relationship, boundaries are relationship specific (see Chapter 2). In other words, there are only six boundaries in every human relationship, but the specific boundaries vary greatly from one person – or group of people – to the next.

You will not equally share with everyone the same amount of time, the same conversation topics, the same environments, the same investment of your energy and resources, the same third-party relationships, or even the same communication tools.

In this chapter, I'll share my boundaries when it comes to dating, or more specifically, dating apps.

Dating apps themselves are a communication tool for singles to form some degree of human relationships with other singles, but these apps are not the healthiest tools at this point in history. I'd rather organize fun and healthy in-person events for singles to meet and determine compatibility to make the experience more real, and it's a goal of mine at this point to try and organize that. However, in the meantime, here's how I protect my peace and sanity as a busy single who is on dating apps because she has very few other tools or environments, and not much time to meet singles otherwise.

Dating is a process of boundary adjustments to keep those green lights aglow.

You probably wouldn't give your home address to everyone you "match" with on a dating app. And you wouldn't respond with "I love you" to everyone on the app who says, "hi!" That is because there is a natural process for each of us to work through as we make decisions about who we'd like to share certain topics with, spend time with, and invest our energy and resources into, and who helps us keep green lights glowing on our Boundaries Dashboard.

Why think of dating as a process? Isn't that too business-like or formal? Whether we like it or not, and whether or not we are conscious of this fact, we go through a process in dating, just as we go through a process of growing from child to adult, whether we like it or not. Either you're unconsciously going through it like an object being pushed along a conveyor belt in the dating factory, or you're becoming conscious of it and owning the factory.

We select our own partner from a sea of strangers who have extraordinarily diverse principles, values, and beliefs about dating and sexual intimacy. Because of this, it's not a simple or easy process to find someone compatible. Rather, there are several stages of learning about someone for that person to graduate from stranger to trustworthy partner.

The process of dating is the process of decision-making, and specifically, that's decision-making about your boundaries. In the modern dating world, it takes a lot of work if we want to keep our sanity, health, and self-respect throughout that process.

As a female on a dating app, statistically I receive more messages than a male would receive. A woman can receive 10 to 20 times the number of messages a man receives – or more. So, what is healthy for me to do when I am on my way home from work, about to get ready for the gym, but then I log in to a dating app to see 17 messages in one day or over 10,000 "likes" on my profile?

Without identifying my dating boundaries, I might neglect my health and fitness goals, stay up too late (which makes me miserable the next day), miss out on my closest human relationships, or jeopardize my career just to make the time to respond to messages and "likes" on a dating app.

Dating apps are ultimately designed to make a profit and generate ad revenue; otherwise, they won't survive. The big dating app companies are not optimized or ultimately designed to ensure the best sexual, emotional, intellectual, and psychological compatibility or reciprocity; they want you on the app as long as possible, even when their marketing slogans say otherwise.

Because of that, there aren't features like automatic replies to respectfully let each sender know that I may not be able to reply to their message. The apps also aren't aiming for psychological safety; rather, they let millions of people experience scammers, identity thieves, and sexually harassing messages, leaving you only able to "report" the behavior after you have experienced it.

If the apps had more legitimate features, filters, and screening processes, there simply wouldn't be as many "matches" and not as much profit for their shareholders. I admit, it's fun imagining that you have so many options. It's a "dopamine hit" for sure.

But, here we are left to do all the safety filtering and screening work ourselves. And this is where dating boundaries come to the rescue. As I make all of those decisions, I check my four Boundaries Dashboard lights to see which boundaries need adjustments.

Battery light (consent): Am I seeking their consent in every reasonable way? Am I expressing my consent in every reasonable way?

Oil light (self-care): Do I find myself neglecting my own self-care needs to make this work? My career, other human relationships, and physical health can suffer if it that is the case. Am I losing myself or learning about myself in the process?

Fuel light (motivators): Am I making decisions that align with my #1 motivator (my number one value)? Are my decisions true to myself and who I am?

Temperature light (emotional state): In our interactions, do I have feelings of inner peace, safety, reciprocated attraction, and a mutual desire to know more about each other?

When any of the above lights go yellow or red, I make adjustments. Most times, those adjustments are to turn all dials down to zero and move on to someone with whom I can clearly see sharing the roads of life ahead of us.

TIME BOUNDARY

Timing is everything, they say, and it's the most important boundary in the beginning of the dating process. The Time boundary is not only the amount and frequency of time you spend, but it also includes questions of sequence or timing, like "When do I share my phone number?" or "When is it safe to share where I work?" or "How long do I wait to talk about (insert private topic)?" or "When does it make sense to introduce him to my friends?"

The answers to some of those and many other questions depend on how many trust behaviors a man demonstrates as I get to know him.

Chapter 27: Dating Boundaries

In any human relationship, what I call a "trust behavior" is a repeated pattern of transparent, reliable, and honest actions toward you over a period of time that gives you proof of a person's character. Yes, people can change, but it's important to discover their patterns at this present point in their life.

A trust behavior makes green lights glow on your Boundaries Dashboard.

A trust behavior is when someone says that they will do something specific for you or for the sake of the relationship, and then they act on it faithfully and repeatedly over a period of time. It can be a big or small action; quantity, quality, and frequency are what matter, not how big or small the act itself.

A trust behavior is specifically what happens inside of your relationship with the other person, not what happens in their relationships with other people or groups.

If someone says, "I will call you tomorrow," or "I will make time for a conversation this week," and they follow through consistently over a period of time with these promises, then you have a trusted behavior.

In a dating relationship, one of hundreds of potential trust behaviors might be the person openly sharing their photo gallery or text messages that come through their mobile phone, without a sense of hiding something. Another example might be honest and humble confessions when they think they may have done something wrong, which shows humility.

So, over time, I look for a series of trusted behaviors, beginning with our first communications.

When it comes to the Time boundary and messages, I generally stick to a rule of 24 to 48 hours maximum to wait for a reply. If there is no reply in that time or no convincing reason why it's taking so long, I like to unmatch and move on. This doesn't mean they're a bad person, but it means they are unable to put significant value on communication.

After no more than one or two days of messaging back and forth in the app, one of the best time investments I make in the dating process is asking for a "five-minute intro video chat" inside of the app. Without giving my number, I can have a quick virtual "face to face," which tells me if their personality is consistent with their profile and, worst case, if they're a scammer or catfish. It gives me a chance to see if I feel safe and comfortable enough to make plans to meet in person.

If we pass the messaging and video chat stages of this delicate process, then I propose a 30- or 60-minute quick coffee or tea to just see what the personality and attraction dynamic is like in person. That amount of time is what makes me feel safe, and if they are not OK with what makes me feel safe, then they're most certainly not OK for me to date.

TREASURES BOUNDARY

Minimal effort *input* usually means minimal effort *output*.

In other words, when looking through profiles on a dating app, in my experience a minimum of 90% of the time, the amount of effort a person is willing to put into their profile correlates with how much effort they are willing to put into the dating process.

When making my own profile, I like to invest a lot of energy deciding what I need to communicate. I create videos and audio in order to share what's important to me, and I think hard and long about what topics to quickly touch on in all of the text parts of the profile. I make sure I find a collection of imagery that offers an honest view of what I look like, including full-length and close-up photos and video clips.

I have seen that the more effort I invest in figuring out my profile, the better quality results I have seen – more sincere men writing me, far better quality conversation, and overall a higher amount of mutual respect. Of course, the quantity of dates is lower, but the quality is higher.

So, for dating app members who don't appear to invest much time or effort in their profile, I turn my Time dial down to zero, even those with an attractive photo. In desperate times when I've forsaken that rule, I've paid the price every time so far. It's not fair for me to expect anything worthwhile from someone who invests the bare minimum energy from the very start.

TOPICS BOUNDARY

It may not be intentional, but the dating app marketing tactic of using words like "matches" and "compatible" psychologically harms members, making many of us think there is a genuine "match" or there is true "compatibility" when, an overwhelming amount of the time, there is neither.

The only thing a "match" means is that both profiles – or maybe a bot – swiped right or tapped a little "yes" button of some sort.

In the general world of marketing, there is roughly a 2% response rate when you send out a mass email to a new group of people. That's what dating app matches are like for me – out of roughly 100 "matches," maybe one or two will turn into a first date. Yes, I estimate that 98 out of 100 of my "matches" go nowhere. We are incompatible either in chemistry, lifestyle, or visions for our futures.

Two people swiping on each other's profiles and becoming what they deceptively call a "match" does not mean compatibility, but it does mean some degree of *potential* for compatibility, even if that potential is less

Part Six: Use the Glove Compartment

than 2%.

Discovering compatibility begins with conversation topics. These are among the most important topics that cross my mind from the first moment I interact with a dating profile, and I aim to find these answers as soon as naturally possible:

Our relationship roadmaps: Do we both value the sacredness of loyalty and exclusivity? How compatible are our current habits and interests? How compatible are our current and future goals in life – health and fitness goals, wishes regarding having children, and career and money goals?

Sexual attraction: How much potential is there for sexual chemistry? This is the distinguishing factor that separates "just a friend" from a partner you want to share a bed and your body with.

It's fascinating how I've felt the butterflies-in-the-tummy "crush" feeling on a first or second date, but then it disappears on the next date because, through a series of conversations, I've discovered information about the other person that my instincts know will not work for me. Incompatibility is not attractive.

TOOLS BOUNDARY

People's personalities are hidden behind text messaging and phone calls because, with those tools, they can speak without sharing facial cues and bodily gestures. In contrast, if 93% of communication is nonverbal, then video chat gives you up to 93% of their personality that you completely miss out on with text. Video gives you a truer representation of the person, an instant insight into basic compatibility, and even general likability.

In a telephone call or text message, you miss out on at least seven nonverbal communication cues. It's true that a voice tells you a lot more than text, but phone calls are too often personality masks for people. It's not a safe or worthwhile way to have an introduction to a potential date, when compared to video chat. One facial expression can say a thousand words, and you miss all of that on a voice call.

Here are at least seven things you lack in a text or voice interaction, which you will get in a video chat:

1. Facial expressions, including both overall expressions and micro-expressions, which reveal true feelings and attitudes.

2. Body language cues, such as eye movement, posture, and hand gestures, that show how engaged and attentive someone is.

3. The use of space, which can signal a person's level of comfort and interest in the conversation.

4. Physical appearance, including energy levels and signs of health like pain or discomfort, that also gives insights into a person's psychological state and lifestyle.

5. The environmental context like simple objects around the person – artwork, furniture, personal items which indicate personal culture, lifestyle, interests, and a narrative of day-to-day life.

6. Visible indicators of confidence, discernible through one's posture and physical movement.

7. The adding up of all of these elements together, which puts all the pieces of the person's story together for a full message and context for whatever they say.

By agreeing to a video chat, a person also proves to me that they are sincere about both wanting to know me and allowing me to know them.

So, I ask if they're willing to have a five- or ten-minute intro video chat.

TERRITORIES BOUNDARY

After a video chat, meeting in person can feel drastically different than seeing them on the screen – for better or worse. The surprising size of the other person towering over me or how closely we sit or seeing their full body for the first time or how they greet me or their scent or odors like bad breath and cigarette smoke (or other things that people smoke).... It can all cause sensory overload and distract me from thinking clearly.

People act differently in different environments. We feel more free to do or say some things in some environments, and we feel less free to do or say some things in other environments. Meeting in a loud and crowded venue might foster banter and surface level behavior, whereas a quiet café or restaurant might inspire deeper listening and more meaningful conversation.

Food and drink are also a part of the environment. Does the place we choose have food that I can eat, given my restricted diet? I've gotten sick after many dates because I didn't think about those factors ahead of time. If it's a bar, will I be more inclined to drink, get tipsy, and make bad decisions?

Remember that territories include not only the environment and all elements in it, but they also include body boundaries. How comfortable do I feel about how close we are sitting? What physical proximity feels safe? If he rests his hand on my leg, how do I feel about that? How does he feel if I want to sit close enough for my leg to rest against his?

Also, of course, when finally sitting in person in front of the stranger I met on a dating app, surprising facts or behaviors can pretty quickly come out of nowhere that can make or break compatibility.

I remember sitting down at a pub with someone I had a video chat with the day before, and as we sat talking, I noticed him looking left and right constantly. I asked him, "is there someone you're looking for?" He then gently let me know that he had just gotten out of jail and was just on the lookout for certain people.

Do not worry about my safety! I have learned since then. And the guy just out of jail did not have any history of violence as far as I knew, but my point is that certain kinds of character traits and behaviors would not come through in a text message, audio chat, or even a video chat.

Sunlight also matters, when it comes to dating boundaries and environments. People seem to behave differently in daylight where everyone can see, as opposed to nighttime.

The environment where a potential date proposes we meet also tells me a lot about his intentions. If he invites me over his place one evening for a first date, it's clear that his topmost priority is probably not to get to know my life goals, hopes, and dreams. He may be prioritizing a physical connection before finding out if there is an intellectual, mental, or psychological connection.

So, when meeting someone from a dating app for the first time, the winning Territories boundary is a public place during the daytime.

THIRD PARTIES BOUNDARY

More than any other boundary, the importance of third parties seems

Part Six: Use the Glove Compartment

to be overlooked in the dating process. Does he have an ex hanging around? What kind of impact do his friends have on him? What part does his family play in his life and dating decisions? Who are the people who influence and inspire him the most? What kind of relationship does he have with the people at his place of work?

Each of those third parties impact him, and they will impact us, if we become an "us."

The most important question I have when it comes to third parties is, "How does he manage boundaries with people in his life?"

I also observe my own third-party influences. How has an ex of mine influenced my opinion of this man? What would my beloved friends say about dating him? Would my dad approve of this guy? How would work impact my availability to see him? When is it ok to start telling people about him?

IT'S ALL ABOUT THE DASHBOARD

It's all about keeping my eyes on the dashboard when I'm dating.

The battery light of consent.

The oil light of self-care.

The fuel light of what uniquely motivates me.

The temperature light of my emotional state.

And based on which of those lights glow red, yellow, or green, I adjust my boundaries.

Part Six: Use the Glove Compartment

CHAPTER 28

FALLING IN LOVE OR FALLING IN EXPECTATION?

(5 minute read)

Sometimes a video on social media leaves an imprint on my soul.

As I was scrolling my feed one day, my heart glowed when I saw someone's big, breathtaking smile celebrating newly-found love, and the words on the screen read, "Finally meeting someone special after thinking I was unlovable."[31]

Someone special.

But then the video suddenly cut to a new scene, when this beautiful soul learned that their newly beloved – their "someone special" – was caught cheating in the bathroom of a bar.

My chest flooded with compassion because I know what it feels like to be overpowered by mind-altering "crush" feelings, where the other person becomes "the one" who suddenly fills an eternity-sized void that you didn't even know you had.

And then that person's most unexpected behavior violently contradicts everything you believed about love, emotions, loyalty, and how the world works.

I didn't know anything about this person's story other than their video. I didn't know if it was a true story or only for entertainment, but that did not matter because I know that same experience is a completely true story for far too many people. I knew there would be many who would watch that video and remember the crush and the life-altering crash afterward, so I felt a need to say something in the comments section.

In my comment, I wrote that a person is not "someone special" until after you have eye-witnessed a pattern of "trust behaviors." As I wrote in the last chapter, a pattern of trust behaviors is a repeated pattern of transparent, reliable, and honest actions toward you over a period of time that gives you proof of a person's character. It depends on which behaviors you're looking for, but only one or two times in a row is not enough.

Think of trust behaviors as rungs in a ladder that go higher and higher, or as ties (the horizontal bars) in a railroad track that lead farther and farther. Yes, rungs break. Yes, ties can be damaged. However, metaphorical ladders and railroad tracks are foundational to a person's character; any human relationship suffers greatly without a firm and reliable series of them.

The longer the period of time, the stronger the character.

An example of a trust behavior is when someone says that they will do something specific for you or for the sake of the relationship, and then they act on it faithfully and repeatedly over an extended period of time. While there is not a hard and fast number to aim for, a particular trust behavior should occur far more than two times in a row.

The more trust behaviors you can name and observe consistently over time, the better and stronger the character, and the more "special" they become.

Chapter 28: Falling in Love or Falling in Expectation?

Are people unbreakable and perfect? No, but some have a far higher quantity, quality, and frequency of trust behaviors than others. And you won't know that quantity, quality, or frequency until you observe and recognize those patterns.

Pattern recognition is how your brain identifies anything, including how you read this sentence right now. You do not truly know if your "crush" will be someone truly special until you've witnessed their patterns of demonstrated trust behaviors toward you.

Many years ago, you slowly learned the patterns of what each of the 26 letters of the English alphabet look like, and now your brain can match every letter you're looking at in this sentence without consciously thinking about it. At one time, perhaps somewhere around five years old, you had to make a painstaking effort to identify the patterns that form each one of the 26 letters.

It requires that same kind of painstaking effort for you to truly identify the character of another person. In a human relationship, behavior patterns identify the general character of the other person and, in turn, the strength of your relationship.

And patterns – including the subtle ones – will also help you recognize if or when that person starts to change.

When it comes to romantic relationships, when we say that we "fall in love," I believe we really "fall in *expectation*" or "fall in *hope*."

In other words, we fall into a pool of expectations or wishes that the person will be who we want them to be and they will follow a pattern of character traits that we desire.

And when we insist that the person is "the one" before they have expressed mutual feelings and before those feelings have had a chance to be consistently demonstrated, it's like a subtle form of dictatorship toward that person. That is because we are, in a sense, directing that person to be something without their consent. We are assuming that the person will create a certain value for us in the future, without allowing them to first consent to that role and then demonstrate it.

Perhaps that's why it's called "falling" — because there is no reliable history of patterns to form a firm ground to stand on.

Falls happen because of instability.

We "fall" when we have nothing stable to stand on.

When you have not witnessed a person's consistent positive behaviors toward you and have not witnessed how you feel with them over time, you are only going by expectations and assumptions.

With a "crush," we have only an unstable assumption that this person is the right one. It's like setting out expensive food on fine china and drinks in crystal glass, all on a table with unstable legs; one slight move, and it comes crashing to the floor.

When we have a "crush" we believe, often with little evidence, that the object of our crush will make us very happy. However, we cannot know the truth about whether or not someone will "make us happy" until we have witnessed first-hand a solid history of realistic and meaningful interactions.

And, healthy or unhealthy, patterns can only be observed and identified over time.

And it is certainly possible that the hopes or expectations that you had in your heart when you felt that crush or "fell into expectations" may prove true, and that does happen sometimes; however, you just don't know until you have personally witnessed enough consistency and repetition.

Considering how often crushes are not reciprocated and how the assumptions we make about them turn out altogether to be untrue, it's a game of emotional Russian Roulette to proceed without adding a little bit of healthy skepticism.

It's the same with professional relationships, too. Sometimes you can "fall in expectations" with the idea of a certain job or company – big dreams of a vibrant future. But then you get hired, and suddenly you start to see patterns of company behavior and management that didn't surface in the one or two job interviews.

It works the other way, too, for managers and business owners: you "fall into expectations with a candidate" in the interview and their track record and first impression personality seems promising, but the character patterns you assumed begin to play out differently after the first few months.

The only reason we can predict the weather to any degree is because many people painstakingly record its patterns. Forecasts take time.

Just like weather forecasts, the more data points, the more likely the accuracy.

That's why consistently doing the Boundaries Health Check can help you think clearly; it gives you the ability to track those patterns that tell you the true story.

CHAPTER 29

FINAL WORDS

(2 minute read)

In order for two lovers to enjoy the chase of each other's hearts, there must be a form of distance or unknowing between them.

By definition, a chase can only happen when there is space in between.

The lovers' chase is perhaps the most exciting example of how distance fuels joy and passion in a human relationship. The power of distance, whether emotional, mental, or physical, also creates joy in all other human relationships, not only between lovers.

With friends, my chase is to find something new to make them laugh or feel a surge of encouragement.

With coaching clients, my chase is to ask questions that trigger clarity and motivated action.

With my favorite funny coworkers, my chase is for that next hilarious comment or joke.

The list goes on.

Part Six: Use the Glove Compartment

Whether you win or lose, chasing a worthy prize moves you out of a feeling of only existing and into a state of feeling alive.

The theory of the Boundaries Dashboard and the practice of the Boundaries Health Check are designed to help you continually identify healthy prizes and then chase after them, and those "prizes" that you drive toward are your destinations.

By now in this book, if you have followed all exercises, you can see your road trip ahead of you. The road trip of a lifetime has begun! I am hoping that the chapters and exercises in this book become a regular part of your life until they become a part of your natural way of thinking, decision-making, and action-taking.

For the easiest way to keep score of the health of your relationship with yourself and others, remember to look out for the Boundaries Health Check app in Apple's App Store or the Google Play Store.

I'm also working on other ways, such as live events, to help you gain control of your dashboard and increase those Boundaries Health Check scores. In the meantime, please find me somewhere online so I can support and encourage you on your road trip.

As your personal coach and author of this book, you and I have now entered into a special kind of human relationship. I have shared with you my thoughts on the topic of human relationship boundaries, and you have shared with me your precious time by listening or reading.

You and I have both invested deeply into this relationship, and for that, I want to thank you.

Our relationship is valuable to me, and I genuinely want to hear from you to know how often you're using your dashboard in your key relationships.

I am waiting to hear from you. On all social media, you can find me as "boundariescheck" or @boundariescheck.

See you there!

ABOUT CYNDI D. MCCOY

(5 minute read)

For those of you who are curious, I'll tell you about the nerdy kind of brain that the theory of the Boundaries Dashboard, the practice of the Boundaries Health Check, and all related ideas in this book were born from.

Throughout my schooling, I was an honors student. In grade school, I remember being a part of the "gifted and talented" program, looking around the room, and feeling like a nerd supreme. So, when I felt like my social status was being impacted, I quit the program.

I nurtured more of my creative side as a teen and managed to graduate high school with a few art awards, including a "Gold Key to New York State" from the New York State Museum. The Gold Key is a symbol of highest achievement in the Scholastic Art & Writing Awards program, one of the most prestigious recognition programs for creative teenagers in the United States.

During my undergraduate studies, I became less artsy and more academic, maintaining a 4.0 GPA for a while and spent my junior year at the University of Oxford in England. A few less-than-perfect scores at Oxford bumped down my previously perfect GPA, but I still graduated *summa cum laude* (highest honors).

I still feel like a geek to this day. I think a lot. I sometimes wake up first thing in the morning attempting to solve complex philosophical problems like if time even exists or how carbon-14 dating can be accurate when the length of a "day" and therefore years has changed over the centuries.

I'm a bit quirky, klutzy, and awkward, and yet somehow I can also come across as cool, calm, and collected. In grade school, I helped lead the dance choreography for our school's talent show two years in a row, where my friends and I were the opening act. I still make fun videos with dance moves for friends. I can appear to have it all together, and yet I find myself accidentally walking into walls and tripping on smooth floors.

I naturally question the meaning of just about everything, but I also love saying or doing absurd things that make me laugh so hard that I'm crying. My favorite thing to watch is nonsense practical joke videos involving unsuspecting strangers, like those from Impractical Jokers or other funny video makers. As long as people are not hurt or scared, it's funny.

I love microphones. I don't remember how I got a tape recorder as a child, but I still remember the deep joy of pressing the record button as a four-year-old girl, leaning into the microphone to sing, talk, or say something funny. I even kept one of those recordings on tape (yes, tape!) with me all these years, and it's still sitting on my shelf right now.

For many years as an adult, I have somehow been able to play the serious corporate role like a soldier, but I also know how to completely let loose and dance on the tables, which I've done many wonderful times.

But one important thing to note in my story is that whenever I have lost sight of the four lights on my Boundaries Dashboard, I've become a very unhappy person and no longer recognize myself. As you might remember from Part Two of this book, the four "dashboard lights" represent consent (battery), motivators (fuel), self-care (oil), and emotional state (temperature).

To lose track of the dashboard is to lose my inner voice, and when I lose my own voice, I lose my joy and am not at all a thrill to be around. I need continuous awareness; so, you might say that I am my number one client of my own boundaries program.

The Boundaries Dashboard is not something that I conceived and have now conquered once and for all. Rather, this theory is like a recipe that I have invented, and no matter how spectacular that recipe tastes, it is something that I must follow the steps for every time I want to enjoy it.

Yes, I made the "recipe" for boundaries, but I too must do the hard work to follow each step and measure ingredients every time.

Every. Time.

Although, great boundaries recipes for some relationships are easier than others.

So, what else should I note? Oh, I love lists and use them in just about every part of life. You'll notice this book is full of numbered lists from beginning to end – the six rules of human relationships, the six boundaries themselves, the 12 ingredients of self-care, and the ten instructions in the "Instruction Manual" at the beginning of this book, to name just a few.

Lists are an essential part of anything amazing that's worth repeating, like a winning recipe's list of ingredients or a checklist before sending a rocket into space or a pilot's to-do list before airplane takeoff, or a surgeon's checklist before surgery.

Making a list means that it's going to be easier to complete the necessary steps to make it as amazing as the last time. Lists also just make information more digestible.

And now for another list! Since this is the "About Cyndi McCoy" part of the book, I leave you with seven other labels I can claim besides author of *The Boundaries Health Check*:

1. Author of *The Science of Personal Coaching* (available on Amazon.com) and narrator for my own audio version of *The Boundaries Health Check*.

2. Professionally trained personal coach. In 2015, I went through a significant process of training and earned professional coaching credentials from the International Coach Federation.

3. Professionally trained singer as well as occasional songwriter, with original music published on Spotify, Apple Music and other retailers. One of my voice coaches was a singer at the Metropolitan Opera House in New York City, and the other was a coach to Cristina Aguilera and Whitney Houston.

4. Creator of an online boundaries workshop (prior to the publication of this book) that earned a rating of 4.6 out of 5 stars. I took that one offline but check boundariescheck.com for when it's available again.

5. Amateur podcaster. (At the time of this book's First Edition, anyway.)

6. Dual citizen. Born in New York City, grew up in New York State, left Staten Island NYC in 2013 to visit Australia but then never returned, and now a citizen of Australia and the United States.

7. Lover of crypto, gym and muscles, God and atheists, love itself, technology that makes life easier, personal development, miracles, sitting on my couch with a blanket, and dancing wildly alone in my flat. That was not in order of importance.

ACKNOWLEDGEMENTS

(5 minute read)

A long list of people have inspired me over the years as I've been developing this theory and writing the pages of this book. That list includes expert and licensed therapist Jo Gore, whose words in the forward to this book were a crowning touch for me, along with everyone who wrote a review, and those who have kindly given me their testimonials. I feel honored and grateful for each of you.

However, here in this acknowledgements section, it's my moment to recognize the other positive people in my life whom I have not yet mentioned in this book but who have encouraged me to get this book done.

First, coach Martha. Our daily coaching conversations got me through the hardest parts of this writing and editing process. I'm so grateful to God for your professional coaching skills, your outstanding persistence over the years, and your belief in me. Oh my, your belief in me!

One of my dearest and longtime best friends, Liz, for being a bright shining north star of wisdom and a gracious example of how to live out and communicate healthy boundaries. Thank you for our few but momentous conversations about boundaries here and there throughout the years. By the way, here on the other side of the world, I still hold dear and wear the scarf you handmade for me.

Michelle D., my clever, talented, and lovely former colleague in Brisbane, Australia, who sat down and gave it to me straight about the state of my book in its early development. You helped me face up to how boring the intro was in that version of the manuscript. Your feedback had me crumple up a large part of my book and start again with more heart-felt directness. I shifted everything after that.

Another one of my personal coaches, Adrian! You have had a uniquely powerful ability to help me cut out what is unnecessary in my dating life so that I could make time to focus again on my book. Your coaching has helped me manage my time, my priorities, my passion, and create the space needed in my life to get this published.

Rachel T., I'm so grateful that you let me read some of these chapters out loud to you. Doing that has helped me make my words a little more natural. You are one of the key people who helped me take a metaphorical stick out of my bum when it comes to my writing. There's probably still some stick left in there, but I'm working on it.

Coach Petar, sitting down with you as your coaching client those few times in that magical café in Southbank was unforgettable. In our coaching conversations, most of all, you gave me more confidence as a coach myself, but you also helped me think through how I can take the ideas of this book that apply to all human relationships and carve them down into a specialized workshop for singles.

I've had only one email exchange with you so far, but hilarious and brilliant author, Ash Ambirge, you inspired me for a long time with only one little email. Your book, blogs, and newsletters inspired me to write more courageously. I emailed you one technical question and never thought that you'd personally write me back, but you did.

And there are so many others I have yet to name who have sprinkled magical encouragement on me to keep me going on writing this book, like my sweet Grandma Nell; my angelic Cousin Marylin from Brooklyn with her messages of love on Facebook; Tammy Lyn's loving and consistently-empowering words; my former iHeartMedia colleague, Michael aka "Happy," and all of his encouragement, including his audio expertise that gave me confidence for The Boundaries Health Check audiobook; my professors from college who still say hi every now and then (Hi Dana!); my neighbors Brad, Sally, Eli, and Adam for our goal-setting and laser-focus meetups; and every person on my social media profiles who has liked or commented on any of my quirky or inspirational or random posts and thereby unwittingly giving me a tiny (or big) dopamine hit to keep me going.

An overwhelming number of podcasts and social media accounts have also given me motivation to keep going over the years, and I've already mentioned some of them in places all throughout these chapters. A complete list would be overwhelmingly long, but as I worked on my book, three have been most consistent. Here they are.

Author Adam Cam, with his soul-penetrating look into the camera and tougher-than-nails big brother style of preaching boundaries.

Joel Osteen, and how he beautifully transcends his haters and pushes forward with his unfailingly enthusiastic style of teaching about the unassailable, impervious, and bulletproof love, grace, and power of God.

Fitness trainer Danny Kennedy of the *Fitness and Lifestyle Podcast*, with his useful, humble, enlightening, and inspiring advice on the relationship between physical and mental fitness.

There are many other people who have inspired my worldview and self-view through our direct and personal interactions or through something they've published. Most notably, two life-changing authors and speakers, Peter Rollins and Rob Bell, take the spot for the most influential humans in my life so far.

Peter, your powerful message about the dangers of putting anyone or anything on a pedestal continually shapes my approach to human relationships, and I must say, it's not easy to keep you off that pedestal.

Rob, thank you for writing *Love Wins*, and thank you for those few days of spending a little time with you and your family on Tamborine Mountain; that experience showed me your integrity, that you're the same in person as you are on the big stage.

Last and most importantly, this book only intends to cover relationships between human beings, not relationships with invisible beings or not-yet-visible beings. So, I don't know what category of intelligence or living organisms to put you in, God, but if you're real and living, as you have seemed to be in countless mind-blowing moments in my life, I love you and thank you for helping me whenever a human has been unable to understand or reach the depths and complexities of my unutterable needs. From the bottom of my heart, I hope you are real and that the story of a resurrected Jesus is true, but even if not, then the idea of you alone – at least the way the book *Love Wins* describes you – shines just enough light to help me navigate my darkest roads. You are my hope.

ENDNOTES

1. The estimated number of minutes to read each chapter is based on the following research of average reading rates, which is an extensively investigated calculation compiled from 190 studies. Research concluded that the average adult reads 238 words per minute for non-fiction. Note that the estimated number of minutes that you see at the beginning of chapters throughout this book (shown as "__ minute read") does not include the time that it will take you to stop and reflect, type, or write out answers to each chapter's exercise. However, estimated number of minutes does include the average amount of time it takes to read through both the chapter and the chapter's exercise. For more information on this research, see: https://www.researchgate.net/publication/332380784_How_many_words_do_we_read_per_minute_A_review_and_meta-analysis_of_reading_rate

2. Robert Waldinger, "What makes a good life? Lessons from the longest study on happiness," November 2015, TEDx Beacon Street, https://www.ted.com/talks/robert_waldinger_what_makes_a_good_life_lessons_from_the_longest_study_on_happiness?language=en. Note: Robert Waldinger is a psychiatrist, psychoanalyst, and director of the Harvard Study.

3. Liz Mineo, "Good genes are nice, but joy is better," Harvard Gazette, April 11, 2017, https://news.harvard.edu/gazette/story/2017/04/over-nearly-80-years-harvard-study-has-been-showing-how-to-live-a-healthy-and-happy-life/.

4. Waldinger, "What makes a good life?" (See Endnote 2 above)

5. John G. Bruhn and Stewart Wolf, *The Roseto Story: An Anatomy of Health*, (The University of Oklahoma Press, 2004).

6. B. Egolf, J. Lasker, S. Wolf, and L. Potvin, "The Roseto effect: a 50-year comparison of mortality rates," *American Journal of Public Health*, 82(8) (1992): 1089–1092, https://www.ncbi.nlm.nih.gov/pmc/articles/PMC1695733/.

7. Debra Umberson and Jennifer Karas Montez, "Social Relationships and Health: A Flashpoint for Health Policy," *Journal of Health and Social Behavior* 51 (Suppl) (2010): S54-66, https://doi.org/10.1177/0022146510383501.

8. Office of the U.S. Surgeon General, *Our Epidemic of Loneliness and Isolation: The U.S. Surgeon General's Advisory on the Healing Effects of Social Connection and Community*, 2023, https://www.hhs.gov/surgeongeneral/priorities/connection/index.html.

9. James Smith, Facebook post, June 26, 2022, https://www.facebook.com/JamesSmithPT.

10. Daniel Goleman, *Emotional Intelligence: Why It Can Matter More Than IQ* (New York: Bantam Books, 1995).

11. "Why We Live: Counting the People You Impact," *Funders and Founders*, https://web.archive.org/web/20170710133817/http://fundersandfounders.com/counting-the-people-you-impact/ (accessed July 10, 2017). The article posits that "On average we live for 78.3 years. Most of us remember people we meet after age 5. Assume we interact with 3 new people daily in cities, 365 days in a year plus leap years days is 365.24. In total it will be (78.3 − 5) x 3 x 365.24 = 80,000 people. Is it a lot? Either way, most of us will

meet around 80,000 people in the course of our lives." My assertion about the percentage of the human population one interacts with is based on this calculation and the current global population at the time of writing this book.

12. "What is motor oil composed of?" *TotalEnergies*, https://services.totalenergies.uk/what-motor-oil-composed.

13. Eckhart Tolle, *The Power of Now: A Guide to Spiritual Enlightenment* (Novato: New World Library, 1999). Note: Originally published in 1997 by Namaste Publishing in Vancouver. The 1999 republished edition reached and remained on the New York Times bestseller list for years afterwards.

14. Daniel G. Amen, M.D., TikTok video, October 7, 2022, https://www.tiktok.com/@docamen/video/7151601822455696682. Note: Daniel G. Amen is a psychiatrist, a 12-time New York Times bestselling author, and has over 2 million followers on TikTok.

15. Rob Bell, *Love Wins: A Book About Heaven, Hell, and the Fate of Every Person Who Ever Lived* (San Francisco: HarperOne, 2011).

16. Christopher Peterson and Martin Seligman, *Character Strengths and Virtues: A Handbook and Classification* (Washington, DC: American Psychological Association, 2004).

17. For more research related to Peterson and Seligman's work, see: https://www.viacharacter.org/research/findings.

18. Eckhart Tolle, *The Power of Now: A Guide to Spiritual Enlightenment*. (See Endnote number 13 above).

19. Massachusetts Institute of Technology, "Detecting emotions with wireless signals: Measuring your heartbeat and breath, device can

tell if you're excited, happy, angry, or sad," *Science Daily*, www.sciencedaily.com/releases/2016/09/160921093924.htm (accessed August 19, 2023).

20. The Healthline Editorial Team, "Hot and Cold: Extreme Temperature Safety," *Healthline* (last updated September 17, 2018). Medically reviewed by Elaine K. Luo, M.D., https://www.healthline.com/health/extreme-temperature-safety#extreme-heat-temperatures.

21. The Editors of Encyclopedia Britannica, "Fever," *Encyclopedia Britannica* (last updated June 23, 2023), https://www.britannica.com/science/fever.

22. Both of these podcasts provided this information:
Huberman Lab, "Dr. Maya Shankar: How to Shape your Identity & Goals," podcast audio (July 24, 2023), 17:15.
Huberman Lab, "Dr. Charles Zuker: The Biology of Taste Perception & Sugar Craving," podcast audio (July 17, 2022), 17:19, https://podtext.ai/huberman-lab/dr-charles-zuker-the-biology-of-taste-perception-sugar-craving.

23. Marcus E. Raichle and Debra A. Gusnard, "Appraising the Brain's Energy Budget," *Proceedings of the National Academy of Sciences of the United States of America* 99 (16): 10237-10239 (2002), https://www.pnas.org/doi/10.1073/pnas.172399499.

24. Michael Nolan, "Using Voice to Maximize Learning," *Friesen, Kaye and Associates* (2017), https://fka.com/using-voice-maximize-learning/. Note: Thank you to the professional learning and performance consultant noted here, whose seven sample sentences I have used and modified.

25. Eric Sprankle, PsyD, Professor of Clinical Psychology (@

DrSprankle), Twitter post "It's a lot easier for couples to blame porn..." (May 21, 2023), https://twitter.com/DrSprankle/status/1659926568939008000.

26. British Broadcasting Corporation (BBC), "Have scientists discovered how to read our thoughts?" (May 27, 2022), https://www.bbc.com/reel/video/p0c9j6wm/have-scientists-discovered-how-to-read-our-thoughts-.

27. Jeff Guenther, LPC (@therapyjeff). TikTok video (July 25, 2022), https://www.tiktok.com/@therapyjeff/video/7124310013224471850.

28. "12 Good Things That Can Go Bad," *WebMD*, Reviewed by Neha Pathak, M.D. (March 2, 2022), https://www.webmd.com/balance/ss/slideshow-too-much-good-thing.

29. Cyndi D. McCoy, *The Science of Personal Coaching* (published through Convosique Pty. Ltd., Brisbane, 2018), Available on Amazon.com: https://www.amazon.com.au/gp/product/B07M5S5VJ4/ref=dbs_a_def_rwt_bibl_vppi_i0.

30. "How Much of Communication Is Nonverbal?" *University of Texas Permian Basin*, https://online.utpb.edu/about-us/articles/communication/how-much-of-communication-is-nonverbal/ (accessed August 22, 2023).

31. Steven James (@stevenjamesnz), TikTok video (May 21, 2022), https://www.tiktok.com/@stevenjamesnz/video/7100044736974654721.

Milton Keynes UK
Ingram Content Group UK Ltd.
UKHW022344201124
451301UK00018B/151/J